ASSESSING AND IMPROVING YOUR TEACHING

**THE JOSSEY-BASS
HIGHER AND ADULT EDUCATION SERIES**

ASSESSING AND IMPROVING YOUR TEACHING

Strategies and Rubrics for Faculty Growth and Student Learning

Phyllis Blumberg

Maryellen Weimer
Consulting Editor

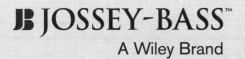

JB JOSSEY-BASS™
A Wiley Brand

Published by Jossey-Bass
A Wiley Brand
One Montgomery Street, Suite 1200, San Francisco, CA 94104-4594—www.josseybass.com

Library of Congress Cataloging-in-Publication Data

Blumberg, Phyllis, date
    Assessing and improving your teaching : strategies and rubrics for faculty growth and student learning / Phyllis Blumberg. — First edition.
        pages cm. — (Jossey-Bass higher and adult education series)
    Includes bibliographical references and index.
        ISBN 978-1-118-27548-1 (pbk.) — ISBN 978-1-118-41953-3 (ebk.) — ISBN 978-1-118-42134-5 (ebk.)
        1. Reflective teaching. 2. College teaching. I. Title.
    LB1025.3.B595 2013
    371.102—dc23
                                                                                    2013013534

Printed in the United States of America
FIRST EDITION

PB Printing 10 9 8 7 6 5 4 3 2 1

Contents

Dedicated with love to my sons,
Adam, Barry, and Noah Kosherick

Preface

THE ORIGIN FOR THIS BOOK came from a department chair's request. He asked me for a comprehensive teaching assessment instrument that could objectively measure teaching effectiveness that he could also use to help his faculty to improve. His professors were largely summarizing student course evaluations, and that did not give enough information. I checked the literature and was not able to find one that fit his needs. Thus began my quest for a better model to assess teaching. Since I see myself as a faculty coach and not a judge, I wanted the model to focus on improvement, not high-stakes decisions. Current methods of evaluating teaching do not generate the data needed to make good choices about how to teach more effectively. This book addresses that need. It emerged from my faculty development experiences and my convictions about what is good teaching.

This book is intended for all teachers in higher education, including those who teach in experiential settings. It offers suggestions for teachers at all stages of their careers. The overarching purpose of this book is to promote teaching excellence. Effective teaching promotes both deep and intentional learning.

This book describes a comprehensive plan for teacher development. It's not something that should be done all at once, and it is not a quick fix for struggling instructors. This is a systematic process for career-long development of teaching effectiveness. I propose a hierarchical development and self-assessment model, but it is not necessary to do all of the steps; doing even one step helps instructors teach more effectively. In fact, making ongoing improvement may be more important than achieving excellence. The hierarchical model is based on essential principles in the literature on faculty development and cognitive sciences. The strength of this model places the locus of control with readers who want to improve rather than with external audiences who want to judge. Thus, this book deals with formative self-assessment rather than summative assessment.

The book begins by building the rationale for the assessment model and methods. It offers broad improvement strategies for career-long growth, describes a formative assessment model, and finally introduces self-assessment rubrics (see figure P1). Throughout, I offer many suggestions to increase student deep and intentional learning through better teaching. The cases describe how five professors improved their teaching. The appendix contains self-assessment rubrics.

Part 1 describes a hierarchical approach to teaching better that integrates four well-supported, but previously separate, effective teaching strategies. An introduction and orientation to this approach is in chapter 1. Chapter 2 discusses misconceptions about teaching and recommends alternative ideas about teaching. Chapter 3 defines the essential aspects of teaching. Studying each of these aspects is the first effective teaching strategy. Chapter 4 discusses the role of critical self-reflection and the need for documentation of this reflection, the second effective teaching strategy. The third strategy for more effective teaching involves evidence-based decision making to guide practice and is the topic of chapter 5. Since many professors may not know the appropriate literature to support teaching, I devote chapter 6 to how to find such literature in your discipline and in general.

The last strategy is using self-assessment as a continuous improvement process. To assist in this process, I describe a constructive, self-assessment model in part 2 that assesses all of the essential aspects of teaching discussed in chapter 3. Chapter 7 describes principles of assessment to foster learning.

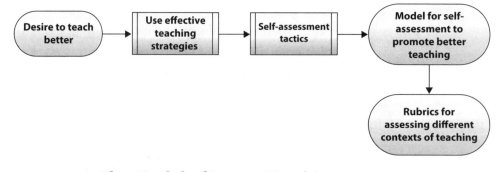

FIGURE P.1   The Model of Better Teaching to Increase Learning Used throughout This Book

Chapter 8 applies these principles to a new assessment model that fosters better teaching. Through critical self-assessment, evidence-based decision making, and rigorous data collection, instructors employ a broad-based and layered support for their teaching effectiveness.

This self-assessment model leads to a catalogue of critical reflection, self-assessment rubrics as I discuss in part 3. Chapters 9 and 10 describe how to understand and use the self-assessment rubrics, which assess many types of teaching and identify specific components of these types of teaching. The discussion shows the types of data that can be used to support claims of teaching quality and how the assessment standards provide suggestions for enhancement. This model and the resulting rubrics will change how you assess your teaching while raising the standard for what is effective teaching.

The five cases, which focus on faculty who have used the rubrics to assess their teaching, show the richness and variety of ways that teaching can promote better student learning. Reading these cases can show you how to improve your teaching and assess your effectiveness largely on your own, as these professors have done.

Acknowledgments

This book was possible only through the collaborative efforts of many people who helped me develop and refine my ideas, validated the rubrics, edited drafts, and offered suggestions for improvement. I offer them my sincere gratitude. Maryellen Weimer, my trusted friend and mentor, read many drafts of this book and offered insightful criticisms in the spirit of improvement.

People who collaborated on the development of the rubrics include faculty at the University of the Sciences, especially the Department of Mathematics, Physics, and Statistics: Linda Robinson, Annemarie Flanagan, Thomas O'Connor, Amy Jessop, Paula Kramer, Carlos Moreno, Thomas O'Connor, Steven Sheaffer, Elisabetta Fasella, Preston Moore, Cathy Poon, Fred Schaefer, Ruy Tchao, and Shanaz Tejani-Butt. Linda Nilson of Clemson University and Shirley Mier of Century College were especially helpful in formulating the rubrics. I also acknowledge the assistance of art faculty from other institutions who assisted in the development of the rubrics for the performing and visual arts, including Nicholas Morrison of Utah State University, Monica Ines Huerta of University of Michigan, Gail Rathbun of Indiana Purdue University at Fort Wayne, and Martin Springborg of Academy of Art University.

James Yarrish crafted the rubrics template.

Paul Halpern, Lia Vas, Susan Wainwright, Kay Scanlon, Gregory Theilman, Madhu Mahalingam, Roger Ideishi, Therese Johnston, Elizabeth Amy Janke, Bo Sun, Lindsay Curtin, Carol Maritz, Amy Jessop,

Ruth Schemm, Shanaz Tejani-Butt, Pamalyn Kearney, Laura Pontiggia, Salar Alsardary, Alice Levy, and Maria Brown participated in the rubrics validation study. Linda Robison, a psychometrician who worked with me consistently throughout the development of the rubrics, also took the data submitted by these professors and completed rubrics on them for the validity study.

Many people offered wonderful advice on the wording and organization of the book, especially Maryellen Weimer, David Brightman, and Halley Sutton of Jossey-Bass, the two external reviewers, and the production staff at Jossey-Bass, Susan Geraghty and copyeditor Bev Miller. My sister, Ella Singer, proofread the final drafts and corrected the smallest mistakes that I overlooked. I also want to acknowledge the many instructors who are named throughout the book who willingly shared examples of their teaching reflections and self-assessments.

August 2013   Phyllis Blumberg
                                       Bala Cynwyd, Pennsylvania

The Author

PHYLLIS BLUMBERG has dedicated her career to improving teaching in higher education and to increased learning. She has taught first-year college through graduate and medical students. She has been working with instructors in the health sciences and the sciences as a faculty developer for thirty years. Blumberg has worked with faculty at five universities in the United States and Canada on a one-to-one basis to help them change their teaching so that their students will learn more.

She is currently the director of the Teaching and Learning Center and professor of social sciences and education at the University of the Sciences. Faculty value teaching at this university and want to teach better. More than 80 percent of the instructors at her university voluntarily participate in at least one faculty development event or consult with Blumberg individually every year.

Blumberg is the author of more than fifty articles on active learning, learning-centered teaching, problem-based learning, and program evaluation, including a guidebook on how to implement learner-centered teaching, *Developing Learner-Centered Teaching: A Practical Guide for Faculty* (2009, Jossey-Bass). She is a frequent presenter at POD, the Teaching Professor, Lilly-East, and other higher education conferences. She has given workshops at numerous colleges and universities across around the world.

Blumberg earned her doctorate in educational and developmental psychology from the University of Pittsburgh, Learning Research and Development Center, in 1976.

ASSESSING AND IMPROVING YOUR TEACHING

Chapter 1

Growing Your Teaching Effectiveness
An Overview

DOES THE FOLLOWING DESCRIPTION FIT YOU?

You want to know how you are teaching, so if need be, you can make appropriate changes that will improve your teaching and students' learning. Like most other teachers, you start by looking at your most recent student evaluations and see that less than 40 percent of the students completed the online course evaluation. Is this a representative sample? Did more of the disgruntled group complete the evaluation than those who were satisfied? Did the really bright students who worked hard in the course evaluate it? Do the answers to the items on the survey instrument address those questions? Your summary scores on the quantitative questions indicate slightly above-average scores compared with other faculty in your department and college; however, the range on some of the questions is fairly large. Moreover, the comments do not offer any real insights. Several students say you are a nice person or a good teacher who treats students fairly. A few students remark that that the course was challenging. To students, "challenging" implies that the instructor made them work hard (Lauer, 2012). Is that a compliment or a complaint? One student did not like how you dress. A few felt the course would be better if it had been scheduled at a different time. What can you learn from feedback like this?

Feeling a little frustrated at the lack of concrete feedback from students, you look at the recent peer observations of your teaching (provided this feedback is available). The comments consistently say that your class was well organized, you know the material, and you maintain a good pace. Your peers note that your rapport with the students is good considering the size of the class, but they suggest that calling on students more by name might help. One suggests using a bit more humor. Another observed that most of the students were paying attention most of the time, but from time to time they got distracted, talking with each other and texting or checking Facebook. Other than trying to use student names, you did not learn much else from this feedback.

What to do now? Your department chair does not offer advice because she has not made classroom visits, so you decide to talk with an esteemed senior colleague in your department. He attributes his success to respecting students as individuals. But what does that mean, and, more pragmatic, how does a teacher show respect for students and with more than two hundred of them spread across three classes?

If you have concluded that the common practices for seeking information to help teachers become more effective does not work, I agree. Current methods of evaluating teaching do not generate the data needed to make good choices about what and how to change teaching. We urgently need new strategies and new tools to provide information for this process.

The Goal: Promoting Excellent Teaching

The overarching purpose of this book is to promote teaching excellence, specifically your teaching excellence. When students are learning and the educational experience is going well, both students and teachers are invigorated. This book identifies many ways in which you can gain insights that will foster better student learning. Learning can be defined in many ways. To clarify, in this book, I am using the term to mean deep and intentional learning. Deep learners gain understanding of the content as opposed to just memorizing it. They form many associations with the concepts and can recall the information and use it to solve problems in the future (Ramsden, 2003). When students purposefully gain knowledge and skills, and learning is not just an incidental outcome, they are intentional learners. Intentional learners spend more effort than what is needed to complete a task in a superficial way (Bereiter & Scardamalia, 1989). Intentional learning is the goal of all higher education, especially the general education curriculum according to the Association of American Colleges and Universities (2002). Effective teaching promotes both deep and intentional learning.

Many professors have not been trained how to teach. In graduate school, they learned the knowledge and skills of their disciplines and engaged in research. But they know little about how students learn generally or how they learn content. It is not surprising that some of these instructors are dissatisfied with the quality of their teaching. They aspire to be excellent teachers (Austin, Sorcinelli, & McDaniels, 2007) but discover that good teaching takes a lot of time—time that they may need to devote to do research. For professors who experience this stress, this book offers constructive ways to teach and how to improve it.

Are you hesitant about spending time developing your teaching skills? Given the pressures to conduct research, advise students, serve on committees, and respond to family responsibilities, you may think there is not enough time left to devote to developing your teaching. However, research shows that developing your teaching is an investment that pays off (Austin et al., 2007). This is an ongoing process, and you can devote a little time to teaching growth each month. In fact, small amounts of time continually are probably better than thinking you will focus on your teaching only during semester breaks.

After identifying ways to change how you teach, as suggested in this book, you may find that your faculty development or teaching and learning center are very helpful. These centers regularly offer programs that address specific aspects of teaching, and chances are good that you'll meet other instructors concerned about improving their teaching. They may become colleagues to work with as you continue your quest for excellent teaching.

Better Teaching throughout Your Career

Academics need different kinds of instructional information at various times during their careers. Those at the very beginning need basic help in how to teach. Junior faculty members may spend too much time on their teaching without being very effective (Austin et al., 2007). Feedback is most helpful in the early years of academic careers if it is oriented more to development than evaluation (Rice & Sorcinelli, 2002). A few years later, as assistant professors approach tenure review, they may find using a systematic way to assess their teaching particularly useful, especially if it offers clear explanations of standards for good teaching (Austin et al., 2007). After tenure and sometimes when teaching the same courses repeatedly, though, professors can find their teaching becoming a little stale, so they may want some fresh ways of doing what has become perhaps overly familiar.

This book offers suggestions for teachers at all stages of their careers. It is a book for every teacher in higher education because every teacher can improve and every teacher should want to be the best teacher possible. The methods and tools described in this book can be especially helpful for assistant professors because they offer an organized and ongoing self-development process that can have huge payoffs if it is begun early in one's career. Midcareer faculty, even very effective teachers, can use the model proposed in the book to continue their development as teachers. It works as well for teachers who may be struggling. Thus, faculty across the entire teaching career can benefit from this book.

Effective Strategies That Promote Better Teaching

I believe that a hierarchical approach that places the locus of control with the instructor who wants to improve, rather than with others who need to judge teaching performance, provides a robust teaching enhancement process. This process best fosters the kind of teaching that promotes deep and intentional student learning. The approach I advocate integrates four well-supported and effective, but previously separate, teaching strategies. Each successive level is based on a separate strategy and incorporates data and insights for better teaching from the previous level. While much literature exists to support each of these strategies individually (Brew & Ginns, 2008; Brookfield, 1995; Kolb, 1984; Kreber, 2002), no one has yet suggested that the strategies be used together. Figure 1.1 shows how I integrate the strategies. Although the concepts of critical reflection with documentation, evidence-based decision making, and self-assessment are consistent with the standards of practice used in other professions and with accreditation standards, they are not commonly used to improve teaching. Using these four best practices strategies in a hierarchical way yields new insights that inform ways to advance teaching and learning.

In the following sections I summarize this process and note where you will find a detailed discussion of these concepts in this book.

Growth Strategy 1: Define the Essential Aspects of Teaching

In order to study teaching, you need to establish criteria that define teaching standards. Of the many descriptions of teaching, in this book I use Barr and Tagg's (1995) learning-centered approach to teaching. They focus on what the instructor does to promote student learning, and not on the instructor's behaviors as ends in themselves.

I categorize the essential aspects of effective teaching into three higher-order learning-centered guiding principles: the structure for teaching and learning itself, the instructor's design responsibilities outside the direct teaching responsibilities, and assessment of learning outcomes. Each principle entails various components:

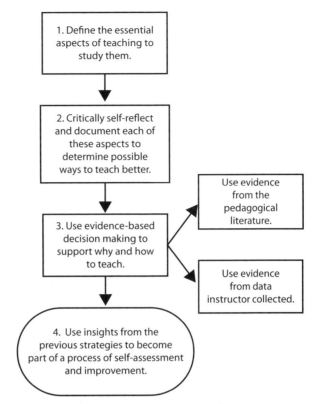

FIGURE 1.1   Four Effective Strategies for Improving Teaching: A Hierarchical Approach

Guiding Principle of Structure for Teaching and Learning

1. Plan educational experiences to promote student learning.

2. Provide feedback to students.

3. Provide reflection opportunities for students.

4. Use consistent policies and processes to assess students.

5. Ensure students have successful learning experiences through your availability and accessibility.

Guiding Principle of Instructional Design Responsibilities

6. Conduct reviews and revisions of teaching.

Guiding Principle of Learning Outcomes

7. Assess student mastery of learning outcomes relating to acquisition of knowledge, skills, or values.

8. Assess student mastery of higher-order thinking and skills: application, critical thinking, and problem solving.

9. Assess student mastery of learning skills and self-assessment skills that can transcend disciplinary content.

These aspects of teaching are shared whether the teaching is didactic instruction, offered online, or experiential, as in clinical or studio settings. Chapter 3 discusses these essential aspects of teaching and the various experiential contexts for teaching.

Growth Strategy 2: Begin and Integrate the Study of Your Teaching with Critical Self-Reflection

Critical self-reflection and documentation of each of these aspects helps determine possible ways to improve teaching. The analysis of teaching through critical self-reflection promotes better teaching, which leads to increased student learning (Brookfield, 1995; Kreber, 2002).

I recommend analyzing your teaching philosophies and classroom policies to understand how your teaching affects student learning and attitudes. With a solid understanding of what, how, and why you teach, you can begin to see how to enhance your teaching. Critical self-reflection yields insights into your teaching that you can use to identify possible areas to change (Weimer, 2010). With those identified, you can prioritize the list and decide which ones to work on now and which ones can wait. This critical self-reflection is not the same as self-assessment of teaching. Chapter 4 describes the literature supporting critical self-reflection and how you can use it to promote better teaching.

Documentation of this self-analysis is a vital part of the process. This documentation should include a description of your rationale, how you communicate it to students, directions for assignments, and evidence that students achieved the learning outcomes. All of parts 2 and 3 of this book discuss this documentation process and the many benefits that accrue from using it.

Growth Strategy 3: Use Evidence to Support Teaching

A system that incorporates evidence-based decision making is superior to relying on perceptions alone (Brew & Ginns, 2008). The concept of evidence-based decision making is consistent with the literature on higher education (Shulman, 2004a, 2004b; Smith, 2001) and with the accreditation standards that professional and regional accrediting agencies use. Yet most instructors do not integrate these practices into their teaching (Handelsman et al., 2004). One reason is that current evaluation tools do not require or even suggest their use. Unless they are motivated by evaluation results, faculty frequently feel little reason to adopt practices that require more effort. The approach to better teaching described in this book uses evidence-based teaching as a standard criterion for all teaching. This strategy has two separate aspects: it recommends reading the literature on teaching effectiveness and advocates collecting data on your own teaching.

Use Pedagogical Literature

Perhaps more than any other strategy, reading the pedagogical literature on teaching and learning in higher education and in your own discipline can improve your teaching (Brew & Ginns, 2008; Weimer, 2006). Lee Shulman (2004a) defines teaching that is designed based on this literature as scholarly. Knowing this literature enables teachers to make better decisions about the instructional design of their courses (Handelsman et al., 2004). This is analogous to health care professionals using their clinical literature to inform clinical decisions. Chapter 5 discusses the argument for why evidence-based teaching leads to improved deep and intentional student learning and identifies the steps you can take to become an evidence-based teacher. Chapter 6 describes how to find and evaluate appropriate literature.

Since the major goal of improving teaching is to increase student learning, it is necessary for teachers to understand how students learn effectively. Educational and psychological research offer many insights into how students learn. The following classic resources, which use less psychological lingo and synthesize many studies, may help you understand the learning process better.

Recommended Resources on the Learning Process

- American Psychological Association. (1997). *Learner-centered psychological principles: A framework for school reform and redesign.* www.apa .org/ed/governance/bea/learner-centered.pdf
- Alexander, P., & Murphy, P. (1998). The research base for APA's learner-centered psychological principles. In N. Lambert & B. McCombs (Eds.), *How students learn* (pp. 25–60). Washington, DC: American Psychological Association.
- Ambrose, S., Bridges, M., DiPietro, M., Lovett, M., & Norman, M. (2010). *How learning works.* San Francisco, CA: Jossey-Bass.
- Bransford, J., Brown, A., & Cocking, R. (Eds.). (2000). *How people learn: Brain, mind, experiences and School.* Washington, DC: National Academies Press.
- Lambert, N., & McCombs, B. (Eds.). (1998). *How students learn.* Washington, DC: American Psychological Association.

Collect Data Systematically

Collecting data on your teaching entails asking questions about the effectiveness of your teaching practices. For example, students can be asked to complete a survey about how much they learned from various activities in the class. The SALG online tool provides a straightforward structure to obtain this kind of information (www.salgsite.org). It is easy to develop a simple survey that asks students what is working, what could be improved, and any suggestions for improvement. Cross and Steadman (1996) offer many suggestions for collecting data from students. You can also ask peers to review your course materials and offer feedback on specific aspects of your teaching, such as clarity of directions on assignments or if your grading rubrics are objective and fair. Follow-up data on how well students performed on certain assignments or examinations in more advanced courses can also be useful feedback.

Growth Strategy 4: Self-Assess Your Teaching as a Development Vehicle

Document formative self-assessments of teaching as a continuous quality improvement process. The insights you gain from analyzing the information gathered in the first three strategies become part of the self-assessment and development process (Weimer, 2010). If you conduct this assessment in the spirit of fostering better teaching, you will reap many benefits. When information is provided as nonjudgmental feedback, you can more easily use the data to change what you are doing. These formative assessments of teaching have two primary goals: to increase student learning and enhance your teaching. The latter is really a subgoal of the former because the objective of improved teaching is more learning for students. When assessments include suggestions for improvement, they can motivate good teachers to become excellent teachers.

Constructive Assessments of Your Teaching

Comments made by students, peers, or chairs tend to be general and do not help with decisions about what or how to change. Students may offer feedback that the material was difficult to learn, but that feedback does not make clear whether the issue is with your teaching skills, the inherent nature of the content, or the amount of material to be learned. Furthermore, most assessment feedback is high stakes in that it is used to make summative decisions such as annual reviews or promotion. A fellow faculty developer underscored the need for useful assessments of teaching to help instructors to develop with this comment: "I was reminded of all the assistant professors who are forced to use comments from a summative review committee [e.g., a third-year review committee] to try to improve teaching. But a summative review committee is frequently not an effective source of feedback, in part because the feedback is usually too general and in part because criticism from a decision-making body is often too threatening to people's self-esteem for them to be able to hear and use that feedback."

This book proposes a more productive way to assess teaching while using the information gained from many sources. Most assessments focus on summative evaluations that others will use to make decisions. This book does not do that; instead it describes ways to conduct your own formative assessments of your teaching that generate feedback and thereby foster your development (Smith, 2001). You will explore your teaching processes using an integrated model that focuses on teaching that promotes increased student learning. This is not a top-down or one-size-fits-all evaluation of teaching.

Tactics for Better Teaching through Assessment

The goal of this assessment is to identify specific ways to change your teaching so that it fosters greater deep and intentional learning for your students. Figure 1.2 shows how it works.

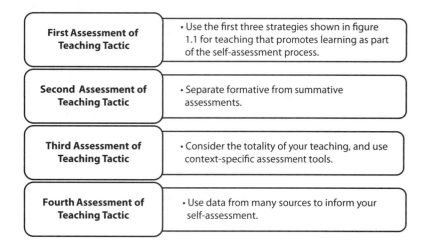

First Assessment of Teaching Tactic	• Use the first three strategies shown in figure 1.1 for teaching that promotes learning as part of the self-assessment process.
Second Assessment of Teaching Tactic	• Separate formative from summative assessments.
Third Assessment of Teaching Tactic	• Consider the totality of your teaching, and use context-specific assessment tools.
Fourth Assessment of Teaching Tactic	• Use data from many sources to inform your self-assessment.

FIGURE 1.2   Four Tactics for a Self-Assessment Process to Promote Faculty Growth and Student Learning

Assessment Tactic 1: Use the Growth Strategies to Promote Better Teaching in the Self-Assessment Process

You can critically self-reflect and document (strategy 2) each of the essential aspects of teaching listed in strategy 1. This enables you to identify which aspects of teaching that you can change to promote better teaching. Using evidence-based teaching as described in strategy 3 will reveal many possibilities for changes. With these steps taken together, you can construct an integrative self-assessment of your teaching. The last section of this chapter summarizes this assessment model. Parts 2 and 3 of this book show how all of these separate elements lead to an assessment model and tools for self-assessment.

Assessment Tactic 2: Separate Formative from Summative Assessments

Most assessments are summative because data are usually collected to inform promotion and tenure decisions. For example, when assembling a teaching portfolio, teachers try to select material that puts their teaching in the best light. They select the most positive comments for inclusion in the portfolio and include only the highest course evaluation scores. But formative assessments are conducted for the purpose of improvement. Here the feedback identifies both strengths and weaknesses. Current evaluation methods do not make adequate distinctions between these two purposes. Instructors often use the same tools, such as student evaluations of courses and peer observations, for both formative and summative assessments (Dewar, 2011).

Current assessment procedures rarely identify what specifically needs to change because they don't ask the right questions (Weimer, 2010). Summative assessments do not ask probing questions that yield detailed information on specific aspects of teaching. Since the purposes of the intended assessments in this book are to increase student learning through better teaching, the focus is exclusively on formative assessments. I will show how to use data from current tools in a more critical and reflective manner and also how new tools offer other insights that will lead to better teaching.

Assessment Tactic 3: Consider the Totality of Your Teaching, and Use Context-Specific Assessment Tools

Teaching is far more than just what happens in the classroom. Teachers design courses, develop syllabi, prepare for each class session, grade assignments, and work with students individually. Yet most assessments of teaching focus on what happens in class. Student course evaluations generally assess only teacher performance. Peers observe only one or two class sessions and might not look at course materials. Thus, these kinds of assessments do not provide data that consider teaching holistically.

Furthermore, many now teach in places outside the traditional classroom. Online teaching requires different skills and assessments needed to consider these unique aspects of teaching. Some teachers supervise students in experiential settings such as in community fieldwork or service-learning, mentoring students in research, or work completed in studio settings. Most teaching assessments ignore these other types of teaching despite their importance and role in student learning (Kuh, Kinzie, Schuh, & Whitt, 2005).

To examine all of these teaching roles, we consider these various contexts for teaching: I will introduce specific tools to reflect the unique aspects of teaching in different contexts in part 3. These tools look at the same essential aspects of effective teaching as listed in strategy 1. There are also components that are unique to specific situations. I include examples of instructors who teach in different contexts and have used this system to gain insights into how they can teach more effectively.

Specific Types of Teaching or Teaching Contexts

- Teaching a course face-to-face or online where teachers have autonomy
- Teaching a course face-to-face or online where teachers have limited autonomy
- Mentoring undergraduate, graduate students, or postdoctoral fellows in research or an engineering project
- Precepting or supervising students in clinical, field, or community settings
- Teaching in studio settings in the visual or graphic arts
- Teaching in theater or music or conservatory settings in the performing arts
- Directing clinical work, experiential education, or service-learning

I introduce specific tools to reflect the unique aspects of teaching in different contexts in part 3. These tools look at the same essential aspects of effective teaching as listed in strategy 1. There are also components that are unique to specific situations. I include examples of instructors who teach in different contexts and have used this system to gain insights into how they can teach more effectively.

Assessment Tactic 4: Use Data from Many Sources to Inform Your Self-Assessment

These four strategies for effective teaching suggest many possible sources of data to inform self-assessments. Critical self-assessments should integrate information from all these sources: students, peers, chairs, the literature on how learning occurs, and your own insights. This book shows how you can integrate data about teaching so that your understanding of how your teaching has an impact on student learning. That insight then makes it possible for you to implement changes that will produce the deep and intentional learning you and all other teachers desire for their students.

Informative and Constructive Assessment Model for Better Teaching

My analysis of what happens now and my ideas for strengthening the formative nature of assessment led me to construct a layered hierarchy. This hierarchy is represented by an inverted pyramid in figure 1.3 and reflects the four strategies to promote better teaching in classroom, online, and experience settings. I used an inverted pyramid to reflect the lack of support most faculty have for their current ways of studying their teaching. Each layer on the hierarchy going up the pyramid increases the support for the teaching assessment. Currently most instructors uncritically summarize what others say about their teaching as the main method to determine their teaching effectiveness. Generally this information does not lead to insights into how to teach better. Therefore, I place the nonreflective summaries at the bottom of the pyramid, with the least support. As instructors move up the inverted pyramid, they must incorporate the lower levels.

Furthermore, I integrated the strategies for better teaching, the layered hierarchy, and assessment tactics into an informative and constructive formative assessment model. If you collect data from many sources and not just from student course evaluations, you will have a much richer database on which to base your assessment of what is working and what you could change. Once you use pedagogical literature to support your teaching decisions, you will be using best practices in your teaching, and your teaching will be evidence based. Finally, if you conduct rigorous and systematic research on your teaching, you will know how effective your teaching is. You can visualize this model as a formative assessment matrix for classroom, online, and experiential teaching as shown in table 1.1. The columns in table 1.1 are a progression. Table 1.1 shows that the increasing quality of teaching standards can be applied to the essential aspects of effective teaching.

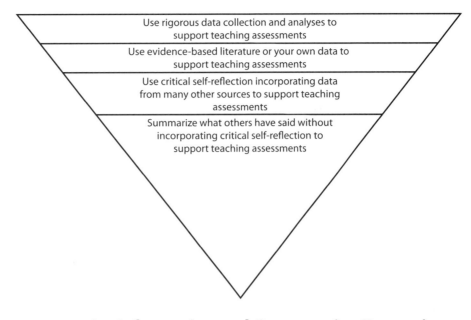

Use rigorous data collection and analyses to support teaching assessments

Use evidence-based literature or your own data to support teaching assessments

Use critical self-reflection incorporating data from many other sources to support teaching assessments

Summarize what others have said without incorporating critical self-reflection to support teaching assessments

FIGURE 1.3   An Informative and Constructive Formative Assessment Model for Faculty Growth and Student Learning

TABLE 1.1   Formative Assessment Matrix for Didactic and Experiential Teaching

Essential Aspects of Teaching by Context as Defined by . . .	Increasing Quality of Teaching Standards			
	Summarize what others have said without incorporating critical self-reflection to support teaching assessments	Use critical self-reflection incorporating data from many other sources to support teaching assessments	Use evidence-based literature or own data to support teaching assessments	Use rigorous data collection and analyses to support teaching assessments
The structure for teaching and learning				
The instructor's design responsibilities				
Assessment of learning outcomes				

Rubrics as Self-Assessment Tools

I use this matrix to create self-assessment rubrics. The essential aspects of teaching are the criteria to be assessed on the rubrics. The layered hierarchy can easily be transformed into the standards or levels on rubrics for assessing teaching, as table 1.1 illustrates. The column headings represent the layers of the hierarchy and become the standards or levels on self-assessment of teaching rubrics. The lowest level (on the left column of the hierarchy) does not contribute to personal growth efforts. Using any of the strategies required for the top three levels can lead to increased insights into effective teaching. Moving to the right or to be rated at a higher level requires meeting all of the criteria in previous levels; thus, they are cumulative. Effective teaching occurs at the second level (use critical self-reflection) and at the two higher levels. Most professors probably cannot do rigorous data collection for the majority of their teaching, but it is possible to use relevant literature and make your practice more evidence based. Part 3 describes these rubrics and how they can be used in more detail. The seven sets of rubrics can be found on online at www.jossey-bass.com/go/Blumberg.

Summary

Teaching is composed of many different skills that can be learned. Just like other skills, such as playing the piano or driving a car, instructors can improve their mastery of these skills with feedback and practice (McKeachie, 2007). This book describes a systematic, ongoing process model that faculty members can use throughout their career for continuous growth. This model is a comprehensive growth plan, not a quick fix. Easy ways, just like promised miracle cures or diets, rarely work. Using this model helps teachers in ways that lead to increased learning for most students. It is not necessary to complete all of the steps at once. Periodic critical reflection of teaching can lead to growth. Furthermore, reading a few good review articles on effective teaching methods can inspire you to change your teaching. The ongoing commitment and continuing but small efforts can have a large impact on your teaching effectiveness.

This process for systematic growth places the locus of control with instructors who want to improve rather than with external audiences who want to judge, and it deals with formative rather than summative assessment. Using this model, all faculty members will be able to teach so that students will acquire deep and intentional learning.

PART 1

A TEACHING MODEL THAT PROMOTES BETTER LEARNING

Chapter 2

Beliefs Leading to Better Teaching

TEACHING IS AN INTEGRAL part of every academic career. At some institutions, such as community and liberal arts colleges, it is the most important part of the academic job. Even at research universities, faculty are expected to teach, and not to teach poorly. Higher education's many stakeholders—parents, legislators, future employers, and, especially, students—all expect teaching to be excellent.

Nationally instructors spend more time on teaching than on all aspects of research and service (Carey, 2009). Universally, faculty believe that the most essential role of teaching is to foster student learning (Smith, 2001). In higher education, this learning is not defined as just memorization of facts, but a higher level of learning. For example, the 2007–2008 Higher Education Research Institute survey reports that 95 percent of instructors feel that fostering student development in critical thinking and knowledge acquisition is an essential or very important part of their jobs in academia (Higher Education Research Institute at UCLA, 2009). These are noble goals, but they are often hard to achieve.

Effective Teaching

Effective teaching helps students to learn more and reach the desired learning outcomes. Your expectations for students are related to your own expectations and beliefs about your teaching. When you maintain high expectations for your students, the students tend to rise to these elevated standards. Furthermore, when you believe you are capable of effective teaching, your students make the highest gains in their learning (Miller, 2009). The concept of efficacy, or the perceived ability to produce the desired result, interacts with faculty development efforts. Instructors with a high sense of self-efficacy probably work hard at teaching, often adapting their methods to their students' varying characteristics and abilities. Unfortunately, instructors with low teaching efficacy often do not engage in teaching renewal efforts but continue teaching the same way they have previously. But there is good news: all instructors can learn to be effective.

Most instructors need concrete guidance to make these changes. Very effective instructors make an ongoing commitment to faculty development and improvement (Miller, 2009). This development involves exploring new teaching methods, experimenting with different educational technologies, and learning how the latest cohort of students differs from previous generations. Professors may seek ways to improve teaching while also increasing efficiency in teaching time and effectiveness. Research also shows that when teaching is improved, students learn more (Miller, 2009).

Misconceptions and Accurate Beliefs about Teaching

Many academics harbor misconceptions about teaching that hamper their ability to teach better. Just as it is important to help students overcome their misconceptions about content, we need to replace our misconceptions with more accurate ideas. Table 2.1 lists common misconceptions about teaching and alternative, accurate beliefs that foster growth. The following sections discuss each misconception and its alternative. These beliefs have important implications for how to teach better. Instructors employ different approaches depending on their notions about teaching.

Teaching Model

Currently there are two general approaches to teaching: traditional instructor centered and learning centered. In the older approach, *teach*, as its definition implies, is a transitive verb in which one person imparts knowledge or skills to others by instruction or example. While many professors are adopting the newer learning-centered approach to teaching, others have not changed their teaching practices. I like to view these approaches on a continuum from teacher centered to learning centered. I advocate for instructors to strive to implement more learning-centered approaches because they promote greater student learning. (Blumberg, 2009a).

TABLE 2.1   Ideas about Teaching

Teaching Construct	Misconception	Belief That Fosters Growth
Teaching model	Teaching by its definition focuses on what the instructor does.	Teaching should focus on the intended outcome: student learning.
Teaching is not intuitive	Faculty members in higher education intuitively know how to teach since they are subject matter specialists.	Effective teaching is not intuitive. Faculty members can learn effective techniques.
Teaching is a scholarly pursuit	Teaching is not a scholarly pursuit like research.	Effective teaching should employ scholarly approaches.
Teaching uses evidence-based practices	Many faculty members do not read the literature on the scholarship of teaching and learning and pedagogy. This literature is confusing and misunderstood, perhaps a reason for its lack of universal acceptance.	Effective teaching uses evidence-based practices.
Teaching contexts	Teaching takes place in the classroom; teaching is didactic.	Varied contexts for teaching; teaching and learning are integrated.

In 1995 Barr and Tagg proposed a paradigm shift in what we consider effective teaching. They began an international movement toward the implementation of learning-centered teaching. It is not just their idea that students' learning is inherently related to good teaching, it is also scientifically based. A large body of educational and cognitive sciences research supports the use of learning-centered teaching (Doyle, 2011; Weimer, 2013). As a result of this shift in paradigms, centers for teaching excellence enlarged the scope of their work as faculty developers to include more emphasis on student learning (Johnson, 2009). Since the purpose of this book is to improve student learning, I frame how to teach better using learning-centered teaching. The essential aspects of teaching, discussed in chapter 3, assume this learning-centered approach and summarize some of this literature.

Implications for Better Teaching

The traditional approach focuses on what the teacher does. Generally the locus of development efforts is improving the dissemination of information, since that is considered the primary role of professors in the traditional, teacher-centered model. Therefore, efforts to improve teaching usually concentrate on improving lectures. Using that model, the instructor alone, or with a colleague or a faculty development expert, might analyze a video recording of a class to identify strengths and weaknesses of the lecture. For example, when professors use the teacher-centered model, they might try to develop more elaborate presentation slides or work to eliminate the "ums" or "you knows" in their lectures. Efforts to teach better using learning-centered approaches would include other considerations.

While improving the quality and appeal of presentations to students remains important in the learning-centered approach, instructors also focus on learning outcomes or on ways to increase student learning. When striving to teach better with this approach, instructors consider how they might redesign their courses, how and what they teach, and how they assess students. Using the learning-centered model when they are endeavoring to teach better, instructors will create an environment that facilitates learning for all students, helps students to assume responsibility for their learning, and gives students frequent feedback on their mastery of content and skills before assigning final grades.

Teaching Is Not Intuitive

Unlike teachers in primary and secondary school, faculty members traditionally did not receive any training or become certified as teachers. When I was in my first year of graduate school as a teaching assistant, I conducted recitation sections and graded assignments. After a year, I was assigned to teach an evening course entirely on my own. I was in my mid-twenties. All of my students were older than I was, and many had years of real-world experience that I lacked. I felt intimidated and ill prepared to teach them. Yet I received no formal training in teaching and little supervision.

Although there was a writing center where I could get help in writing my dissertation and a statistical consulting center, there were no supports for teaching, especially for inexperienced teachers. Teaching was assumed to be intuitive. After all, I had attended over sixteen years of school and had the opportunity to observe many teachers. It was deemed more important for me to have a command of the subject matter I was teaching.

My experience was similar to that of many other graduate students in the 1970s. Many of my North American cohorts of graduate students are still teaching in higher education. Therefore, many experienced professors and adjunct instructors have not been trained how to teach. They may not have been required to think much about the teaching process either.

The situation is improving for graduate students and faculty today. Teaching is no longer considered intuitive for inexperienced or even experienced faculty. Many doctoral institutions sponsor Preparing Future Faculty programs, where graduate students learn effective teaching techniques and are supervised in their teaching experiences. Instructors interested in teaching better can seek the advice of experienced or well-regarded senior professors. Now, most colleges and universities have faculty development support in the form of a teaching center or at least faculty members who can be called on for advice on teaching. Many institutions run orientations to assist new faculty to teach better.

Implications for Better Teaching

Many people assume that faculty members in higher education intuitively know how to teach since they are subject matter specialists (Blumberg, 2011). Faculty members often taught and perhaps continue to teach how they were taught, probably without giving much thought to the teaching/ learning process in general or in their discipline. Using this seat-of-the-pants approach, many professors focus their thinking about teaching on the content to teach and how to deliver it clearly, not on how to maximize student learning of the content. Thus, they may often use lectures that encourage student passivity. These methods are becoming increasingly less effective with the millennial or totally wired generation and with the greater diversity of students in higher education (DiPietro, 2012; Howe & Strauss, 2007). Moreover, professors may not know there are more effective techniques to foster learning.

You can learn effective teaching techniques that improve student learning. In addition to teaching and learning or faculty development centers, you can read from a large collection of print and online resources on teaching effectively. You can attend conferences that concentrate on teaching in higher education or attend educational sessions at your discipline-specific conferences. Today there is a much greater emphasis on teaching effectively than there was at the beginning of my career.

In the rest of the book, I discuss many techniques for effective teaching, some of them derived from the psychological and cognitive sciences. I also describe models of teaching that have been widely used and the experiences of individual successful teachers.

Teaching Is a Scholarly Pursuit

Traditionally professors saw research and teaching as different aspects of their jobs. They did not have to consider teaching methods before teaching as they would consider research methods before beginning a scholarship project. Teaching, unlike research, was not a common topic of discussion with others (Shulman, 2004a).

Over twenty years ago, Ernest Boyer (1990) argued that academics should employ the same scholarship standards in their teaching that they use with their scholarly research work. Boyer was a former commissioner of education for the United States and president of the Carnegie Foundation for the Advancement of Teaching when he began promoting this entirely new idea, which met, and continues to meet, resistance from those in academia. However, since then, other influential people in higher education have been advocating the incorporation of systematic methods, literature, and data-driven support into teaching (Cross & Steadman, 1996; Shulman, 2004a, 2004b; Weimer, 2006). In line with what they say, we should be basing how and why we teach on sound research, which makes the practice of teaching more objective. When all of this happens, teaching becomes part of our scholarly work. More effective teaching is anchored in investigations of what is working and why (Shulman, 2004b). Investigations of a particular topic, such as how students learn their discipline or effective grading, are based on pedagogical literature. Consequently teaching quality is enhanced (Shulman, 2004b; Weimer, 2006). Scholarly approaches to teaching and learning can help us to become distinguished teachers and can improve teaching overall in higher education (Shulman, 2004a, 2004b). In chapter 5 I discuss a developmental approach to integrating scholarly attitudes in teaching.

Although the argument for using scholarly teaching is quite sound and logical and is consistent with the literature on higher education and the accreditation standards that professional and regional educational accrediting agencies use, most academics do not implement this best practice (Shulman, 2004a; Weimer, 2006). Even authors who propose its use lament that the academy at large has failed to embrace these scholarly approaches as the norm for teaching expectations. Many professors in fact may question why teaching needs to be research based.

Because most instructors do not consider teaching as a perpetual experiment, teaching in higher education has not improved as much as it could have (Edgerton, 2004). Perhaps because teaching is not as valued as research at many institutions, instructors may teach without knowing how to teach effectively or even that a growing literature explores how to teach to maximize learning. When faculty members do not know research-supported, effective teaching methods, they may make decisions based on tradition or on how they experienced teaching.

Implications for Better Teaching

Faculty development efforts without a scholarly approach often involved trying to change teaching on the basis of course evaluations completed by students and peer or chair observations of teaching. Instructors who desire to teach better would rarely think of looking in the literature on teaching in higher education. However, with a scholarly approach to teaching, faculty development is based on literature or systematic investigations into effective teaching. If you want to teach better, read the literature on teaching in higher education in general or teaching in your own discipline. A faculty developer might assist you to identify this pedagogical literature.

Shulman (2004a) called teaching a solitary activity because faculty members rarely share teaching experiences to try to improve their teaching. An advantage of using a scholarly approach to teaching is that instructors talk about teaching more with colleagues. You can model your changes based on what others have found to be effective. Shulman (2004a) says this moves teaching from a solitary activity to community property in that more people discuss their teaching and it becomes more valued by the academy (Shulman, 2004a). These informal discussions can also provide opportunities for faculty development.

Teaching Use Evidence-Based Practices

Few instructors routinely read the literature on teaching in higher education for many reasons. Many believe that the scholarship of teaching and learning and pedagogy are intimidating concepts because they were not trained how to teach or how to do research on their teaching (Blumberg, 2011). The literature may appear off-putting to them since it is unlike what they usually read. Instructors may not feel eligible to be a scholar about their teaching or even read the scholarly literature since they believe they lack the right research skill sets. After all, they did not learn these skills in graduate school and have not been required to learn them until now. Furthermore, they probably perceive a lack of time to acquire an additional research domain.

In addition, the literature on pedagogy and the scholarly approach to teaching is confusing because the nomenclature in this area is not consistent and clear. For example, authors do not even agree on what pedagogy is. Some people believe that *pedagogy* refers only to teaching children since it has the same prefix, *ped,* as *pediatrician.* Therefore, they believe, it does not apply to higher education. These authors, especially Malcolm Knowles (1984), prefer *andragogy,* which means teaching to adults. The role of personal data collection in scholarly approaches to teaching is another component of this confusion. Some authors use the term *scholarship of teaching and learning* only when the faculty member engages in research on teaching; others use the term when people base their teaching on data-driven best practices even if they did not collect the data themselves. The literature does not answer the question, "Do professors have to engage in their own data collection, or can they rely on the data reported in the literature to be considered using scholarly approaches to their teaching?"

This confusion can be alleviated by not using the terms *pedagogy* and *scholarship of teaching and learning*. In their place, I use *evidence-based decision making*. While the term *evidence based* is not new, it does not carry the baggage that has come to be associated with the other terms. For a variety of reasons, *evidence-based teaching* more accurately reflects my goals for effective teaching than *scholarship of teaching*. *Evidence* is not an educational term, but one widely used in many disciplines. Currently many professionals make decisions based on research-supported best practices. Just as is routinely done in medicinal practice, we should be basing how and why we teach on sound research-based evidence (Alberts, 2012).

Using evidence to support teaching has similarities to the research process that instructors might use in their own area. The most striking parallel is that inquiry in either the discipline or in teaching begins with a review of the literature. Evidence-based decision making is systematic and rigorous, just as research in the academic disciplines is. Furthermore, the type of research done in the disciplines, such as qualitative or quantitative, can inform the study of teaching (Shulman, 2004a).

Implications for Faculty Development

Faculty development involves learning about different types of satisfactory evidence on teaching. Instructors, often with the assistance of faculty developers or librarians, can identify relevant pedagogical literature in higher education to guide their improvement process. Evidence can offer different ways to teach, even best practices, that instructors may not have known about before. (In chapter 5 I discuss evidence-based instructional methods that can be used in most courses.) A further step for instructors is to systematically gather data on their own teaching effectiveness. Faculty developers may collaborate with instructors on how to obtain evidence on effective teaching. Not all faculty will gather their own data, but all faculty can benefit from evidence reported in the literature.

Once instructors know about evidence-based decision making, they can incorporate such practices into their own teaching. Faced with evidence and a desire to improve teaching, they probably will want to use the best teaching methods that lead to the most learning. When instructors use evidence to support their teaching, they can feel supported in their teaching. Thus, the use of evidence should lead to better teaching and improved accountability.

Teaching Contexts

Within classroom teaching, there are many different teaching approaches, from lectures to seminars to small group discussions. Yet many people have the stereotype in higher education that teaching means didactic instruction because classes are often called lectures. Today many instructors are not lecturing but actively engaging students in the classroom. In learning-centered teaching, the students are actively participating in the class.

Online Learning

Increasingly instructors engage in many other kinds of teaching, including using online and blended or a combination of face-to-face and online pedagogies. Here, the concept of lecture needs to take on unconventional forms. In today's connected world, students can access information online from many sources. Therefore, recording a lecture for students to view is not the most effective way to disseminate information. In blended courses, students meet with their teachers fewer hours per week than in the past, and the students do more work on their own outside class.

Instructors need to structure their courses so that students take responsibility for their learning and successfully meet out-of-class obligations. Keeping students engaged is a major task for online instructors. Professors also need to address the questions of students individually without the course consuming too much of the their time. Online courses often assess students through projects where they apply the knowledge and skills gained instead of traditional multiple choice tests. The line between learning and assessment is often blurred as learning activities get graded.

Teaching in Experiential Settings

Authors of textbooks often use straightforward, streamlined, and clear problems. In didactic instruction, instructors prefer well-defined problems and situations because they illustrate a point and are easy for students to master. However, the real world is complex and often ill defined. In courses, learning is compartmentalized by disciplines, whereas in authentic settings, it is organized around problems or practice. There is a lack of congruity between how students learn in traditional classrooms and how they will need to learn once they are out of school (Resnick, 1987). Ideally, experiential education complements the desired course-specific learning outcomes because it helps student bridge what they learned in courses to real-world situations. During experiential education, students usually encounter ill-structured problems that do not have one correct answer or even any solutions. They need to tolerate ambiguity and make judgments with incomplete information in these settings.

Research studies consistently show that when students participate in enriching educational activities, they are more engaged with the learning and graduation rates increase (Kuh, Kinzie, Schuh, & Whitt, 2005). Many of these enriching educational activities take place in experiential education such as in field placements. In fact, the Association of American Colleges and Universities has identified service-learning, research in laboratories and in the community, cooperatives, and internships as educational practices that research shows have a high impact on undergraduate student learning in the liberal arts (Freeland, 2009). In these high-impact practices, academic knowledge is transformed into knowledge-in-use that leads to effective action (Eyler, 2009). Experiential learning is also referred to as *situational learning* because it takes place in real settings under the guidance of experts or practitioners in the field (Bransford, Brown, & Cocking, 2000). Psychologists consider situational learning to be effective, powerful education. During these experiential learning encounters, students apply what they learned in courses to new situations as they move from theory to practice. These experiences help students to synthesize and integrate their learning. Experiential learning leads to deeper and better understanding of content because it was used in a real situation (Eyler, 2009). This learning is exactly what we are seeking: deep and intentional.

Experiential opportunities have always been a major part of professional or clinical education; now they are also common for undergraduate students. The National Survey of Student Engagement, which surveys thousands of American students in their fourth year of college, found that more than half of the senior respondents participated in some form of experiential experience, including practicums, internships, or clinical assignments (Carey, 2009). Examples of experiential teaching are

- mentoring students in research or engineering design projects,
- precepting or supervising clinical, community field work, cooperatives, or service-learning,
- supervising students in practicums or internships, and
- teaching in conservatory, visual, performing, or fine arts.

In addition to traditional classroom teaching, many instructors engage in supervising students in experiential learning because these pedagogies lead to increased student engagement and learning (Kuh et al., 2005). Yet most administrators and faculty see them as marginal to the whole curriculum (O'Neill, 2010). Although it is time-consuming and labor intensive, it is beneficial to students. Experiential teaching can be individualized and intense, and the ratio of teacher to students is often lower than with didactic instruction. About one-third of all faculty members, many of whom are at the lower ranks of academia or are adjunct faculty, and are often women or people of color, supervise students in community or clinical settings (Astin & Vogelgesang, 2006). When professors who mentor student research or teach in nonclassroom settings in the arts are included, probably about half of the teaching staff in higher education is involved in experiential teaching.

As we are increasingly recognizing the important learning that takes place in experiential education, we need to recognize that individuals in these settings are also engaged in vital teaching. In all of these experiential settings, instructors can benefit from guidance to help them teach more effectively.

Implications for Faculty Development

Just as many believe that most teaching occurs in the classroom, most efforts to improve teaching are also concerned with the didactic aspects of teaching. Yet teaching and learning increasingly occur outside the classroom. Because the demands on professors who are teaching in online and blended courses are unique, they need training in these areas to be effective teachers (Palsole & Brunk-Chavez, 2011). Furthermore, some untrained instructors in experiential settings supervise students without giving adequate consideration to the teaching and learning process. If instructors in experiential or online settings desire to teach better, they must consciously create ways to maximize student learning. We know this is not often the case, however, because students sometimes complain that they do the same jobs again and again, probably because these jobs need to be done in experiential settings and also because the instructor has not planned realistic educational experiences. Perhaps the most important faculty development efforts for experiential instructors are improving and increasing the opportunities for students to reflect on their experiences to make their learning more meaningful (Eyler, 2009; Qualters, 2010).

Beliefs about Teaching and Their Corollary Implications for Better Teaching

I discussed five teaching misconceptions and have proposed an alternative set of beliefs central to this book. An ongoing commitment to faculty development and improvement should lead to better teaching. However, if instructors have misconceptions about teaching, their faculty improvement efforts may not be entirely productive. When more accurate alternative beliefs about teaching form the basis for growth efforts, better teaching is a more likely outcome. Table 2.2 summarizes and integrates the misconceptions and accurate beliefs and their corollary implications for better teaching. Start reading this table from the center column, "Question about Teaching Construct," and then read toward the margins.

TABLE 2.2   Beliefs and Corollary Implications When Striving to Teach Better

Misconception		Question about Teaching Construct	Belief That Fosters Growth	
Corollary Implication for Better Teaching	← Idea		Idea →	Corollary Implication for Better Teaching
Better teaching is primarily concerned with how information is disseminated.	Teaching by its definition focuses on what the instructor does.	What should effective teaching focus on?	Teaching should focus on the intended outcomes, especially student learning.	Efforts to teach better expand to include many ways to improve the environment for learning.
There is no need for organized faculty development efforts.	Faculty members in higher education intuitively know how to teach since they are subject matter specialists.	Is teaching intuitive, or can instructors try to learn effective teaching approaches?	Effective teaching is not intuitive. Faculty can learn effective teaching strategies.	Efforts to teach better help instructors learn, implement, and assess effective teaching strategies.
Efforts to teach better do not need to be based on literature on the scholarship of teaching and learning and pedagogy.	Teaching is not a scholarly pursuit like research.	What roles do the literature on scholarship of teaching and learning and pedagogy play in teaching?	Effective teaching should employ scholarly approaches.	Efforts to teach better include knowing the pedagogical literature in higher education and in one's discipline.
Efforts to teach better do not need to be supported by evidence-based pedagogical practices.	The literature on scholarship of teaching and learning and pedagogy is confusing and misunderstood.	What roles do pedagogy and evidence-based practice play in teaching?	Effective teaching uses evidence-based practices.	Efforts to teach better should be supported by evidence-based pedagogical literature or investigations into effective teaching practices.
Efforts to teach better are primarily concerned with didactic teaching.	Teaching takes place in the classroom; teaching is didactic.	How does the context of teaching affect how instructors teach?	There are varied contexts for teaching; teaching and learning are integrated.	Efforts to teach better expand to many varied teaching contexts.

Suggestions for Better Teaching Coming from This Chapter

- Misconceptions of teaching inhibit better teaching; therefore, instructors should confront these misconceptions.

- Consider alternative beliefs of teaching that can foster better teaching.

- Use a learning-centered approach to teaching because it focuses improvement efforts on what instructors can do to promote more student learning.

- Teaching in all contexts is not intuitive; instructors can learn effective teaching techniques and practices.

- Use teaching practices that are based on the pedagogical literature in higher education in general and in your own discipline and best educational practices.

- Effective teaching uses evidence-based practices.

- Your faculty development efforts should be context specific.

Chapter 3

Essential Aspects of Effective Teaching

USING A LEARNING-CENTERED approach to teaching, I integrate the various components of teaching into three higher-order guiding principles: the structure for teaching and learning, instructional design responsibility, and learning outcomes. From reviewing the literature on teaching in higher education and my work with faculty in different contexts, I have characterized these guiding principles by their essential aspects. This chapter summarizes the psychological and educational literature for eleven essential aspects of learning-centered teaching, listed in box 3.1. As you read these literature synopses, consider how to teach better using these components. If you are unfamiliar with any of the terms I use, refer to the literature cited for more descriptions.

Box 3.1. Essential Aspects of Teaching Common to All Learning Contexts

Guiding Principle of Structure for Teaching and Learning

1. Plan educational experiences to promote student learning.
2. Provide feedback to students to foster learning.
3. Provide reflection opportunities for students.
4. Use consistent policies and processes to assess students.
5. Ensure students have successful learning experiences through your availability and accessibility.

Guiding Principle of Instructional Design Responsibilities

6. Align learning outcomes.
7. Organize content to facilitate learning.
8. Conduct reviews and revisions of teaching.

Guiding Principle of Learning Outcomes

9. Assess students' mastery of learning outcomes relating to acquisition of knowledge, skills, or values.
10. Assess students' mastery of higher-order thinking skills: application, critical thinking, and problem solving.
11. Assess students' mastery of learning skills or self-assessment skills.

These components are essential facets of effective learning-centered teaching in traditional classrooms, online courses, and experiential settings. Although differences between teaching in these varied settings exist, there are many more similarities. These essential aspects are not discipline specific; they apply to all kinds of teaching. In my view, it is the contexts of teaching that direct the teaching process and not the disciplines.

Structure for Teaching and Learning

Although many instructors believe that their primary function as teachers is to cover content, that is not enough to foster learning. Learning-centered instructors consciously structure the teaching and learning environment so that students have opportunities to learn by constructing their own meaning of the content (Blumberg, 2009a). When new instructors ask me how to plan courses, I often give them a rough rule that less than half of their planning for their classes involves deciding on the content and its order. More than half of the planning for teaching is actively developing an environment that is most conducive to learning. The next section discusses ways instructors can develop such an environment.

Educational Experiences to Promote Student Learning

Effective instructors plan educational experiences to promote student learning using these common elements:

- develop learning outcomes to direct course planning,
- relate these learning outcomes to students' acquisition of knowledge, problem solving, critical thinking skills, and values, and

- use these outcomes to select appropriate teaching and learning methods and educational technologies.

Learning Outcomes

Learning outcomes are central to the teaching and learning process (Biggs, 1999; Fink, 2003). Developing learning outcomes is the first critical step in course planning as they set the direction for the entire learning process. They frame the content to be learned and guide appropriate assessments of learning. Learning outcomes inform students of intentions and direct student study efforts. Finally they help both instructors and their students monitor their progress (Ambrose, Bridges, DiPietro, Lovett, & Norman, 2010).

A Note about Interrelated and Confusing Terms: Learning Outcomes and Learning Objectives

Learning outcomes are the big picture, often complex goals that instructors expect students to achieve or learn by the end of the course. They should be stated in terms of student performance, not what the instructor hopes to achieve, such as what content will be covered. *Learning outcomes* are also called instructional goals (Diamond, 2008; Nilson, 2003). *Learning objectives* are smaller units of learning that flow directly from the learning outcomes. While a course may have about five larger learning outcomes, each learning outcome may have a few learning objectives associated with it. For example, learning objectives may describe what students will learn from the discussion in a specific class. The literature often interchanges *learning outcomes* and *learning objectives*. In this book, I am referring to the larger learning outcomes.

During the last half of the twentieth century educators developed objectives using Benjamin Bloom's taxonomy to describe learning experiences (Bloom, 1956). This taxonomy reflects the behaviorist psychological theories of learning that were accepted in the 1950s and 1960s and identified a hierarchy of levels of cognitive learning from recall to evaluate. Objectives could also be in the psychomotor or affective domain. Courses often had such a long list of behavioral objectives that faculty became frustrated and limited their teaching innovations (Diamond, 2008). With the move toward more accountability and the focus on learning as opposed to teaching, educators are now using learning outcomes.

You have various learning taxonomies to choose from when developing learning outcomes. Some of Bloom's original team, along with other scholars (Anderson & Krathwohl, 2001), modified Bloom's taxonomy to be more consistent with current theories of learning and considers a hierarchy of types of cognitive processes (similar to the verbs used in Bloom's taxonomy) required to learn and four nonhierarchical types of knowledge: factual, conceptual, procedural and metacognitive. L. Dee Fink (2003) offers a very different taxonomy of learning by identifying six types of significant learning: fundamental knowledge, application, integration, human dimension, caring, and learning how to learn. Choose the learning taxonomy that best suits your learning goals.

Teaching/Learning Methods

I call this element of this aspect *teaching/learning methods* because I see them combined into one process with a learning-centered approach. Learning is now an integral part of the teaching process. Instead of only lecturing to students, instructors now engage students in many different active learning activities, including role playing, simulations, debates, case studies, small group learning, and problem-based learning (Fink, 2003). Learners need to interpret content in ways that make it meaningful to them, not just hear or read it. Teaching/learning methods can also occur out of the classroom as assignments or in online learning.

Active learning methods that foster deep and intentional learning often involve interactions with others. In these situations, students take control of their own learning. Active learning through discussing the content or solving problems in small groups leads to better long-term retention and the ability to use the material in new situations in the future. When students articulate their ideas to their peers, hear what others have to say about these ideas, and collaborate on an instructional task, their conceptual learning improves (Bransford, Brown, & Cocking, 2000; Fox & Hackerman, 2003; Kuh, Kinzie, Schuh, & Whitt, 2005; McKeachie, 2007; Resnick, 1991).

Most concepts and tasks in higher education are complex, involving different component skills, cognitive processes, and many different facts. To help students learn, instructors need to break down these complex concepts or tasks into their component parts, provide students opportunities to perform these skills or cognitive processes separately, and then allow them to practice the integrated tasks before assessing them. Instructors can point out the key aspects of the task so students know where to concentrate their efforts (Ambrose et al., 2010). Reading the educational literature on this topic can be useful as others may have conducted research on how to teach this concept. Sometimes instructors have trouble seeing these components as distinct because they appear so integrated. An advanced student or teaching assistant can help unpack these components.

When students engage in authentic learning, defined as solving real-world problems, they become more motivated to learn deeply and with intention. Often students work collaboratively and use technology as they carry out these tasks. Authentic learning promotes the development of critical thinking and the ability to organize and use information and creativity (Doyle, 2011).

Acquisition of Knowledge, Skills, and Values

The contemporary view of learning is defined as knowledge construction. Psychological research shows that the most effective learning occurs when students build their own associations between new information and their previous knowledge base, not when they memorize how others have framed it (Alexander & Murphy, 1998; Mayer, 1998). An individual's prior knowledge about a topic influences what and how he or she learns new material; it can help or hinder new learning. Students' prior knowledge may include appropriate and inappropriate conceptions or beliefs. Effective teachers find out if their students have incorrect prior knowledge, such as misconceptions or stereotypes, by assessing students' understanding when they begin the course or unit. Instructors address any erroneous knowledge by challenging the misconceptions directly. This is especially important in the physical, biological, and social sciences. Experiences with previous students and the literature in the field further identify common misconceptions and stereotypes (Ambrose et al., 2010; Fox & Hackerman, 2003).

Motivational theory and cognitive psychology describe conditions that foster this acquisition of knowledge, skills, and values. The relationship between the difficulty of a course and student learning is curvilinear. The best learning occurs when the course is perceived as difficult enough to be challenging, but still seen as achievable. Under these circumstances, students are motivated to try. If a course is too easy, students do not put forth any effort. If the course is perceived as too difficult, students are not motivated to try because they think there is no way they will succeed (McKeachie, 2007). After three decades of research on college students, Ernest Pascarella and Patrick Terenzini (2005) conclude that the student's amount of effort and level of involvement is one of the best predictors of the impact of higher education on him or her. The more involved and engaged students are with their educational program, the more they will be influenced by their college experience.

Problem Solving and Critical Thinking

Employers and society in general expect college graduates to be able to apply the facts for critical thinking and problem solving. These skills are almost universally required in all careers today (Jones, 2005).

Problem solving depends on in-depth knowledge of the discipline and the context. Apt problem solvers generate detailed and correct representations and individualized contexts for problems that accurately represent the dilemma. These representations and contexts are highly specific according to the organizing structures of that discipline. Good problem solvers employ discipline-specific procedural skills (Bransford, Brown, & Cocking, 2000; Wittrock, 1998). For example, graduate students in chemistry can solve chemical problems, but their education does not increase their ability to solve problems in other disciplines.

Effective problem solving draws on different processes: selecting the appropriate strategy, applying this strategy to solve the particular problem, and monitoring the success of that strategy. All of these processes are essential to successful problem solving. The task is to give students opportunities to learn and practice different strategies in different types of situations. Good problem solvers try another strategy when they find that the initial tactic did not work; weaker problem solvers continue to apply same approach even if it is not working (National Research Council, 2001).

Educational Technologies

With the increasing availability of a wide variety of technologies, it is crucial to select technology that helps students learn better. The adoption of educational technologies needs to be supported by sound pedagogy and evidence-based practices. Furthermore, the use of technology should not be just for its own sake or appearing to appeal to a stakeholder group such as students (Diamond, 2008). And it should not drive decisions of the choice of teaching and learning methods to use.

Technology can be an effective aid to increase learning in various ways because it allows students to build on and strengthen their learning, as a few examples illustrate:

- Software can provide students with three-dimensional cascading models to help them see complex processes in the sciences.
- Computers can provide students with far more practice with feedback of foreign language vocabulary, grammar, and pronunciation than instructors can provide in a class or a textbook can describe.
- Educational technologies can provide paths for increased engagement of students both in and out of the classroom.
- Students can have access to ideas, people, and places from around the world through Internet sources or specialized databases.

- Educational technologies can help students perform difficult or complex tasks more efficiently.

- Online quizzes can offer students opportunities for learning from their mistakes and immediate feedback on their mastery of content.

- Computer-enabled communications tools such as discussion boards, blogs, podcasts, wikis, and other forms of synchronous and asynchronous communication have great potential for changing student and faculty interactions.

- The online environment is appropriate for collaboration and group interaction (Vonderwell, 2003).

Feedback to Students to Foster Learning

Many psychologists recommend providing frequent feedback to students as an effective way to foster learning (Ambrose et al., 2010; Bransford et al., 2000; Fox & Hackerman, 2003). To be effective, this feedback needs to be well structured and useful to the students.

One of the most important functions of assessment, neglected by some instructors, is to provide timely and constructive feedback to students. When teachers do this often during instruction, they help their students learn more effectively and efficiently. Formative feedback is targeted to specific aspects of performance so that students can improve. Feedback is most helpful when students can revise their thinking as they are working on a project or before they take an exam.

Frequent opportunities for formative feedback increase student learning and their ability to apply the content in the future. Giving formative feedback to students who are struggling may help them to improve the quality of their learning or motivate them to revise their work significantly (Miller, 2009). The more students get formative feedback, the more they come to value it.

Ambrose and others (2010) offer these ways to embed feedback within the learning process:

- If instructors use classroom assessment techniques such as asking students to write a one-minute summary paper of a class or reading or to list the muddiest point from a class (Angelo & Cross, 1993).

- By asking questions and requesting that the students use audience response systems or clickers, both the instructor and the students will know if they mastered a concept or made a correct prediction.

- Many computer learning management systems (e.g., Blackboard) allow students opportunities to take quizzes repeatedly until they master most of the content. After the instructor develops or selects the pool of questions, the computer can give students different quizzes and grade them. Instructors might also provide an explanation of the correct answers and why other answers are wrong.

- By reviewing drafts or allowing students to hand in parts of an assignment, instructors can give feedback that students can use to demonstrate greater mastery or proficiency on the final version.

- Instructors can give feedback to the class as a whole on common mistakes or show examples of excellent papers and discuss why they are such high quality.

- If instructors develop explicit criteria, guidelines, or a rubric, students can offer constructive feedback to each other.

Instructors can make minor midcourse corrections to their teaching if they monitor student progress routinely. When feedback from students indicates that they did not understand or did not learn a procedure or skill, instructors can revisit that content, offering students further opportunities to practice before being tested on it. Reviews can be more focused on what students need to learn better, thereby eliminating the need to go over everything. When students do well, instructors know their teaching has been effective (Bransford et al., 2000).

Student Reflections on Their Learning

Instructors who ask students to reflect on their learning or on their experiences are helping those students construct knowledge from the concepts they are learning and the experiences they are having (Fink, 2003). Since reflection facilitates better learning, instructors should provide frequent, well-structured opportunities for students to reflect on their education (Bonwell & Eison, 1991). Reflection is especially helpful when students struggle with ill-structured problems, complex issues, or tasks with no obvious solution (Moon, 2006). As this situation characterizes situational learning, reflection is considered an essential aspect of experiential education (Eyler, 2009; Qualters, 2010).

Although reflection seems like a personal, introspective event, most people find that their reflection is more effective when it occurs interactively (Rodgers, 2002). These interactions expose students to different ideas, perspectives, and new or richer meanings. Reflective discussions are not open-ended free-wheeling dialogues. Instructors can make interactive reflection more effective by using targeted questions. Debriefing after a problem-solving or simulation exercise is an effective reflective exercise that fosters learning from this activity. When students reflect together, they also build a sense of community, which enhances the quality of the learning experience (Fink, 2003). This interactive aspect of reflection also distinguishes it from metacognition, which I describe in the learning outcomes section of this chapter.

Professors need to foster student reflection for several reasons: few students realize that they should reflect, it is hard to do well, and students rarely do it well alone or even in class. Therefore, instructors need to model how to reflect effectively and guide students in these ways:

- Guide or frame how students reflect in their learning journals through specific questions, or ask them to do a particular task.

- Request that students create concept maps (graphic representations of the content showing the relationships and hierarchies among concepts) representing their understanding of a particular concept. People can create a concept map of the relevant content by placing the main idea at the center of a hub and connecting subordinate concepts as they relate to this hub (Novak, 1998).

- Ask students to write about critical incidents that occurred in class or in online discussions and reflect on their reactions to these incidents and what they learned from them (Brookfield, 1995).

- Require students to assemble a learning portfolio that contains the work they did in the course and then reflect on their learning and the progress they made toward achieving the learning outcomes (Paris, 1998). They can address the value of what they did or learned and how they will be able to apply it in the future (Fink, 2003).

Just as students learn more by reflecting on their learning, you can use this same reflective process to learn more about your teaching. The next chapter focuses on how to use this kind of reflection to improve teaching.

Assessment Policies, Methods, and Processes

For most students, assessment is the driver for their learning, not a separate process from learning. Instructors can integrate assessment within the learning process and learning into the assessment process (Blumberg, 2009a). Assessment can enhance the quality of the learning itself at the same time it demonstrates the extent to which mastery of the content has occurred.

Robust assessment processes accurately determine what students know. Possibilities beyond tests include peer and self-assessments, mastery learning involving repeated attempts, authentic assessments, and student portfolios. Authentic assessments require students to complete real-world tasks, sometimes in simplified situations (Suskie, 2004). Just as with authentic learning, students can be more motivated to do a good job on an authentic assessment than on a test as they see its inherent value. Simulations can be authentic assessments too. While developing a portfolio of what they have done and what they have learned, students engage in meaningful self-assessments. The assessment methods chosen should fit the learning outcomes.

Ensure Availability and Accessibility

This is more of an issue for online classes and experiential settings than for classroom-based courses. If students come to class, they should have access to teachers. If they do not come to class, instructors should not have to ensure individual availability to them. Online students can become very frustrated when they try to contact their instructor and wait days for an answer to their questions. Instructors who are serving multiple roles in experiential settings may be too busy or too preoccupied with their other roles to make sure they spend quality time with their students.

Instructional Design Responsibilities

These responsibilities refer to ways instructors can improve that are not directly related to day-to-day teaching. They tend to occur before the course starts, outside interactions with students, and after the course ends. Again, they reflect a learning-centered approach to teaching that is consistent with contemporary cognitive science and pedagogy.

Align Learning Outcomes

Learning outcomes require different levels of student cognitive processing depending on what is expected. The cognitive processes, often represented by different types of verbs, can be divided into three major categories: low level of cognition such as recite or identify, medium level including apply or analyze, and high level of cognition involving synthesize, evaluate, or create. Instructors should align learning outcomes internally with teaching and learning activities and assessments and within an educational program. Figure 3.1 shows how a course can be aligned internally, within an educational program, and with the larger goals of the institution.

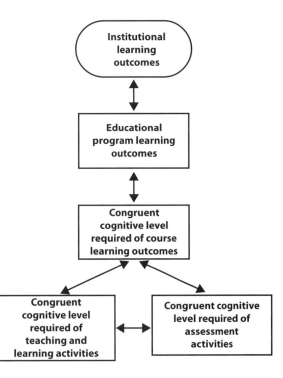

FIGURE 3.1   Alignment of a Course Internally and within an Educational Program

Align Learning Outcomes within a Course

Internal alignment means that the learning outcomes of the course, the way it is taught, how the students learn, and the assessment procedures are all consistent and interrelated. Consistency refers to the uniformity of the students' cognitive processes necessary to achieve each of these major elements of the course: the learning outcomes, the teaching/learning methods, and the assessment methods (Blumberg, 2009a, 2009b; Fink, 2003). Cognitive processes are represented by verbs. Thus, the verbs should be congruent with the three course components. If a course specifies high-level learning outcomes, instructors need to ensure the students have opportunities to practice these skills through their teaching/learning methods and that they assess them at this same level. It may also be necessary to teach at a lower level as a foundation and also do some basic or lower-level assessments. (The cases and the rubrics later in this book give tables showing course alignment.) Demonstrating this alignment in the syllabus helps students understand the rationale for teaching/learning methods and how they are assessed.

This component is not only calling for high-level learning outcomes; rather, consistency is what is required. An introductory course in medical terminology at my university is aligned with all low-level learning outcomes (e.g., the ability to correctly use medical terminology, including Latin and Greek prefixes that are commonly used), teaching/learning methods, and assessments (multiple choice and short answer tests). The instructor uses competitive games in class to maintain the students' motivation with such dry but essential material.

Aligned courses lead to maximum student learning (Biggs, 1999; Fink, 2003; Wulff, 2005). This is a hard concept to implement but well worth the effort. Many instructors, especially those who teach large classes, rely on multiple choice questions almost exclusively to evaluate their students. While the learning outcomes are at a high level, multiple choice questions may be at lower level because they are easy to write. For example, if learning outcomes require students to evaluate information from patients to make treatment decisions, the students practice these skills through computer simulations, but the multiple-choice exams require only lower levels of cognitive processing, this course is misaligned. Such exams might instead ask students to identify signs and symptoms and select appropriate clinical tests in the answer options with the diagnosis listed in the question stem.

Align Learning Outcomes within an Educational Program

Courses fit into a larger sequence of a curriculum or an educational program. A close fit between courses and the entire program facilitates student learning. This fit is achieved by paying attention to the integration among the courses. Yet curricula, educational programs, and courses are often designed without considering how they are aligned. If your department does not look at the curriculum holistically, you can begin the process by mapping your courses onto the introductory course that is a prerequisite for your courses and the courses that require your courses as prerequisites. You could also look at the other courses that students usually take at the same time and see how they integrate with each other in terms of learning expectations.

Organize Content to Facilitate Learning

Subject matter expertise uses well-organized knowledge of facts, concepts, and ways of thinking in the discipline and not just isolated knowledge (Bransford et al., 2000; Ambrose et al., 2010). Unfortunately most students acquire the facts and concepts without inherent unity because they do not see this organization. Lacking the inherent organization, they can easily forget isolated facts and concepts. Instructors who present material as an organized, coherent body of knowledge can foster greater learning and retention because students then see the big picture.

Psychologists refer to discipline-specific overriding themes or frameworks as organizing schemes (Bransford et al., 2000). In my experience working with faculty in different disciplines, I have noticed that most disciplines have fewer than ten organizing schemes that connect the vast majority of the knowledge in that discipline. In some disciplines, faculty often think of these organizing schemes, whereas in others, they rarely use this concept. It is a useful framework to try to use. The structure-function relationship is an organizing theme of biology, homeostasis is an organizing theme in physiology, individual differences in behavior are such a scheme in psychology, and the movement toward modernity is an organizing theme in history. Instructors can provide the frameworks, explicitly discuss these organizing schemes in their teaching, and select texts or other readings that use such frameworks. To help beginning students in a discipline to succeed, instructors can provide them with organizational frameworks (McKeachie, 2007). Once students acquire these organizing schemes, they will have the framework in place to be able to answer new questions, solve problems, and acquire additional content.

When instructors place concept maps in syllabi and discuss these maps so that the various relationships are clear, students can see the big picture of the course more easily (Nilson, 2007). Professors can then refer to this concept map as they move through different units so students can see the relationships among the units. They can also ask students to develop their own concept maps to illustrate how they have created their own meaning of the content.

Reflect on Teaching as Part of a Review and Revision Process

Skillful instructors continuously assess their own effectiveness with their students, reflecting on what went well and making modifications if necessary (Bransford et al., 2000). Questioning assumptions about teaching and viewing educational practices from different perspectives, especially those of students, leads to critical reflection on teaching (Brookfield, 1995).

This review process helps instructors set realistic and appropriate goals, so those who use it can learn to be more effective (McKeachie, 2007). Instructors can conduct this active review of their teaching and revision process alone, with a colleague, or with a faculty development specialist. However they engage in the process, doing it conscientiously will make them better teachers. Even though this process is what this entire book is about, the next chapter focuses on reflection. Part 3 provides the tools to assist in reviewing teaching.

Assessment of Learning Outcomes

Learning outcome statements identify what students should be able to demonstrate or produce as a result of their learning. Using multiple methods of assessment is advantageous over a single assessment of learning outcomes because assessments are only inferences about the depth and nature of learning (Fox & Hackerman, 2003). Assessment methods are either direct or indirect. Direct methods include using national standardized tests and inventories such as subject tests developed by testing services; locally designed tests and inventories; and authentic, performance-based methods. Indirect methods focus on student perceptions of their learning; they complement direct methods by offering insights into the learning process. Focus groups, interviews, surveys, and questionnaires are examples of indirect measures of learning (Maki, 2004).

In addition to determining the assessment method, instructors should clearly establish the criteria and standards on which the assessment is based. These criteria and standards should be congruent with the learning outcomes and also be explicit and clear. These requirements do not mean that instructors must use only objective tests. When instructors assess with a nonobjective measure, they can create a grading rubric.

Rubrics make the grading decisions explicit because they list the criteria and standards used to measure student performance (Fink, 2003; Fox & Hackerman, 2003). They also reduce grading time and students' arguments about their grades (Walvoord, 1998). (See http://rubistar /teachers.org for many examples of grading rubrics.) Sharing rubrics with students before they complete the assessment promotes intentional learning. Because students know what they will be evaluated on, rubrics help them prepare effectively and can motivate them to perform better (Reddy & Andrade, 2010). Students also perceive that they will be graded consistently and without bias. Without rubrics, some students, particularly nontraditional or ethnically diverse populations, feel that some instructors grade them more harshly than other more traditional students.

From a learning-centered perspective, a major goal of assessment is to increase learning. This is especially true of formative assessment, but ideally could also apply to summative assessments. Using this paradigm, instructors could design summative assessments that function both for accountability and to foster improvement. For example, if students assemble and review portfolios of their work, this assessment meets these dual goals of accountability and fostering learning, provided the students use the feedback they received earlier. For assessment to be effective, students need to understand the purpose of the assessment.

Instructors may consider the assessment and grading process as classroom research as it can be a systematic investigation of the relationship between teaching and learning. Results of student assessments can inform future teaching. Instructors need to ask questions that not only determine student mastery but offer insights into how well they are teaching. Assessing students can provide useful information to improve teaching, which leads to improved student learning. This process can also serve the institution's accreditation data needs if instructors provide information on what students learned and not just final grades (Walvoord, 1998). Since grading can serve all of these important functions, the time investment seems appropriate, as efforts can pay off in ways beyond just assigning grades to students.

Assessment of Knowledge, Skills, or Values

Most assessments in higher education measure students' abilities to acquire knowledge or understand basic concepts (National Center for Education Statistics, 1995). Even if instructors want to assess higher levels of cognitive processes, they still need to see if students mastered the basic knowledge or skills. Objective questions can be used to assess students' acquisition of declarative knowledge because they are an efficient way to determine comprehension of a broad range of topics (Suskie, 2004). Objective questions can be graded by a computer or a nonexpert in this discipline with an answer key. Common examples are multiple choice, matching, and fill-in-the-blank items. Before constructing an objective test, plan the parameters of the test through a test blueprint—a plan to match the desired learning outcomes with the number and type of questions to be asked on the test. Then specify the number of questions desired at each appropriate cognitive level (Suskie, 2004). After scoring the test, you can analyze how the students did on each aspect of the blueprint to see how to improve your teaching or assessing.

In addition to asking factual, objective questions, instructors can ask questions about students' organization of their knowledge. Those who have attained deep learning have developed their own organizing scheme or assimilated into their own knowledge those schemes taught to them. Instructors can ask objective questions about patterns because students use organizing schemes to see trends quickly. Ask students to explain or diagram how they organize the content through more open-ended questions. Students can describe the algorithms used with skills, for example, or how to solve problems (Marzano, 1998).

Instructors also can assess students on their knowledge, skills, and values by using performance tasks in which students develop a product. They are especially appropriate for disciplines that involve procedural knowledge, such as mathematics or business writing. Performance tasks expand what can be assessed and become more authentic assessments (Marzano, 1998).

The acquisition of values is best assessed by analyzing what students say about values in their learning journals. Instructors can determine how well students are questioning their assumptions, recognizing alternative perspectives or breaking down stereotypes. If a goal of the course is to develop students' own value system, instructors can determine the extent to which they developed over time through student reflective writing. Teachers may also ask students to state their values several times during the course and then, for the last assignment, ask the students to assess how their values changed during the course and what influenced these changes. Giving students the scoring rubrics in advance of being graded on values helps them understand the importance of developing values (Walvoord, 1998).

Assessment of Higher-Order Thinking Skills: Application, Critical Thinking, and Problem Solving

Authentic or performance assessments where students demonstrate critical thinking or how they apply content to solve real-world problems should characterize these assessments. Since many of these assessments have nonobjective aspects, instructors need to specify their expectations and criteria explicitly. These assessments lend themselves naturally to being learning centered.

Learning-centered assessments have three characteristics. First, they assume a commitment to helping students acquire the knowledge, skills, and values they will need in their careers or to function in society. Some of them are specific to disciplines, such as the application of content or problem-solving skills, and others are constant across higher education, such as the ability to work in groups. Second, they are learning events, as students learn while performing these assessment tasks. This is often accomplished when the students have to apply, integrate, or transfer their knowledge. Third, students can monitor their own progress on stated performance criteria. With student self-assessment, instructors need to explain these performance standards, identify the different levels of performance, and show examples of outstanding performance. In addition, they should help students own these standards so they are meaningful for them (Baron, 1998).

Assessment of Learning and Self-Assessment Skills

This component has discipline-specific and generic skills that students can apply in many courses. Learning skills help students make their study time more efficient. There are many such skills, and they change as expectations within higher education increase. They may include time management, monitoring the progress one is making or self-regulated learning, goal setting, how to read textbooks or primary material independently, how to conduct independent research, and information literacy skills (Blumberg, 2009a; Pintrich, 2000; Zimmerman, 2000). Developing good learning skills can promote lifelong, self-directed learning (Ambrose et al., 2010; Candy, 1991; Fink, 2003).

Psychologists consider many of these skills metacognitive skills because when individuals use them, they become aware of their thinking processes. Students may have an internal conversation about what they are doing or learning, and they may monitor their level of mastery, the progress they are making toward their goals, and their time management, and assess if the resources or strategies they are using are appropriate (Bransford et al., 2000). Strong metacognitive skills foster success in both higher education and throughout one's life. Since many students are unaware of the importance of metacognitive skills or even know they exist, instructors need to be explicit about them, showing how to use them and explaining why they are so helpful, before their assessment.

Metacognitive skills are often divided into two components: knowing one's own mental capabilities and the ability to evaluate one's progress. Instructors can assess both of these two components. For example, when asking students to solve problems, they can also ask these students to judge their ability to solve the problem, identify the limits of their knowledge, explain why they chose to apply certain procedures or rules, and predict the correctness of their actions. Although these aspects may not be graded, they can help identify student limitations and provide ways to help students learn better. To evaluate progress, instructors can ask students to estimate how long they think it will take to solve a problem and how much progress they are making toward successful solution. Good problem solvers can explain which strategies they used to solve problems and why. They monitor themselves and their progress continuously. Less competent problem solvers monitor their own progress occasionally, if at all, and they do it ineffectively. They have incomplete explanations for their thoughts and action (National Research Council, 2001; Zimmerman, 2000).

Unlike other assessments, self-report data are crucial to assessing these learning and metacognitive skills. Learning is an internal process, and the learners need to describe their self-perceptions of their abilities (Candy, 1991; Marzano, 1998). Students' understanding about their learning conveys important data surrounding the conclusions about their work and their achievements (Blumberg, 2000). Instructors cannot judge learning skills in the same way as other skills, because there is often not one single correct answer. However, students have better and worse learning skills. Professors can assess students on their skills when they complete rubrics on their use of metacognitive skills such as planning work, awareness of available resources, or how hard they try to do difficult tasks (Marzano, 1998).

The ability to self-assess is an essential learning skill. Once students leave school, they need to assess their achievements and determine when they need additional resources or help. Because most students think the purpose of self-assessments is to boost their grades, they normally give themselves top marks. However, when instructors explain the purposes of these self-assessments, ask specific questions, and encourage a trusting environment, students can begin to be more honest in their self-assessments. After modeling how to engage in this personal reflection and examination, instructors can evaluate students on their ability to rate the quality of their own work. The points students earn on self-assessments might be a measure of the accuracy of a student's assessment with external standards such as the instructor's assessment.

The premise of this book mirrors the process instructors ask their students to do when they monitor themselves through self-assessments. If you engage in the critical self-reflection model described in this book, you will be applying metacognitive skills to gain insights into your teaching. Going through this study of your teaching to monitor your progress toward increased student learning is a big metacognitive exercise. Just as it is hard for your students, it may be hard for you. However, it is worth it for both students and instructors.

Teaching in Experiential Settings

Janet Eyler (2009) recommends that the same procedures instructors use for effective teaching in classrooms should be applied to create meaningful experiential learning. I think they might be even more important because the main purpose of these authentic environments is not teaching and learning, but rather creating art, performing a service, or conducting research. These concepts need to be adapted to these experiential teaching situations because of these setting differences. I elaborate on these adaptations to experiential teaching in chapter 10. Here are a few examples of nuances in expressing the same essential aspects of teaching as they relate to experiential contexts:

- Relate experiential learning opportunities to specific goals of the experience to define the learning outcomes.

- Define expectations and roles clearly in nonclassroom settings as a way of planning learning opportunities for the students.

- Deliberately insert meaningful teaching and learning activities for intentional learning to occur while students engage in the activities of the site such as community service or rehearsing for a play.

- Consciously build in ways to show how practice uses theory.

- Provide structured reflection opportunities. Most researchers emphasize the essential role of critical reflection for learning to occur in experiential education (Eyler, 2009; Qualters, 2010).

- Plan opportunities for growth and new learning because it is easy for students to do the same task, especially low-level jobs, repeatedly.

- Routinely provide formative feedback. Students especially benefit from formative assessments in experiential settings because they may not be able to self-assess their abilities there.

- Develop assessments that demonstrate that the students achieved the learning outcomes.

There are added complexities of teaching in experiential settings. In addition to the usual teaching responsibilities, experiential instructors have other site- or context-specific roles, such as providing care in a clinical setting or conducting the musicians as they perform. Serving as role models for students in the way instructors conduct themselves ethically is an additional essential component of teaching in all experiential education. I discuss the specifics of teaching in particular experiential settings in part 2 of this book.

Suggestions for Better Teaching Coming from This Chapter

- Consider a comprehensive list of the essential aspects of teaching to understand all aspects of your teaching.

- Analyze all of the contexts of your teaching, and not just those of the discipline.

- Use appropriate literature because it offers many possible ways to teach better.

- Consciously structure the teaching and learning environment so that students have opportunities to learn by constructing their own meaning of the content.

- Address students' misconceptions or stereotypes by forcing them to challenge these mistaken beliefs directly.

- Embed formative feedback within the learning process.

- Continuously assess your effectiveness with students through reflection, and modify your practices if necessary.

Chapter 4

Documenting Critical Self-Reflection of Teaching

FOR A SYSTEMATIC APPROACH to achieving the goal of teaching that promotes more deep and intentional learning, instructors should critically reflect on each of the essential aspects of teaching discussed in chapter 3. This teaching improvement strategy has three vital interrelated facets: reflection, critical review, and documentation. I describe each facet individually and then show the impact of their integration at the end of this chapter, in part 3, and especially in the cases at the end of the book. Reflection, critical review, and documentation are rarely integrated in the literature: authors often describe one facet but not all three together. When they are integrated, they offer rich insights into teaching. Each one is necessary, but no one alone is sufficient for a comprehensive strategy to foster teaching that promotes greater intentional and deep learning.

Figure 4.1 shows a Venn diagram of the relationship of these three aspects to foster insights into better teaching. Critical reflective review with documentation makes this observational process more enduring and permanent. While reflecting, instructors need to critically review their actions. Reflection, critical review, and documentation characterize the second layer from the bottom on the hierarchical model for support for teaching shown on the inverted pyramid on figure 4.2. When instructors do them routinely, they have the power to make lasting changes. Documentation of reflections and critical review of teaching foster changes

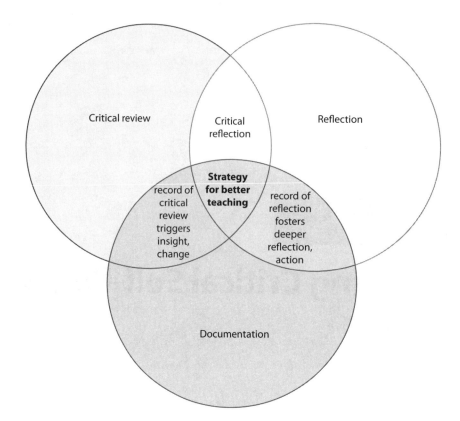

FIGURE 4.1   The Relationship of Three Facets of a Strategy for Better Teaching

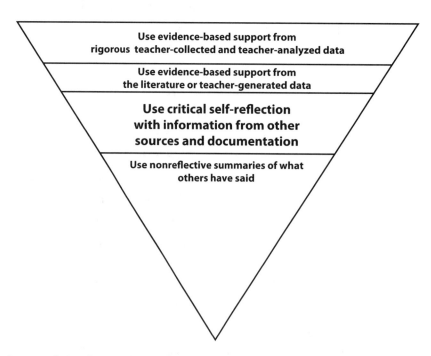

FIGURE 4.2   Hierarchical Model of Support for Teaching

because when ideas are written down, they are more likely to be acted on. These three facets should be incorporated into ongoing self-improvement processes and not seen as ends in themselves.

Reflection

During reflection, people reconstruct and make meaning of their experiences. Developmental psychologists see making meaning as one of the central tasks of adulthood, and it is a fundamental aspect of learning and development (Kegan, 1994). This powerful process leads to insights about oneself. People who reflect on their experiences and actions have a greater ability to produce the desired results, or self-efficacy (Stevens & Cooper, 2009). Self-knowledge is one of the most powerful influences on productivity for academics in all three major responsibilities of teaching, research, and service (Blackburn & Lawrence, 1995).

The concept of self-reflection has a long history. Four hundred years before the Common Era, Socrates noted that the unexamined life is not worth living. By "examination," he meant taking stock of oneself and the direction in which one is headed. The Judeo-Christian religions highlight the role of reflecting on one's deeds as a way to become a better person. A century ago, the great educational philosopher John Dewey emphasized the importance of reflection. More recently, Donald Schön and David Kolb reinforced this concept. However, it seems that today, we reflect less than we did in the past. Terry Doyle (2011) in fact calls it "the lost art of academia." Reflections can focus on day-to-day concerns as well as future aspirations and expectations, and it can help clarify ill-defined situations or problems. I summarize Dewey's, Schön's, and Kolb's thinking because their ideas led to my focus on reflection as an essential tool for becoming a better teacher.

John Dewey

According to Dewey, reflection is an intentional action whereby the individual makes experiences meaningful by using a systematic way of thinking similar to the scientific method. During reflection, people scrutinize complex situations to clarify them. They also examine their beliefs and assumptions and consider their implications, actions that lead to further insights and learning. Reflective thinking fosters the development of open-mindedness, wholeheartedness, and responsibility in facing consequences, attitudes that lead to further reflective habits (Dewey, 1933). If instructors reflect on their teaching with open-mindedness, wholeheartedness, and responsibility, they can become much more discerning about their teaching. Reflection allows instructors to become conscious of what psychologists call tacit knowledge (Rodgers, 2002).

Donald Schön

According to Schön, people require guided practice with reflection to develop expertise. He described two types of reflective processes that contribute to expertise development: reflection while engaged in the experience and reflection after the experience. All instructors can use these reflective processes with their teaching. Reflective practitioners think about their teaching in a disciplined systematic way as part of personal professional development. These reflections allow professors to examine their teaching behaviors and determine if what they are doing facilitates or inhibits student learning (Schön, 1987).

David Kolb

Kolb describes the process that enables people to learn from their experiences. An individual moves from someone who engages in a concrete experience to a reflective observer, to one who makes abstract conceptualizations or thinks about the experience, and finally engages in active experimentation. At each stage, learning occurs because of reflection; for example, during reflective observation, the individual explores the meaning of the experience and tries to connect it to past learning. Lacking reflection, people remain in the concrete experience without learning from it. While people can enter the learning cycle at any stage, they need to complete all four stages (Kolb, 1984).

Since reflection helps adults manage and benefit from poorly structured, complex situations, instructors can use this reflection learning cycle to improve their teaching. As they reflect on their teaching, they are able to observe their own behaviors, think about their experiences, and use the increased insight to make changes.

• • •

Dewey, Schön, and Kolb integrate experience with reflection to form an action-reflection-action cycle. Learning from experience means going back and forth between experiences, observations, and reflections on these experiences and making changes as a result of these reflections. Box 4.1 discusses how a professor used the action-reflection-action cycle to solve students' concern about her availability. This cycle spirals on itself as people reflect more; the better they get at reflecting, the more they learn and the larger improvements they can make.

> **Box 4.1. Using the Action-Reflection-Action Cycle to Improve Teaching**
>
> A nontenured mathematics professor is caught between the demands of her career and her family. She has children in late elementary and middle school who come from school in the middle of the afternoon, and she is also assisting with care for her disabled mother. Students at this college have become accustomed to going to their professor's offices whenever they want and not just during posted office hours. She is present for her required office hours but not in her office in the late afternoon.
>
> This professor used an action-reflection-action cycle in response to complaints from students that she was not accessible to help them and reflected on how she can balance her competing time demands. This reflection led her to increase her accessibility by e-mailing students more regularly using online homework software to check where they had difficulties. She sends many e-mails to students answering their questions about homework.
>
> Her reflection and action led to positive resolution of the accessibility concern. On end-of-course evaluations, she asks if the students feel that she is accessible to them. She has noticed that over the past few years, probably with the increased use of laptops and iPads, her students appreciate her immediate virtual accessibility.

Reflection on Teaching

Many instructors are not self-reflective, for several reasons. First, self-reflection is difficult. It is hard to be objective about our teaching and tough to see what we actually do. Teaching is such an expression of who we are as people that we have a vested interest in what we are doing. Second, we may be so caught up in the day-to-day aspects of teaching that we do not take time to reflect on our behaviors and why we are doing them. Third, reflecting on teaching is not an expectation for instructors, and many never engage in this important information-gathering mechanism. The literature contains examples of the incongruity between what teachers say they value in teaching and what they actually do (Argyris & Schön, 1974).

Dewey and Schön stressed the essential role that reflection plays in continuous professional development and growth. Weimer (2010) applied this concept of reflection directly to what instructors can do to improve: she directs faculty members to ask specific questions about themselves and their teaching: Who am I (as a teacher)? What do I do (as a teacher)? Why do I do what I do when I teach?

Reflection plays such a critical role that it can be considered the engine that drives the learning (Stevens & Cooper, 2009). During this reflective process, instructors reorganize their knowledge and feelings to have greater insights. Reflection leads to self-knowledge and increased efficiency (Stevens & Cooper, 2009). When people engage in a high level of reflection, their understanding can be transformed because it helps them overcome their misrepresentations (Raelin, 2010).

Reflection on teaching is also a good tool to help instructors who feel they have little control over their teaching situation. Sometimes instructors are part of a multiple section course with a common syllabus and common teaching methods or an instructor in a multi-instructor course. Graduate students teaching part of a large enrollment course with a course director may experience the students' complaints, but may not be able to do anything about them. All of these teachers may not have any choice in what is done in the course and may feel disenfranchised. These are difficult teaching situations. Reflection offers these teachers a chance to think about what they would do if it was their course—how they would make it better and teach differently (Boye, 2011).

Reflection is personal, internal, and introspective. In contrast, critical review requires integrating other perspectives in addition to your own. I think critical review is a more data-driven process than reflection. Some people see them as distinct processes; others might combine reflection as a part of critical review. I separate them to help distinguish their characteristics. However, I advocate the combination of reflection and critical review to truly develop your teaching. Critical review incorporates the insights gained from reflection along with how others see the situation.

Critical Review

Critical review incorporates the perspectives of key stakeholders along with the instructor's beliefs. Brookfield (1995) considers critical review so important that it is his most important indicator in judging teaching effectiveness. He bolsters his argument with six reasons that teachers should engage in critical review:

1. *It encourages informed actions.* Informed actions increase the probability that they will lead to the desired outcome. For example, Therese Johnston, an assistant professor of physical therapy, observed, "I need to do better at the end of lectures to keep students involved. It is hard with a three hour block of time." This understanding caused her to replan her classes so that the students were more engaged throughout the three hours of class.

2. *It helps to develop a rationale for practice.* A rationale for practice means understanding and being able to explain why instructors do what they

do. When communicated to students, the rationale conveys confidence in the teacher's teaching abilities. Rationales for practice are context specific and can change over time.

3. *It guards against instructors falling into guilt or self-blame traps.* Some instructors take too much personal responsibility when students do not achieve or don't seem to care about the course, and they blame themselves when many other factors may be at play. When instructors critically review what their students are doing, they come to understand that some students are not motivated to achieve.

4. *It stabilizes the emotional roller coaster of teaching.* Teaching is a mix of successes, frustrations, and failures. With critical review, instructors realize that the results of their actions don't happen by chance but are influenced by a host of variables, many outside their control.

5. *It fosters stimulating and challenging interactions with students.* Instructors should communicate their reviews to their students by discussing their assumptions and questions. This process models critical thinking and encourages students to engage in their own critical thinking.

6. *It increases trust and democracy in the teaching and learning process.* Instructors who engage in critical review know that what they say and do and their policies have a large impact on students. This power can develop or hinder trust in individuals. Instructors can model honesty and respect.

Instructors should try to see the realities of their teaching through their own perceptions; those of their students, peers, or other professional colleagues; and the lens of literature (Brookfield, 1995). Self-review is a good starting place, but it does not give the complete, objective picture. If instructors review their behaviors only from their own perspective, they are confined to their own assumptions and beliefs. That is why the other perspectives play an important role. Considering outside views helps people to see themselves more accurately. While critically reviewing one's actions, instructors need to see themselves as an "other"; that is, they must look outside themselves. When they consider these three external perspectives, they are seeing outside themselves. Once they view their teaching externally, they begin to see the impact of their beliefs and policies on others.

Insights gained from each of the four lenses build on the others. The knowledge achieved by looking through these additional three lenses filters what instructors see through their own and serves as an evaluative check for the professor's own ideas. Instructors need to try to understand how students are learning, what they are struggling with, and how they come to comprehend the material. Student course evaluations rarely offer this kind of information.

Box 4.2 describes how a professor combined this kind of knowledge about student learning and student feedback with her own critical review to achieve better student learning. When instructors talk about their teaching experiences with their professional colleagues, they gain new insights into teaching and realize that they are not encountering unique problems. Teaching is improved when it is discussed (Shulman, 2004a). Box 4.3 discusses how a professor made changes as a result of colleagues' discussing their teaching. Just as self-review alone has limits, so does including only students and peers in this review. Reading the literature on teaching in one's discipline and in higher education in general completes the picture (Weimer, 2006). The literature can suggest alternative methods and question deeply held assumptions. Box 4.4 discusses a statistics professor who used pedagogical literature to inform her teaching and improve student learning. The following two chapters discuss why using the educational literature improves teaching and shows how to find such literature.

Box 4.2. Combining Self-Critical Review with Student Perspectives

Therese Johnston, a physical therapy professor, teaches the second course in a progression that focuses on examination and interventions with patients with neuromuscular disorders. She has taught this course several times, and each time, she reviews student performance and her own observations to improve the course.

She realized that students make common mistakes in examining such patients. Since she wanted to address these mistakes early in the course, she developed an assessment during the second week of the semester in which students observe simulated patient examinations that are not conducted entirely correctly and identify what was done correctly and incorrectly. Instructors then gave students immediate feedback when confusion arose.

This assessment simulation has two simultaneous diagnostic purposes: to assess student learning while identifying areas of weakness and to identify teaching needs. Johnston noted areas of weakness and changed her teaching each semester to focus on these common weaknesses. She also collected feedback about the students' perceptions of the simulation assessment and how it affected their learning. She summarized this entire process as a feedback loop (figure 4.3). By using the student performance data through the semester and the student feedback, Johnston concluded that the more recent students were doing better than the previous ones. She observed an increase in their problem-solving skills and clinical decision making during the practical examination when the students need to conduct neuromuscular examinations (Johnston, 2012).

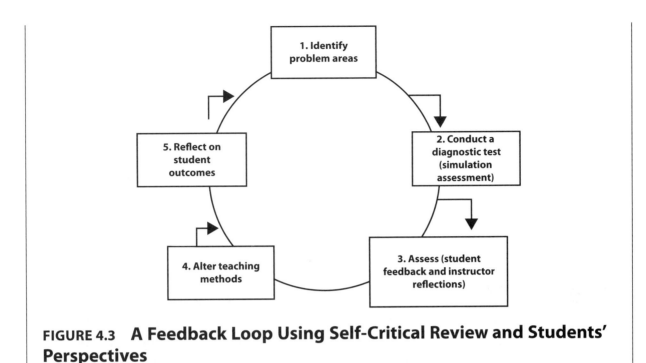

FIGURE 4.3   A Feedback Loop Using Self-Critical Review and Students' Perspectives

Box 4.3. Colleagues Discussing Courses to Foster Greater Integration

Annually the Department of Physical Therapy at the University of the Sciences holds a curriculum retreat where faculty discuss their courses to identify gaps and overlaps. When problems are identified, the professors who teach these courses meet to make appropriate changes. Greg Theilman, an associate professor in that department, wrote, "after the annual course review in 2008–2009, the entire faculty who are involved in teaching the intervention track and the neuromuscular track met throughout the summer of 2009 to analyze these courses. This led me to restructure both of my courses in these tracks in 2009–2010. Additionally I collected student assessment data in the midway point of each course to check on newly implemented approaches. In my neuro course the changes made were welcome, and no further changes were made throughout the semester. In the interventions course, the shifting of course content did not allow enough lab time, which I subsequently added."

Box 4.4. The Epistemology of Discipline-Specific Higher Education Literature Informing Teaching

Seeing the connection among statistical concepts is necessary for truly and deeply understanding the material; without understanding these connections, students may acquire an isolated knowledge of the concepts but often miss the big picture. Laura Pontiggia, an associate professor of statistics, wrote, "There is a growing body of research [she listed three peer-reviewed journal articles coming from the *Journal of Statistics Education* and the *Journal for the Scholarship of Teaching and Learning* and a book on assessing students in statistics] with evidence that shows that after taking an introductory statistics course, students fail to integrate important statistical concepts."

From talking to other faculty and listening to presentations by faculty at the Teaching and Learning Center's programs, Pontiggia learned that concept mapping is a commonly used technique to graphically organize and represent concepts and their connections. "Based on this evidence," she wrote, "in fall 2009, another statistics faculty and I decided to introduce concept mapping in the Introduction to Statistics course. For each of the three main areas covered (descriptive statistics, probability, and inferential statistics) we asked each student to create his or her own map and then, in class, discuss it within a group in order to produce a group concept map. I believe that the use of this concept map exercise helped me to assume more the role of a facilitator in the learning process in the classroom. I do not have hard evidence on the effect of this learning activity, since several other changes were introduced at the same time in the course. However, I believe that the concept map exercise has contributed to the increase in the posttest score gain, compared to their scores at the beginning of the semester on the Statistics Concept Inventory [a standardized test] in the past six semesters."

Documentation

Documentation should note your critical, reflective reviews. These individual records can be conversations you have with yourself about many aspects of teaching while incorporating information from many sources. The main purposes of documentation are to help manage and keep track of a wide range of details related to teaching. While managing these day-to-day aspects of teaching, documentation helps you consider how these aspects fit with your long-term expectations and to develop insights and to establish clarity about your roles.

Documentation helps organize thinking about teaching, the process of writing can foster deeper reflection, and writing encourages review and the reexamination of ideas (Stevens & Cooper, 2009). Box 4.5 shows how an adjunct professor of sociology effectively uses documentation to organize her thoughts about teaching and what she needs to change.

Box 4.5. Documentation of Teaching Practices to Organize Change and an Improvement Process

Maria Brown, a long-standing and dedicated adjunct professor of sociology, is methodical in her record keeping about her teaching. She wrote, "After each class, I note if planned content has been covered and if learning activities and methods seemed to work or not. I take particular note of student participation in class discussion and in small group work. I prepare for the next class with these considerations in mind and, when there's a significant issue, jot down notes on my course materials to inform next semester's planning. I keep a file of course materials that I feel need editing, revision, or expanding before they are used again. I sometimes work on this material over the summer but more often go back to it when the relevant topic comes up in the next round of the course."

One of the most important lessons I learned early in my career, which I try to convey to all new faculty, is the importance of documenting comprehensively. This documentation extends well beyond recording the number of students enrolled in each course and the grade distribution. While numbers are important, qualitative documentation enriches the records. As the examples in the boxes illustrate, reflections on how effective individual assignments and classes are can be very useful when returning to the same material a semester or year later. Recording critical incidents in teaching helps to jog your memory of the situation and can offer new insights into how to handle similar concerns in the future. Instructors can also record the lessons they learned from these situations or problems. Furthermore, professors can note where students have difficulty with content and the need to find additional readings because the textbook does not make the point well.

In this era of social media, people are writing about their lives or their thoughts and sharing them electronically on Facebook and blogs, for example. A positive result of all of this documenting, sharing, and getting feedback from others should be that instructors might become more familiar with and more comfortable documenting their teaching.

Instructors can use many different vehicles to document their teaching, including blogs, personal journaling, notes, and comments on their teaching materials. The important thing is to record perceptions, comments, or feedback from peers or students shortly after the teaching occurs. It does not have to be analyzed when it is first written. When instructors review these notes later, they can be quite revealing.

When I asked professors to list possible sources of information about their teaching during faculty development workshops, they collectively generate a short list. Student course evaluations and peer observations are always listed. Unfortunately instructors rarely get good, helpful formative feedback from them. (I discuss more about the shortcomings of student evaluations and peer observation in chapter 7.) To open up possibilities beyond these commonly used information resources, I generated a comprehensive list of possible sources of information about teaching. I apply Brookfield's (1995) four lenses of self, student, peers, and the literature to identify four important stakeholder groups. Each group can yield many possible sources of data that you can use to support your reflection and critical review of your teaching. Students can provide insights into how they perceived the course, such as its organization and clarity. Furthermore, you can consider the materials you created for the course, such as the syllabi or assignments, to determine how effective these were in facilitating learning. Examples of student products such as their presentations and summaries of performance on examinations measure how well students met the goals of the courses.

Although these lists are long, they can prompt you to think of other possibilities also. Table 4.1 lists sources for documentation of quality of teaching for all teaching contexts, and table 4.2 lists sources for documentation of quality of teaching that are context specific. Both tables illustrate many sources of information for reflection and critical review. To demonstrate the richness of data that you can obtain from each stakeholder group, I identify the box numbers corresponding to the examples given in this chapter that used this source of information.

TABLE 4.1   Sources for Documentation of Quality of Teaching for All Teaching Contexts

Source Perceptive			
Self	**Student**	**Peer**	**Literature**
Personal reflection (boxes 4.1 to 4.5)	Student evaluations of experiences (standard or course-specific form) (boxes 4.1, 4.2)	Peer assessment data	Higher education literature in general
Instructor-developed course materials (boxes 4.2, 4.4)		Chair or unit director report or observations	Discipline-specific (e.g., epistemology of the discipline) higher education literature (box 4.4)
Personal observations after teaching (boxes 4.2, 4.3, 4.5)	Student assessment data (boxes 4.2, 4.4)	Peer observations	
	Recording of student performance or presentation, or explanation of work	Peer review of student products	Professional organizations devoted to higher education (e.g., AAC&U) or discipline-specific organizations that advance teaching/learning agendas
Calendar, appointments documentation		Peer review of instructor-developed educational materials (box 4.3)	
Use of standardized tools (box 4.4)	Review of student products (boxes 4.2, 4.4)	Teaching awards nominated by peers	
Use of assessments that the instructor creates (boxes 4.2, 4.4)	Reports from students (box 4.1)	Peer review of teaching portfolio	Regional accreditation, professional or discipline accreditation agencies
Documentation using critical incident observations	Follow-up data on where students went after graduation	Learn teaching ideas from others (box 4.4)	ETS, GRE discipline exams
Self-review of student products (box 4.2)	Student reflections		
Formative self-assessment tools	Student portfolios		
Summative self-assessment tools	Teaching awards nominated by students		
Self-review of assessment plans			
Teaching portfolios			

TABLE 4.2   Sources for Documentation of Quality of Teaching That Are Context Specific

Context of Teaching	Self	Student	Peer	Literature
Classroom, online	Classroom research data A summary statement about learning outcomes, teaching/learning, assessment methods	Student products developed for the course Feedback from teaching assistants	Comments from coteachers	Discipline-specific higher education literature (epistemology of the discipline)
Mentoring research	Documentation of goals and how project was geared to these goals Documentation that instructor is current on all ethical considerations in this discipline or profession	Review of student lab notebook, reports Review of student presentations at internal lab or research meetings, journal club, or seminar Feedback from graduate assistants Documentation that students are current on all ethical considerations in this discipline	Comments from other researchers on the team	Discipline-specific higher education literature (epistemology of doing research in this discipline)
Supervising or precepting in community or clinical settings	Action research data Documentation that instructor is current on all ethical, continuing education considerations in this discipline or profession	Documentation that students are current on all ethical considerations in this discipline or profession	Comments from other practitioners at the site	Discipline-specific higher education literature (epistemology of this discipline or profession)
Performing and visual arts	Documentation of goals and how project was geared to these goals Instructor's written or recorded oral critiques Documentation that instructor is current on all ethical considerations in this discipline or profession	Students' written or recorded oral critiques Documentation that students are current on all ethical considerations in this discipline or profession	Media coverage of art exhibits and productions or performances Critics' reviews of art exhibits and productions or performances	Discipline-specific higher education literature (epistemology of the performing and visual arts)
Director of experiential education	Documentation that instructor is current on all ethical considerations in this discipline or profession	Documentation that students are current on all ethical considerations in this discipline or profession	Comments from practitioners at sites where students are placed	Discipline-specific higher education literature (epistemology of the experiential education in the discipline or profession)

Integration of Reflection, Critical Review, and Documentation

When the processes of reflection and critical review are done separately, the results can be like the old story of six blind people touching different parts of an elephant, with each coming to a different conclusion. However, when both processes are integrated and documented, the conclusions reached about teaching are likely to be more accurate. This systematic process can also clarify thinking, motivate instructors to analyze data from different sources, and motivate people to resolve to make changes.

Instructors who engage in reflection and critical review examine and evaluate their deeply held assumptions and beliefs. They move beyond questions about what they do and start asking questions about how and why they teach as they do. Answering these rationale-based questions about their beliefs and assumptions can lead to new insights. When instructors critically assess and reflect on their teaching philosophies and policies, they come to understand their impact on student learning and attitudes. Discussion of these rationales can be informative, especially when instructors use the same approach regularly. This kind of reflective analysis is not easily accomplished, but it is well worth the effort and time expended. It also needs to be done over time.

Practical Recommendations

Begin and integrate the study of your teaching with critical self-reflection because it will offer many insights into how to teach better. Explore the assumptions you make about students, learning, and your teaching process. Fully document in writing the results of this study of your teaching. To be more specific, here are some types of questions to consider:

- Why do you use certain instructional and assessment methods?
- Are your policies and practices congruent with or in conflict with your assumptions and beliefs?
- What proportion of content is devoted to building a knowledge base, developing problem-solving or critical thinking skills, and increasing learning or metacognitive skills so students can continue to learn this content after the course?
- Do you explain what you mean by student participation so that students can do this effectively?
- Can the students use student or peer feedback?
- How do you use student feedback?

The answers to these questions inform self-knowledge that can lead to growth and changes in your teaching. While addressing these questions, you begin to develop a sense of what you want to become as a more informed, self-aware, and effective teacher (Weimer, 2010). Next, compare your analysis with data from students and faculty. Using many sources for data and integrating those data leads to a broader and more accurate understanding of teaching processes. If you do it periodically, you will teach significantly better. When you document the products of your reflection and critical review, you are employing the second layer on the pyramid of strategies for better teaching shown in figure 4.2. The following chapter discusses the higher layers on this model, suggesting additional ways to develop your teaching skills.

While engaging in this active review and reflection process, you acquire the habit of documenting teaching that is necessary for summative evaluations. Good records, the product of critical reflection, are also helpful in preparing teaching portfolios for promotion and tenure or when applying for new jobs or other responsibilities.

Integrating Thoughts

Critical self-reflection helps you teach intentionally. This intentional teaching uses the same thought processes we expect from our students when they learn with intention (Association of American Colleges and Universities, 2002). When you teach with intention, you become aware of the reasons for teaching, the teaching process itself, and how what you do has an impact on students and their learning. It is a powerful process. Intentionally reflecting on the teaching helps you to see where you need to change and how you can improve. Through this process, you will deliberately link your discipline-specific content and ways of thinking in your discipline with appropriate pedagogical approaches. Because you have reflected on the teaching methods, you will realize that there is not one perfect method, but some work better in one course or with some types of students and others work better in other situations (Millis, 2009). You will also be able to apply and adapt what worked in different teaching circumstances to current teaching situations and concerns.

Summary of Suggestions for Better Teaching Coming from This Chapter

- Reflect continuously on your teaching practices.
- Perform ongoing critical review of your teaching.

- Begin and integrate the study of your teaching with critical self-reflection.

- Incorporate reflection with critical review of your teaching. This practice can foster insights into better teaching.

- Document your critical reflection and review. Documentation makes your insights more permanent and more likely to be acted on. The documentation process also leads to more profound awareness.

- Perspectives from yourself, your students, your peers, and the literature inform critical review and reflection.

- Consider using data from many sources.

Chapter 5

Evidence-Based Approaches to Enhance Teaching

EVIDENCE-BASED TEACHING HELPS instructors make better-informed decisions about the instructional design of their courses (Blumberg, 2011). Teaching that incorporates evidence-based decision making is superior to instruction that relies only on personal experience because it contributes to student learning (Brew & Ginns, 2008). I introduced the concept of evidence-based teaching as a strategy to promote better teaching in chapter 1. I elaborated on this concept in chapter 2 since evidence-based teaching confronts the misconception that teaching is not a scholarly pursuit like research. I have also discussed advantages of using the phrase *evidence-based teaching* and its implications for faculty development. I continue this discussion of evidence-based practice in this chapter and the next one.

Informed teaching uses evidence-based practices. Instructors do not need to obtain this evidence directly by doing research on teaching and learning. This evidence can come from pedagogical literature in one's discipline, higher education in general or research in the neurocognitive sciences, and data from their courses. When instructors rely on these kinds of evidence, they can explain the reasoning behind how and why they teach. Furthermore, such evidence can point to concrete ways to change teaching.

This chapter discusses the two evidence-based layers of the inverted pyramid highlighted in figure 5.1. Instructor-collected data fit the top two layers on this figure; the distinction between the two levels relates to the

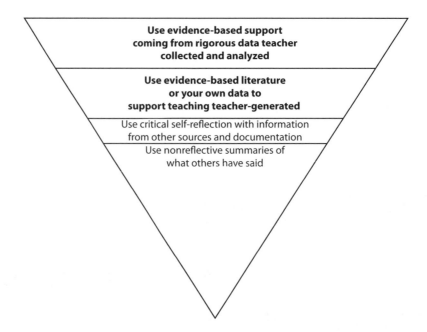

FIGURE 5.1   Hierarchical Model of Support for Teaching Emphasizing the Evidence-Based Layers

amount of rigor and how methodical the study of their teaching is. Using scores derived from student evaluations of the instructor or course or comments made on these forms are examples of the kinds of data that fit the next-to-the-top level of support. Instructors who do research on their teaching, gathering systematic data from their students and receiving peer review on this work, are at the top layer of support for their teaching. When instructors conduct research on how their students learn as a result of how they are teaching, they acquire even greater insights into and understanding of their instructional process and practices. Since the expectation that instructors use evidence-based teaching is new, I explain a step-wise process to help you become an evidence-based instructor.

Evidence-Based Teaching as a Developmental Process

Evidence-based teaching draws on skills that most professors have but do not always think of as being relevant to teaching. This is not their fault: it is not taught in graduate school and instructors have not observed it or had a mentor explain or role-model it. In addition, many senior-level professors do not engage in evidence-based teaching. In this section, I describe seven steps to become skilled in evidence-based teaching. Figure 5.2 summarizes these steps, which you can work through gradually.

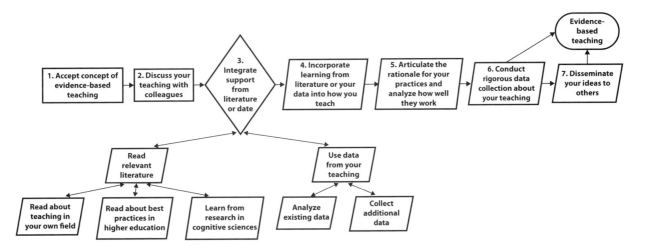

FIGURE 5.2   Steps to Becoming an Evidence-Based Teacher

Step 1: Accept the Concept of Evidence-Based Teaching

The most important of the many benefits to using evidence-based approaches is that teaching is enhanced when it is used. This enhancement leads to deep and intentional student learning that lasts.

Non-evidence-based approaches to teaching conflict with the standards of practice for many professionals. Health care professionals use their clinical literature to inform clinical decisions. Students in law school learn the importance of precedent or finding prior cases to support their arguments. Engineering decisions are made on the basis of calculations from hypothetical or actual data. To be more consistent with these other professions, when instructors know the literature on teaching effectiveness, they can make better-informed decisions about the instructional design of their courses.

We can also expect students to use evidence-based decision making. For example, science, history, engineering, health professions instructors, and those in many other fields as well require students to use evidence consistently in their arguments in class discussions, course assignments such as term papers, and research. In these disciplines, scholarly work done by professors and even students always includes a review of the literature. Students must cite other people's ideas as a basis of their own thinking. Yet we often do not use the same standard of relying on evidence-based ideas in our teaching. Surely we need to be consistent with what we expect of our students and our own work in many of our disciplines.

Regardless of discipline, all academics want their students to graduate with lifelong learning skills. Here again, we should practice what we say we want from our students. Learning more about teaching is one way that we as faculty members can continue learning throughout our careers in higher education. Worthwhile literature describing pedagogy, the scholarship of teaching and learning, and neuroscientific research continues to be published. Committing ourselves to reading this literature on a regular basis shows that we are lifelong learners in an important part of our lives.

When I tried to convince instructors at my university to adopt evidence-based decision making to inform teaching, I encountered some resistance. As an educational psychologist grounded in the scientific inquiry methods, I had a hard time understanding why the idea of evidence-based teaching didn't make sense to them. Humanities professors helped me arrive at alternative terminology. If you also have trouble with the phrase *evidence-based teaching*, substitute *self-conscious teaching*; the essence of the idea remains the same. Instructors can even skip the label entirely and just apply the concept of reading about teaching and studying teaching so that they can grow as instructors.

Step 2: Discuss Your Teaching with Colleagues

The more that faculty discuss their teaching with others, the more valued teaching becomes. Shulman (2004a) feels that this moves teaching from a solitary activity to one where there is greater community responsibility for it. When teaching is a valued activity, instructors feel supported to talk about both what they are proud of and to raise concerns or challenges. Teaching and learning centers or centers of teaching excellence are good places to share teaching experiences and to learn how others are teaching.

Step 3: Integrate Support from Literature or Data

Because evidence-based teaching is either literature driven or data driven, instructors can start with either approach. This evidence may come initially from the literature, which then drives personal research-in-action of teaching (Blumberg, 2011). Or instructors can consider some data about their teaching that leads them to read how others handle similar situations. Each of these two components also offers the following further choices.

Read the Relevant Literature

Reading the research-based literature helps develop teaching and learning methods or adapt what others have done (Weimer, 2006). Following are three practical suggestions to get started using literature to support your teaching:

- *Read in your own discipline.* Research-supported methods that other faculty members in your discipline use may be the easiest to implement. Therefore, begin by reading the educational literature in your field. Box 5.1

Box 5.1. Adapting a Successful, Evidence-Based Model

Almost ten years ago, Frederick Schaefer and Madhu Mahalingam, both assistant professors at that time, wanted to improve their students' mastery of general chemistry. All of their students were required to get at least a C in their course to stay in their preprofessional majors, yet 28 percent of their students were earning less than 60 percent on the exams before they were curved to get a reasonable letter grade distribution. By attending a program hosted by the Teaching and Learning Center, they learned how Dennis Jacobs (2000) had solved a similar problem at the University of Notre Dame: he organized general chemistry students into small groups to solve multiple-step, complex problems, and the number of students receiving satisfactory grades improved.

Schaefer and Mahalingam transformed their ineffective recitation hour, where students had the opportunity to ask questions, into a highly structured small group problem-solving session. Students worked on problems that were more difficult than the ones Schaefer and Mahalingam assigned as homework. Since they implemented the structured group problem solving, the number of students failing the exams without curving them has dropped to 19 percent (Mahalingam, Schaefer, & Morlino, 2008). This recitation structure is now used in all sections of general chemistry. Even though different professors now teach some of the sections, fewer students are earning Ds or Fs, and more students earn Bs and Cs in all sections (Mahalingam et al. 2008).

---

describes how instructors learned about a successful model for teaching general chemistry elsewhere that they adapted to their courses. You can also learn how others teach using best practices in your discipline by attending the educational sessions at your professional conferences.

- *Read about best practices in higher education.* Try implementing teaching and learning methods well supported by research and widely used in many disciplines. Many successful techniques, such as small group discussions (Springer, Stanne, & Donovan, 1999), larger group discussions (Brookfield & Preskill, 1999), and collaborative learning (Millis, 2010), can apply to part of the course. Later in this chapter, I discuss my favorite best practices that change the way entire courses are offered. Instructors who have not read material on teaching and learning may find locating good material a bit challenging. I provide advice and guidance on how to find suitable literature and how to evaluate if the literature indicates best practice models, and not isolated studies, in the next chapter.

- *Learn from research in the neurocognitive sciences or psychology.* Solid evidence coming from psychological and neuroscience research, as well as classroom-based investigations, shows that actively engaging students to construct their own meaning of content instead of passively listening and memorizing what they heard promotes greater learning and long-term retention of content (Bransford, Brown, & Cocking, 2000; Fox & Hackerman, 2003; Kuh, Schuh, & Whitt, 2005; McKeachie, 2007;

Resnick, 1991). Instructors do not have to read the primary neuroscience literature; many good books summarize it for nonexperts. Some of these books include those published by the National Research Council (Bransford et al., 2000; National Research Council, 2001), the American Psychological Association (Lambert & McCombs, 1998), and individual authors (Ambrose, Bridges, DiPietro, Lovett, & Norman, 2010; Zull, 2002). Becoming familiar with this literature is an important and concrete step toward better teaching.

Use Data from Your Own Teaching

Here are two possibilities:

- Analyze existing data such as exam results or projects to determine how well students learned a specific concept or can solve problems. This goes beyond the typical grading of papers or tests but is not a big extra step. For example, instructors could determine the relationship between the amount of time students spend on online exercises and how well they did on the exams.

- Collect some data to get further insights. This could be a simple online survey to ask students a few questions. Sometimes professors are intimidated by the concept of course assessment and think they need to employ complicated methodologies to assess their courses. This is not true. Instructors can do a pre- and posttest and measure gain scores. Box 5.2 explains how an instructor gained insight into how her students perceived novel teaching methods by asking the students to take a small survey.

Box 5.2. How Analyzing Existing Data and Collecting Data Give Insight into Student Learning and Their Perceptions of Their Learning

Associate professor Alison Mostrom teaches upper-level biology courses without lectures. During class, the students create concept maps representing their knowledge about specific content-rich topics. They construct their concept maps based on readings from their textbook and primary and secondary literature.

In her ecology course, Mostrom asked students to construct a concept map at both the beginning and midpoint of the semester to address the basic question, "What is ecology?" She found that all of the students' midpoint maps contained much more hierarchical structure and complexity than their first map, showing their knowledge gain. Students stated that constructing concept maps was superior to attending lectures for understanding the scientific literature, but ranked these two methods equal for understanding material presented in the textbook (Mostrom, 2008).

Share such data with your students so they can see that you are using what you learned from them. For example, Salar Alsardary's students in his Discrete Mathematics course complained that his course was highly time-consuming. The following semester, he asked students to record how much time they were spending each week on this course and another three-credit course. To their surprise, the averages were about the same. Alsardary now tells his students that previous students spent about the same amount of time on this course as they do on other three-credit courses.

Step 4: Incorporate Learning from the Literature or Data into How You Teach

The purpose of using evidence-based practices is to teach better. The insights gained can be incorporated into teaching even within an ongoing course, as well as the next time the course is taught. Box 5.3 shows how a professor used the data she collected to teach better.

Step 5: Articulate the Rationale for Your Practices and Analyze How Well They Work

Just as teaching leads to consolidation of content, articulating ideas about teaching can elucidate the rationale for teaching. This process makes implicit or even unconscious ideas about teaching more explicit. (I elaborate more on how to do this in part 3.) Furthermore, instructors might express ideas about what is effective or not as effective and personal teaching aspirations. Instructors can do this by discussing them with a

---

Box 5.3. How Studying Teaching Improves the Learning Outcomes

Lia Vas, a professor of mathematics, has been an excellent teacher since she was a graduate student. In the past, she never investigated the reasons she was such a skilled teacher. She did not conduct any classroom-based research and was skeptical of conducting educational assessments on the effectiveness of her teaching, as she admitted in a presentation on assessment of courses to other faculty members. Yet as she explained in this presentation, her thinking and her actions changed, driven by several factors: realizing that data professors routinely collect can be turned into meaningful assessment data, interacting with colleagues can inspire and produce novel ways of assessment, and surveying students' attitudes can drive course innovations.

In particular, she decided to survey students' attitudes in her courses. Several years ago she compared the attitudes of students toward learning mathematics, desire to take more mathematics courses, appreciation of the use of the graphing calculator, and comfort level when using a computer to solve mathematical problems. Her analysis of the results changed how she teaches. For example, when students in one course had lower comfort levels with the computer for solving mathematical problems, Vas increased their exposure to computers. She now shares her analyses of her teaching with colleagues outside the department.

colleague, a mentor, or a faculty developer. This analysis of what is working or not working can stimulate instructors to collect data.

Writing about these insights can transform teaching. Box 5.4 shows the power of writing for one professor.

Step 6: Conduct Rigorous Data Collection about Your Teaching

Conducting systematic investigations into teaching helps develop or refine an individual's pedagogical framework or teaching philosophy. This process yields profound reflections and insights into teaching that may free instructors from continuing to teach the same way because they never thought about alternatives previously (Brew & Ginns, 2008). With data, instructors will be able to explain why their practices are effective or look at new ways to make their teaching more effective. If instructors are going to collect data from their students that go beyond the normal assessments, they should obtain Institutional Review Board approval.

Systematic study of teaching leads to enhanced teaching and increases student learning (Brew & Ginns, 2008; Hutchings & Shulman, 1999). When

---

Box 5.4. How Writing Makes Tacit Knowledge More Explicit

For years Roger Ideishi, an associate professor of occupational therapy (OT), incorporated service-learning into some of his courses and received good to excellent teaching evaluations from his students. However, it was when he started to articulate his rationale by writing about his service-learning experiences that really gained insight into why he was so committed to this time-consuming teaching and learning method. His writing, along with a more thorough review of the literature, made explicit the centrality of service-learning to his philosophy of teaching and teaching practices.

In 2006, spearheaded by the chair, all of the faculty members in his department wrote an article describing how their educational program's curricular themes of clinical reasoning, critical thinking, innovations in practice, and engagement were expressed in different teaching methods (Kramer et al., 2007). Ideishi wrote that the values of service-learning contribute to the foundation of these themes for beginning professional students: "Service-learning promotes critical thinking through deep reflections of the social, cultural, political, and economic contexts of occupational therapy practice. Service-learning promotes innovations through challenging future OTs to create or expand rich occupational therapy practices. Service-learning promotes engagement through regular participation in civic, health, and educational needs of a community" (Ideishi, 2009, p. 240).

Since then, he has written more scholarly articles describing the role of service-learning in occupational therapy education overall, including one on how his students work in a therapeutic preschool program for developmentally delayed children. In these articles, Ideishi systematically incorporated relevant literature into his rationales and descriptions of the service-learning experiences. He explained the evidence-based decisions for the student roles, how the students perform valuable service for the agency, student reflection assignments, and assessment.

professors collect data to determine how or why students are learning, they treat their courses as laboratories or field sites (Cross & Steadman, 1996). They can develop some formal hypotheses that they can test or questions that they would like to formally answer. Then they collect evidence documenting how the method has an impact on student learning.

The Carnegie Foundation for the Advancement of Teaching offers many excellent resources, including how-to-do-it advice and case examples (Huber, 2002; Hutchings, 2000; Hutchings, Huber, & Ciccone, 2011; Hutchings & Shulman, 1999). They describe four defining features of this rigorous study of teaching: framing questions about teaching, collecting and analyzing data, implementing different or innovative practices while teaching, and sharing what was done and learned with others (Huber & Hutchings, 2005).

Weimer (2006) explains various legitimate approaches or methods for this type of research. The most common research on teaching is descriptive: instructors collect survey data on teaching practices or attitudes and describe the results. Research can rely on the paradigms commonly used in the instructor's discipline, such as quantitative methods involving experimental design and qualitative investigations in naturalistic, educational settings. Box 5.5 describes how an instructor used qualitative observations about what occurred in her classroom to improve her teaching. Weimer (2006) offers practical advice for getting started, such as how

---

Box 5.5. Using Naturalistic Observations to Improve Teaching

Susan Wainwright was an assistant professor of physical therapy when she wanted to incorporate more active learning in her classes. Trained in evidence-based decision making from her clinical discipline, she decided to gather baseline data on what was actually occurring prior to making some changes. She audiotaped several classes to determine how much active learning the students were doing and was surprised at how much she talked and how little the students engaged in active learning. So she decided to require the students to come to class prepared, and classes would be more discussion than lecture. At the same time, Wainwright was enrolled in a PhD program at another university. While in the process of changing her teaching, she realized that she needed to learn more about qualitative research methods, so she enrolled in an elective class on this topic.

Wainwright used well-established educational qualitative research methods to code the types of interactions from her second series of audiotapes. She analyzed who spoke and the types of remarks they made. This analysis revealed that she was still more directive than she wanted to be. These data pushed her to completely revise how she taught her classes.

The next semester Wainwright introduced clinical cases for the students to discuss in small groups. Analyses of the audiotapes from classes conducted in this format showed that the frequency of her own directive comments dropped significantly while the informative and clarification questions made by the students markedly increased. This rigorous qualitative study of classroom interactions led to a publication in a higher education journal (Wainwright, 2009).

to craft a research question, and lists resources to consult in different disciplines. Faculty developers can also assist throughout all of the steps in this research process.

You can do systematic study and data collection of your courses and not publish the results, but still obtain great benefits. Systematic data collection and analysis might be the most meaningful and enduring example of critical reflection and review. If instructors complete the first six steps and do not engage in step seven, they are still using evidence-based teaching.

Step 7: Disseminate Your Ideas to Others

Once instructors engage in this process of seeking explanations for why their teaching is effective, they probably will want to share it with others. This can be accomplished through informal discussions with peers or formal professional conferences, educational newsletters, and peer-reviewed publications. However, formal dissemination through peer-reviewed publication is optional in evidence-based teaching. Do not be discouraged by the daunting prospect of doing data collection so that it can be published. The goal is greater knowledge and understanding of your teaching.

Integrated Instructional Techniques That Are Evidence-Based, Best Practices

Throughout this book, I discuss instructional techniques that professors can use to teach or assess students as a way of illustrating a concept. In this section, I discuss five evidence-based best practice methods that have specific learning activities. All are well supported by literature and can help instructors move from discussion of teaching to using the literature. Although there are other equally good techniques, these can be used with most disciplines.

These models have been used in various disciplines and with different levels of students. All use the concept of flipped classes to define the way the entire course is organized. Flipped classes move most of the information dissemination out of the classroom so that class time can be spent on faculty-student interactions or various forms of active learning (Bergmann & Sams, 2012; Fink, 2003). So much research supports these methods that they have been labeled evidence based (Buskist & Groccia, 2011). The research supporting these integrated instructional techniques is directly connected to these methods, whereas with the other examples, the research comes from more diffuse educational or cognitive sciences research.

I have taught using these learning-centered methods or have worked with faculty who use them and can say that they work to engage students and promote learning. I include brief summaries of these integrated instructional techniques to provide examples of evidence-based approaches to the organization of entire courses. Instructors may also want to read the sources and the supporting research.

Problem-Based Learning

Problem-based learning (PBL) has been used extensively in the health professions, engineering, and other professional education since its inception in the 1960s. Instead of instructors lecturing, students use an iterative process to discuss real-world problems in small groups.

When students encounter a new problem, they raise questions about the content that they will need to answer to understand it. They read many resources, ranging from textbooks to primary literature, to answer their questions. They share their newly acquired learning to discuss the concepts at a deeper and more integrated level when they reconvene. Assessments are often authentic exercises where students apply their knowledge to a similar problem (Blumberg, 2007).

The results of meta-analyses and individual studies showed that students in traditional courses did better than students in PBL courses on knowledge-based, traditional multiple choice tests at the end of the courses (Prince & Felder, 2006). I believe this is due to the PBL students' being exposed to less content. However, the literature on the long-term effects of type of instruction indicated that graduates of PBL programs retained more knowledge and applied concepts better several years later than graduates of traditional, largely lecture-based programs (Allen, Donham, & Bernhardt, 2010). Students in PBL courses acquired a variety of self-directed, lifelong learning skills, including information literacy, better than students in traditional courses did (Blumberg, 2000). (The University of Delaware maintains a peer-reviewed clearinghouse of problems in various disciplines: http://primus.nss.udel.edu/Pbl/.)

Team-Based Learning

At the first class of a new unit, students take a short multiple choice quiz twice assessing their comprehension of the facts and concepts within that unit. First, they take it alone, and then they take it in their small groups or teams. As they record their group answers, they get the results either by taking the quiz online or by using answer sheets that reveal the right answer by scratching alternatives on a special answer sheet (like a lottery ticket) (Epstein et al., 2002). For the rest of the unit, the teams work together to solve challenging problems that require students to make decisions based on the concepts in the unit. Students provide formative and summative assessments to their team (Michaelsen, Knight, & Fink, 2004).

Educators who use team-based learning have found many positive results: increased attendance, higher test scores, better long-term retention, improved attitudes toward group work, and student satisfaction with their learning experiences (Michaelsen & Sweet, 2011). (For examples of how team-based learning has been implemented in many different disciplines and empirical studies of its effectiveness, go to the team-based learning clearinghouse: www.teambasedlearning.org.)

Just-in-Time Teaching

In courses employing just-in-time teaching (JiTT), students respond to web-based questions that require thought and often are open to interpretation, the night before class is held They also write an explanation of their answer. The purpose of these types of questions is to get the students thinking about the content and checking their comprehension before class. Thus, with JiTT, students come prepared to class to engage meaningfully with the content. The instructor analyzes the student responses and adjusts what will happen in class depending on the student responses. If the students seem to understand the material well, the instructor will not need to cover it in class.

Nevertheless, because the questions are demanding and one clear answer is not obvious, the instructor will spend time on the relevant content. Instead of the traditional lecture, he or she uses a variety of techniques to focus on the content—perhaps give a short demonstration, lead a discussion after displaying some different answers, pose a problem and have the students work on it in small groups, or use audience response questions with clickers, or any combination of these methods. Students' responses to the questions posed in class and their answers on the JiTT questions prior to class and class work count toward their grade.

Attendance increases with JiTT. Although students often complain about the extra work involved, they realize there are many benefits, including better preparation and staying focused on the subject (Simkins & Maier, 2010). When JiTT is implemented properly and students fully participate, they can make dramatic gains on standardized pre- and posttests of understanding of concepts compared to much smaller gains with traditional lecture methods (Novak, 2011). Simkins and Maier (2010) provide case studies of how JiTT has been used in the sciences, social sciences, and humanities.

Blended or Hybrid Learning

This instructional method integrates the best aspects of face-to-face teaching with the advantages of online learning. Technology can disseminate information quite well. When instructors prerecord short content presentations, they can check that they were clear and incorporate materials that experts have developed that are available on Web 2.0. Popular Web 2.0 resources include presentations of experts on Khan, TED talks, and Academic Earth. Merlot and iTunesU give examples of how others explain concepts and often have excellent three-dimensional examples or interactive aspects. Students can view aspects of society in exotic places or visit a museum or a nature reserve through resources on the web. They can take online quizzes repeatedly until they master the content. Face-to-face time, which is reduced by about 50 percent over traditional classes, is well spent with small group work, instructors answering questions, discussions, or laboratory work. Students should interact with each other, their instructor, and the content both online and in the classroom.

When blended learning is done well, students learn more than they would have in either total face-to-face or entirely online environments (US Department of Education, Office of Policy, Evaluation, and Policy Development, 2010). Instructors teach more effectively in blended courses when they receive training on this method (Palsole & Brunk-Chavez, 2011).

Service-Learning

In service-learning, students participate in an organized service project that relates to the course content. The service project benefits the community organization as students gain valuable skills. This is not the same as volunteering in a community service project. Instructors who include service-learning need to collaborate with the community partners to identify projects that are mutually beneficial to all parties involved, with stated desired outcomes for the community organization and the students. Students write and discuss critical reflections of their experiences to document their learning, a critical aspect of service-learning (Eyler, 2009). The assessment process involves input from the staff at the community organization and the instructors; it considers whether the service outcomes have been met, as well as the student learning. Service-learning promotes deep learning and personal growth in undergraduate students (Kuh, 2008).

Melanie Oates, a business associate professor at Carlow University in Pittsburgh, requires service-learning in nonprofit organizations because she feels that the principles of marketing and management are the same regardless of the setting, and community organizations benefit from the students' time and expertise. During service-learning, students are often required to analyze complex situations from various perspectives, which promotes the development of higher-order cognitive skills such as critical thinking and the understanding of contemporary social issues (Felton & Clayton, 2011). Participating in service-learning leads to greater long-term civic engagement as well (Pascarella & Terenzini, 2005).

Transformative Results from Evidence-Based Teaching

When instructors begin to read the literature in higher education, they learn so much about teaching that it can be transformative for their teaching (Brew & Ginns, 2008; Smith, 2001). Few express this as clearly as Barbara Millis, an internationally known faculty developer, writer, and speaker. In an issue of the journal *Peer Review* devoted to good teaching, Millis (2009) reflects that her own teaching improved only after she began to use pedagogy and research literature to inform her teaching. She notes several successive breakthroughs, including hearing about various techniques to make cooperative learning effective, reading about deep learning, and reading the literature on how the brain works to facilitate learning. With each breakthrough, Millis thought about how she taught and why she taught the way she did, and she made changes to reflect the new knowledge she acquired. As a result of these transformations, her teaching improved. She concludes from her teaching experiences and her work as a faculty developer that effective teachers internalize what they learn about pedagogy from reading, mentors, and working with faculty developers. Furthermore, their teaching continues to evolve as they engage in more reading and discussions (Millis, 2009).

When Roger Ideishi and Susan Wainwright began inquiry into their teaching, their careers were transformed: they went from being effective teachers to teacher-scholars. Ideishi reinforced his ideas on why and how he taught using service-learning. He was so intellectually curious about explaining ideas that he launched a new research direction for his clinical work. He now conducts field research on helping autistic children function in museums, airports, and others public places. This research stems from supervising students in their service-learning where they worked with developmentally delayed children in inclusive community programming.

Wainwright recently changed jobs and became the head of the Physical Therapy Department at Thomas Jefferson University, where she is cochairing an initiative on promoting the scholarship of teaching and learning in the School of Health Professions. She has introduced qualitative assessments to this project, where others were considering only quantitative surveys to study the development of professional attitudes and behaviors. Not only were Ideishi and Wainwright transformed, but once their ideas began to be disseminated in writing beyond their immediate peers, they, like all other teacher-scholars, had an impact on people, both instructors and students, they never will meet. This is the most transformative aspect of conducting rigorous study of one's teaching: presenting and publishing the findings to larger audiences (Smith, 2001).

Why Conduct Inquiry about Your Teaching?

This type of evidence-based teaching advances the profession of teaching in general (Hutchings & Shulman, 1999). Weimer (2006) discusses many reasons that systematically studying teaching improves learning outcomes. When instructors investigate what interests them, they can change how they teach as a result of what they learned through their investigations. Just as in all other fields of inquiry, the question-and-answer cycle about teaching always leads to more questions, widening the intellectual curiosity about teaching. When instructors engage in systematic data collection, they are doing it because they want to learn more about specific aspects of their teaching, not because they have to or because they are trying to get higher scores on their course evaluations.

When I was in graduate school, a senior professor in a completely different field gave me good advice: he told me to think of everything I do, including teaching, as an intellectual pursuit or a scientific investigation. That, he said, keeps routine work from getting stale. When I do investigations into teaching, I gain a greater awareness of behaviors and rationales for teaching. These insights are more profound when coupled with the critical reflection discussed in the previous chapter. When instructors investigate their teaching, they have interesting and substantial things to discuss with other faculty members and not just complain about their students. Doing systematic inquiry into teaching brings instructors out of their departmental silos and helps them meet and interact with people from other disciplines and perspectives (Weimer, 2006).

These investigations can be renewing and invigorating for experienced teachers (Weimer, 2006). I learned this from a colleague at least twenty years older than me at a departmental holiday party many years ago. All semester I had been working with this full professor on research relating to his teaching. The project was going well, and our work was headed toward a publication in a higher education journal. At the party, my collaborator made a point of introducing me to his wife, who said she was so glad to meet me because her husband seemed happier this semester than she had seen him in years. Several weeks earlier, when she remarked about this to him, he replied that he was pursuing a line of research and it was very exciting to be learning in a new field. He enjoyed his teaching more and felt renewed.

Promoting a Transformative Culture of Evidence-Based Teaching

When instructors use either the literature or data collection to support their evidence-based teaching, they tend to share their good ideas and teaching challenges with their colleagues. This leads to the benefit that teaching is more of a public practice than a solitary activity (Shulman, 2004a). When a cohort of faculty members uses evidence-based teaching at an institution, the culture changes to where good teaching is valued. Instructors readily share how they teach.

I am proud that this culture exists at my university. Last year, over a third of the full-time faculty and additional adjunct faculty presented their ideas in well-attended presentations on campus through various venues sponsored by my Teaching and Learning Center. Each spring for thirteen years, I have hosted an educational innovation poster session, and abstracts of these posters are compiled into annual editions of "A Document of Innovations" (www.usciences.edu/teaching /innovations). The many case examples I use throughout this book summarize some of these presentations. My university now embraces Shulman's notion of teaching as community practice (Shulman, 2004a). As a result of this evidence-based culture of sharing teaching, many University of the Sciences faculty members now present at national peer-reviewed conferences on teaching in higher education. For example, the fewer than two hundred full-time faculty members at my university presented 13 percent of the thirty-nine posters at the peer-reviewed and highly competitive Lilly Conference: College and University Teaching and Learning, in Washington, DC, in 2011. A second-year assistant professor's poster was voted the best poster at that conference.

Suggestions for Better Teaching Coming from This Chapter

- Consider your teaching as a legitimate area to study systematically.
- Use evidence to inform your teaching.
- Read the literature or learn about effective teaching practices in your discipline.
- Read the literature on teaching in higher education in general.
- Consider adopting evidence-based effective practices.
- Become informed about how the brain works, how people learn, and how they remember and use information.

- Become curious about your own teaching to develop your understanding of the teaching/learning process.

- Study a specific aspect of your teaching to explain how effective it is for student learning.

- Incorporate what you learned from your reading and your own inquiry into your teaching practices.

- Continuously consider how to teach better through evidence-based decision making.

Chapter 6

Finding and Using Literature to Promote Better Teaching

YOU ARE READY TO DEVELOP your teaching by using the literature to support your instructional practices. Using research and research-informed literature gives you the potential to excel in your teaching because you will be using best practices that work with similar students. When you start reading the literature on teaching, you are beginning a fascinating journey that will show you new ideas of teaching and skills that lead to better teaching. There are many unpredictable side paths along the way, and they are worth pursuing. Figure 6.1 illustrates this path, which consists of reading for general purposes and seeking answers to specific questions that you may have.

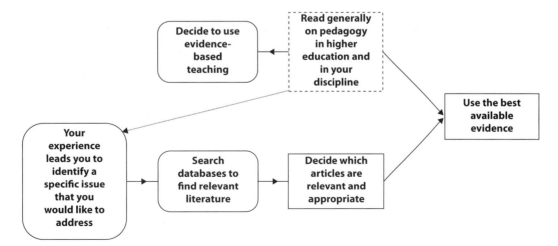

FIGURE 6.1 **Pathways to Using Evidence-Based Teaching**

Sources about Teaching in Higher Education

To begin understanding how to teach using the research literature, read higher education literature in general and in your discipline. Weimer gives an excellent overview on how and why to read different types of professional educational literature. Her book, *Enhancing Scholarly Work on Teaching and Learning* (2006), and Cathy Bishop-Clark's and Beth Dietz-Uhler's book, *Engaging in the Scholarship of Teaching and Learning* (2012), list many appropriate journals to consider in both higher education and in specific disciplines. You might cultivate a habit of reading a few journals or the educational sections of journals in your discipline on a regular basis. Because their peer-reviewed articles have a general appeal, I recommend these journals:

- *Assessment and Evaluation in Higher Education*
- *College Teaching*
- *Innovative Higher Education*
- *Journal of Excellence in College Teaching*
- *Journal of Faculty Development*

In addition, I suggest a worthwhile non-peer-reviewed resource, *Teaching Professor Newsletter* that Weimer edits, as a general way to find out about effective teaching techniques. She summarizes literature from many diverse disciplines. If you find an idea that you want to read about in more detail, you can access the full article that is referenced at the end of the summaries in this newsletter.

Attending conferences is another way to learn about current ideas in teaching in higher education and to be directed to appropriate authors and literature. Most large discipline meetings offer some education sessions. Some offer teaching and learning tracts within the conference, and some fields have teaching and learning conferences—for example, the annual meeting of the American Society for Engineering Education and Biennial Music Educators National Conference, which is sponsored by the National Association for Music Education. There are also conferences dedicated to excellent teaching in higher education, such as the six Lilly Conferences on College and University Teaching held in different regions of the United States, and the Teaching Professor Conferences. Finally, you can consult with the staff in the teaching and learning center or center for excellence in teaching, if your institution has one, for educational literature.

Number 128 of the *New Directions for Teaching and Learning* series (Buskist & Groccia, 2011) discusses nine approaches to teaching, from lecturing to service-learning to online education, that have a great deal of evidence-based support. This monograph is a good place to begin your reading about teaching. Another option is to read a good book on teaching in higher education. Because there are so many available, I recommend books written by Stephen Brookfield, Terry Doyle, L. Dee Fink, and Maryellen Weimer, all of them excellent examples of accessible, evidence-based pedagogical literature that faculty can read and apply their ideas to their own teaching. Perry and Smart (2007) summarize the evidence-based literature on specific topics, such as student evaluations of teaching and student motivation.

Specialized journals may be relevant to your interests. Educators in most disciplines have been conducting systematic research for years. For example, physicists have reformed how introductory and general physics should be taught based on such research (Mazur, 1997). Most disciplines have peer-reviewed, pedagogical journals, such as *Teaching Sociology*, that publish research on effective teaching in that discipline. Although *CBE* focuses on teaching the biological sciences and *Journal of Management Education* focuses on business education, I often find articles in them that can apply to other disciplines. Also, several journals are devoted to online education (e.g., *American Journal of Distance Education*, *Educause Quarterly*).

Some journals are devoted to specific themes, such as the first year of college, general education, or teaching English as a second language. Two series, *New Directions in Higher Education* and *New Directions in Teaching and Learning*, focus on a different theme or topic each issue. Reading the list of topics covered in the past couple of years gives you a good idea of what topics are being researched. Each issue has about a dozen short chapters that summarize different perspectives and the literature on that topic.

Reading Directed to a Specific Topic

Most likely your critical reflections about your teaching or the literature will lead you to specific questions or problems that you would like to address. This calls for a different method to access the literature. In this case, you will need to conduct a directed search to find specific literature.

Figure 6.2 lists the steps to follow when you are trying to answer a specific question about your teaching. These steps are modified from evidence-based decision making in medicine (Guyatt, Haynes, Jaeschle, Cook, & Green, 2000).

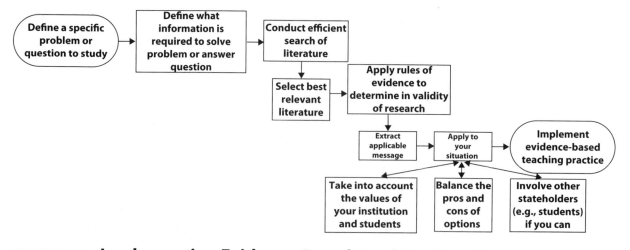

FIGURE 6.2   Implementing Evidence-Based Teaching Practices Using the Literature

Source: Modeled after Guyatt et al. (2000).

How to Find Supporting Evidence

In today's information age, it is easy to find supporting evidence in the literature using search engines and databases. In fact, doing searches in the education literature is similar to how searches are done elsewhere. I offer some basic background and then discuss how these basic principles apply to searches in the education literature.

There are two main databases for pedagogical literature that pertains to higher education: ERIC (US Department of Education, 2012; www .ERIC.ed.gov) and Professional Development (www.EBSCO.com), which is accessed through EBSCO. ERIC, a US Department of Education database on teaching from infancy through adult education, allows unlimited access to 1.4 million bibliographic records of journals (indexed since 1966) and other print materials. Anyone with Internet access can find materials in ERIC. Due to its scope, ERIC contains peer-reviewed and non-peer-reviewed materials, and the quality of the record varies. To find a specific journal, you enter the word to retrieve the list of journals containing that word. There is also a complete listing of the many journals it indexes. ERIC is striving to have many of these records linked to full text in Adobe PDF format if the publisher allows that. The extensive nonjournal collection includes presentations at key conferences, curriculum guides, self-studies done for accrediting agencies, and reports.

The Professional Development (EBSCO, 2013) database is a specialized collection of more than 500 complete text education journals, over 350 of them peer reviewed. It also contains 200 education reports. You may specify that you want peer-reviewed literature. If you do not select that feature, the results of a search indicate the type of reference, including academic journals, which most likely are peer reviewed; periodicals, which are not peer reviewed; or books. Professional Development is accessed through EBSCO, a subscription service that many higher education and public libraries subscribe to. You need to access EBSCO from a library site; therefore, the URL would be library specific. The results of the search will tell you how you can access this reference through your library, such as full text or a PDF file. The availability of articles varies depending on what your library subscribes to.

I also recommend the search engine Google Scholar (Scholar.google .com) to locate articles, books, theses, and abstracts from academic publishers, professional societies, and higher education websites. This is a good search engine if you want to look for literature beyond your own discipline. Within Google Scholar, you can search by author or title. I use Google Scholar when I remember hearing about some research or an author but lack enough details to locate the information. Use advanced Google Scholar to define your search further. You can limit the phrase you are looking for to the title or anywhere in the article or book. The citations in Google Scholar list the publications citing this article, so you can find more up-to-date literature on the topic. However, the majority of the full text articles that I want to access after reading the abstract are available only by subscription or a pay-per-view method and not immediately available.

Conduct an efficient search. Because education has such a wide range, it is always a good idea to include the words *higher education* in the search. All of these databases and search engines use Boolean logic, which means they use combinations of connectors such as *and*, *or*, and *not* to determine the relationships among concepts in their advanced search options. Start with *or*, and if you get too many hits, you can limit the search with *and*. Place quotes around a specific phrase in your search if you want an exact match of those words. For example, I was looking for information with the question, "Does using learning-centered teaching lead to grade inflation?" I knew that if I searched *learning-centered teaching* or *grade inflation*, I would get an unmanageable number of citations to read because the search would yield resources on both topics. Therefore, I searched *learning-centered teaching* and *grade inflation* using both of the databases and the search engine; these searches led to no citations. If you find that you are not successful with the words you selected, try looking in the database's thesaurus for similar words. I did this by looking in the database's thesaurus for similar words, like s*tudent-centered learning* and *grade improvement.* The answer to my question was that there were no published articles or presentations that showed a relationship between learning-centered teaching and grade inflation.

Librarians can be extremely helpful in making your search more productive. After you have obtained the results, save them. If you have developed a good search strategy and want to keep up without having to constantly search, direct the database to update you regularly using the RSS feed options available.

How to Select the Best Relevant Literature

After using these databases and search engines, you have to decide what is worth reading. If your problem is too many citations, you can quickly reduce the size of your list of possible sources since many of them will not be relevant based on the title of the article. Next, read the abstract to decide if you want to read the entire article. Instead of relying on an isolated study, it is better to look at interventions that have been applied to multiple populations and settings (Dolan, 2007). An efficient way to become knowledgeable about the issues on a topic is to scan your list for reviews of research literature articles. Read those articles early in your information gathering; then read the relevant original articles discussed in these review articles.

Table 6.1 lists guidelines for evaluating the quality of specific articles. You probably are familiar with these guidelines because they transcend disciplines. Lynn Worsham, an editor of *JAC*, a scholarly journal of rhetoric, culture, and politics, warns faculty to avoid what she calls "fast food scholarship" (Worsham, 2011). Articles that have characteristics that would place them largely on the less preferred evidence column in table 6.1 could be called fast food scholarship.

Studies with the most rigor or preferred evidence include systematic review or meta-analysis of related studies using similar methodologies (Tomlin & Borgetto, 2011). Meta-analysis is a statistical technique that combines the results of separate research studies to provide an estimate of the treatment effect. These articles are more common in clinical investigations than in educational research. In some of the most researched educational topics, such as problem-based learning, you can find a meta-analysis of the literature (Vernon & Blake, 1993). In addition, the more specific the question is, the less likely it is that someone has done a meta-analysis of the literature. Since few topics in education have meta-analyses, relying on critical and systematic reviews of the literature is quite suitable. Active learning (Prince, 2004) and small group learning (Springer, Stanne, & Donovan, 1999) are topics with many critical reviews.

Research-based articles are preferred because they are more objective than the more subjective experience-based literature (Weimer, 2006). Table 6.2 lists guidelines to select the best available research evidence.

TABLE 6.1   Guidelines for Evaluating the Quality of Articles

Criteria	Less Preferred Evidence	More Preferred Evidence
Publication source	Listed in increasing order of strength of evidence • Blog, nonauthored website • Popular press • Newsletter • Non-peer reviewed	Peer-reviewed, high-quality journal
Credibility of the author	No author credentials given Not an expert in the discipline, not the primary researcher	Primary researcher with professional expertise did the research and wrote the article
Potential bias of authors or researchers	Listed in increasing order of strength of evidence • Has clear conflict of interest • May have a conflict of interest	No conflict of interest Objective researcher and reporter of research
Introduction of article, review of the literature	Few citations Only older citations Citations that only directly support this study	Literature is critically reviewed Current citations referring to peer-reviewed journal articles Contrasting perspectives reviewed
Methodological rigor: Applicable if a research article (see tables 6.3 and 6.4)		
Strength of data	Other factors may contribute to outcomes or confound results or conclusions	Data show a strong or highly statistically significant relationship between the intervention or teaching method and the outcome; results did not occur by chance
Results: Applicable if a research article (see tables 6.3 and 6.4)		
Discussion, implications, results	Implications for practice are not discussed Author makes illogical conclusions or conclusions that do not follow from the data	Discussion and implications follow logically from the data Contains a discussion of what the reader could do about the results
Fidelity of report	Unclear record, missing details Sections are not internally congruent	Record is clear enough to replicate Entire report appears consistent and congruent

However, much of the literature in higher education continues to be experience based, and much of it is well worth reading.

Determining the Quality of Research Literature

I offer several methods to help make this judgment. The three main types of research are quantitative, qualitative, and outcomes. Table 6.3 lists guidelines for evaluating the strength of evidence given in these different types of research articles.

TABLE 6.2 Guidelines for Selecting the Best Research-Based Available Evidence

Criteria	Less Preferred Evidence	More Preferred Evidence
Amount of data available	Listed in increasing order of strength of evidence • Single study • Small sample size • Few isolated studies	Many studies finding consistent results in various settings Literature systematically reviewed that leads to consistent results Meta-analysis
Impact or effectiveness of teaching methods	Listed in increasing order of strength of evidence • Observational, descriptive studies • Studies that test hypotheses	Listed in increasing order of strength of evidence • Efficacy studies or experimental studies to test hypotheses in controlled environments • Effectiveness studies in authentic environments
Ability to generalize findings	Special unique population such as honors college, study occurs in another country or culture, or with nontraditional students	Diverse types of students studied
Ability to extract implications that are relevant to specific teaching issue; relevance to your teaching question	Loosely related	Close fit between study and specific teaching situation

TABLE 6.3 Guidelines for Evaluating Strength of Different Types of Research

Research Method or Study Design	Advantages of This Type of Research	Less Preferred Evidence	More Preferred Evidence
Quantitative research	Can determine cause and effect Can carefully control variables	Listed in increasing order of strength of evidence • Single-subject study • Variables not controlled • Quasi-experimental	Listed in increasing order of strength of evidence • Experimental design • Controlled trial • Randomized, blinded controlled trial
Qualitative research	Offers insights into perspectives of various stakeholders Can measure student satisfaction with teaching methods Can identify unintended consequences	Listed in increasing order of strength of evidence • Study with one informant • Limited number of sources of data	Extensive data coming from many people, many observations
Outcomes research	Can determine feasibility of intervention effects Can determine applicability to various groups in real environments	One group, pretest and posttest study	Measure immediate and long-term effects in diverse populations Compare covariables Teaching occurred in authentic environments

Source: Modeled after Tomlin and Borgetto (2011).

Strong substantiation shows consistent evidence that the educational practice is associated with large improvement and the effects can be generalized to a range of students and settings. Moderate evidence provides one but not both of the above characteristics. Minimal evidence comes from indirect sources of support or in related areas (Slocum, Spencer, & Detrich, 2012).

Research to determine the impact or effectiveness of teaching methods occurs in three stages:

1. Educators make systematic observations about what is effective in their teaching, which may lead to hypotheses. These descriptive studies are the most common research done by individual faculty.

2. Researchers might do more experimental studies to test these hypotheses. These might be called efficacy studies. In efficacy studies, variables are controlled and usually are done in controlled, simulated environments, not real classrooms.

3. Researchers conduct effectiveness studies. Because effectiveness studies are conducted in real educational environments, there is less strict control over variables. However, they often allow more generalizations to other populations (Slocum et al., 2012). If possible, try to find effectiveness studies.

You can use evidence-based decision making to determine the quality of the literature. This idea originated in medicine and spread to many caring or service professions, including social work, counseling, and education. Deciding if an article is evidence based is not straightforward, and the answer is not either yes or no. Instead readers need to judge the strength of the evidence-based support from the research described in an article. Evidence-based decision making is defined as the integration of three essential components: best available evidence, professional judgment, and client values and context (Sackett, Richardson, Rosenberg, & Haynes, 2000). Professional judgment, client values, and context complement best available evidence. Best available evidence considers two essential characteristics: the methodological quality of the evidence available and the degree of relevance to the specific educational situation

Determining the Quality of Research Methods

"Methodological quality" refers to the procedural or research rigor of the evidence available. Tables 6.3 and 6.4 describe some general guidelines to help you judge the quality of the research methods. Table 6.4 lists relevant research quality considerations. This is a suggested list and not a firm checklist, and you can modify it to suit your own needs. If you need more help, ask a faculty member who teaches research or statistics.

TABLE 6.4   Methodological Considerations When Reading Research Literature

Aspect of Research	Methodological Considerations: Appropriate Study Design	Applicability to Your Situation: Description Should Allow You to Judge Similarity to Your Situation
Participants in the study	Sample size should be adequate to measure effect.	Evaluate similarities and differences in the type and level of students compared to your students. Judge if the type of students is similar enough to believe that this intervention would work with your teaching.
Context of the study	Description should be adequate to understand context.	Evaluate similarities to and differences from your teaching the discipline studied and the desired learning outcomes. Judge if the setting is similar enough to believe that this intervention would work with your students.
Analysis of data or statistical tests	Sufficient data to support the author's claims. Appropriate for study, type of data. Accuracy and credibility of the data. Statistically significant results for quantitative research. Correlations imply associations among variables, not causation. Data comes from a number of sources in qualitative research	Unable to apply data directly to your situation. Can use same data analysis and statistical tests in your research.
Significance of findings	Ability to generalize to other populations. Context and population study may play a large role in strength or significance of the findings.	Judge if the significance of the findings is similar enough to believe that this intervention would work with your students.

Source: Modeled after Dolan (2007); Tomlin and Borgetto (2011).

Degree of Relevance to Your Situation

Table 6.4 describes how methodological considerations relate to applicability to your situation. You can screen for relevance in your search for literature; however, do not be surprised if you find few extremely similar contexts. In that case, broaden your search to include fewer similar contexts, and evaluate this literature on how similar it is to what you are seeking. Then judge if the findings might apply to your situation.

Use Best Available Evidence

For some academics, the concept of evidence-based decision making implies extremely high standards of research methods, such as those used in laboratory or clinical sciences. Research in education, however, rarely reaches the highest level of evidence-based support, especially to scientists who are used to laboratory-controlled research. Within the health professions, multisite, blinded, randomized-controlled trials are the gold standard. But this methodology is usually not appropriate in education because students are not randomly assigned to classes, and it is hard to conduct blind trials where the instructor does not know the intervention his or her students are receiving. Faculty in higher education therefore are not able to conduct these types of studies. Using the same, unrealistic standard needlessly deters some from even trying to use evidence-based practices (Slocum et al., 2012). It is better to be more pragmatic and use the best evidence or support that is available.

Studying teaching and learning is different from studying occurrences in the physical sciences. Most educational research is done in the dynamic milieu of the classroom where variables are much more difficult to control than in laboratories. Learning is, after all, a human phenomenon with lots of variation. Neuroscience research explains how learning occurs, which can apply to all types of teaching in higher education. This certainly should lead faculty in higher education to accept the standard of best available evidence, combined with professional judgment. If the concept of best available evidence is used, then many more faculty can use evidence-based decision making to direct their teaching.

Faculty should strive to rely on research with the highest extent of confidence that is the most relevant to their teaching context; this would be an ideal situation (Spencer, Detrich, & Slocum, 2012). However, such ideal evidence rarely exists. Some professors may feel they cannot use evidence-based education unless the research is the highest quality, relevant, and plentiful (Slocum et al., 2012). If faculty in some fields may be uncomfortable calling the kind of literature available in higher education as "evidence based," they can instead refer to it as "research–based or empirical support for teaching."

Far more large-scale, experimentally controlled research occurs in primary and secondary education than higher education. Yet even in K–12 education, most practice guides rely on far less than strong support (Slocum et al., 2012). Although there is not a lot of really high-quality research literature in higher education, there is sufficient "good-enough" writing to justify looking at the literature that does exist in most areas.

Decisions can be made on the basis of the literature that exists now. Instructional practice could and should be much more evidence based than it is. If empirically supported research is not available on your topic, then you might consider other types of literature to support your teaching, for example, narrative reviews such as might be found in edited books and reports of expert panels that may be published in conference proceedings or practice guides (Slocum et al., 2012). Sometimes best practice committees or consensus conferences of experts have developed documents that offer practical recommendations for implementation. Experts may make recommendations for best teaching practices based on their own research, experience, and reviews of the literature. Here the reputation and credentials of the experts need to be considered. Textbooks and teaching support guides often identify well-supported teaching techniques.

You should strive to use the best available evidence coming from literature to support your teaching. When you read the literature, you will find ways to develop your teaching. Using evidence gives you confidence that you are implementing effective teaching methods. You can also use evidence in assessments of teaching. Part 2 of this book applies the same concepts described in this section to self-assessments of teaching. Evidence-based teaching citing literature is a powerful way to show that you are an effective teacher. I illustrate with a concrete example in box 6.1.

Box 6.1. Applying the Steps in Figure 6.2 to Finding and Using Literature to a Real Teaching Situation

I want to show that learning-centered approaches are effective or perhaps even more effective than traditional teaching methods in my courses. A search of the literature using the strategies I have outlined can tell me if there are any studies that can guide my assessment of my teaching that are not just looking at how well students did in my courses. Final grades may not be a good indicator of learning.

I found thirteen studies that assessed the impact of learning-centered practices on students achieving learning outcomes. All of them used valid and reliable methods. I classified these studies into four types: using a pre- and posttest design; comparing two sections of the same course taught using traditional and learning-centered approaches; using a combination of the first two by using pre- and posttests in different sections; and looking at the long-term effects of the teaching methods (Mostrom & Blumberg, 2012). This is the only section of this course, so I cannot use the two methods that compare two different sections of the same course. I could do a follow-up of my students after this class is over, but this is logistically messy, as some of my students are in their last year at my university when they take my courses. Therefore, I decide to use a pre- and posttest measure of knowledge and skills and not go over the answers to the pretest. I will ask the same questions on the tests given at the beginning and the end of the semester. These questions mirror the learning outcomes for the course but are not the same as the final exam. I will seek Institutional Review Board approval to do this assessment and give students some credit for taking the extra two tests so they will approach them seriously. This study will implement the best evidence-based practices that are relevant to my situation. Figure 6.3 shows the steps I use by applying the steps given in figure 6.2.

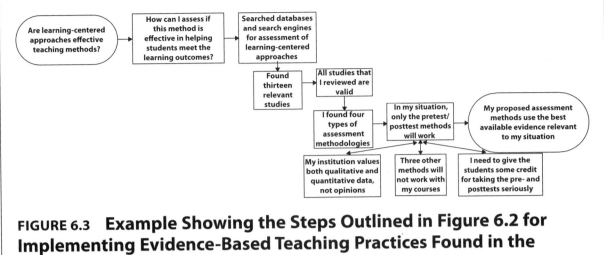

FIGURE 6.3   Example Showing the Steps Outlined in Figure 6.2 for Implementing Evidence-Based Teaching Practices Found in the Literature

Suggestions for Using Literature to Promote Better Teaching

- Teach using evidence-based literature.

- Read the pedagogical literature in general and in your discipline.

- Address specific teaching questions through a database search.
  - Select appropriate resources to read based on filtering guidelines.
  - Read critical reviews of the literature.

- Use the best available evidence to support your teaching.

- Considerations for the best available evidence include:
  - Many consistent studies showing the effect
  - Research that is methodologically valid and rigorous
  - Various research methods showing that specific teaching techniques are effective
  - A research context similar to your own situation

- Do not be discouraged if you cannot locate much directly relevant literature. This allows you to do the groundbreaking research on this topic.

- In the absence of directly relevant literature, apply general, evidence-based, best practices.

A MODEL TO ASSESS TEACHING TO PROMOTE BETTER LEARNING

The two chapters in part 2 should be read together as a unit.

Chapter 7

Principles of Assessing Teaching

TEACHING CAN BE ASSESSED for formative purposes of improvement or summative reasons to make high-stakes decisions including continued employment. This book is concerned only with improvement goals, not with the summative functions of assessment. For our purpose, assessing teaching has two primary goals: to increase student learning and to enhance or invigorate teaching. The second is really a subgoal of the first because when teaching improves, students learn more. Because of the power of assessments, they can be critical for promoting the use of effective teaching behaviors. Although summative assessment is legitimate and widely used, it does not offer much to improve teaching for the following reasons: It does not

- Provide the kind of information that allows teachers to determine if they are effective in the classroom.
- Help professors learn how to teach better. The tools available for evaluating teaching do not offer practical and specific suggestions for improvement.
- Increase student learning since the focus is not on learning outcomes. Unfortunately, many assessments of teaching still focus on teaching style and personality characteristics and give no insight into how effectively students are learning.

Just as academics teach based on misconceptions, they also have misconceptions about assessing teaching that can hamper their ability to teach better. Half of these misconceptions about assessing teaching follow from misconceptions about teaching. The other half resides in the assessment process. The following sections discuss each misconception and the more accurate concept that needs to replace it.

Beliefs about Teaching and Their Implications for Assessment of Teaching

The constructs about teaching discussed in chapter 2 have implications for assessing teaching for the purposes of improvement. Misconceptions about teaching lead to fallacies about assessing teaching; alternative, accurate beliefs about assessment follow from the recommended ideas. Table 7.1 lists four common misconceptions about assessing teaching and accurate recommended concepts that are derived from these teaching constructs. (Read this table beginning with the middle column.) This table builds on table 2.2.

TABLE 7.1 Concepts about Teaching and Corollary Formative Assessment Implications

Misconception		Question about Teaching Construct ← Start reading here →	Recommended Concept	
Corollary Formative Assessment Implication	**← Idea**		**Idea →**	**Corollary Formative Assessment Implication**
If teaching is intuitive, then criteria for assessing teaching can be implicit, subjective, and unique to individual faculty.	Faculty members in higher education intuitively know how to teach, since they are subject matter specialists.	*Is teaching intuitive, or should instructors try to learn effective teaching approaches?*	Effective teaching is not intuitive. Faculty can learn effective teaching strategies.	If teaching is not intuitive, then criteria for assessing teaching should be explicit, objective, and uniformly defined and applied.
Assessment tools currently in use focus on teaching styles and characteristics, not student learning. These tools falsely assume they accurately reflect good teaching practices.	Teaching by its definition focuses on what the instructor does.	*What should effective teaching models focus on?*	Teaching should focus on the intended outcomes, especially student learning (Barr & Tagg, 1995; Blumberg, 2009a; Weimer, 2013).	Good teaching practices, such as learning-centered teaching, should drive assessment tools and assess how well the instructor creates a successful environment for learning. They should focus on student engagement and learning.

The current focus on student course evaluations and, to a lesser extent, observations inaccurately defines what is effective teaching. Assessments of teaching therefore do not consider scholarly criteria such as relying on best practices or consistency with pedagogical literature.	Unlike research, or professional practice, teaching does not need to be evidence based.	*What role does evidence-based practice play in assessing teaching?*	Effective teaching should employ evidence-based practices (Boyer, 1990; Shulman, 2004b; Weimer, 2010)	Assessment of teaching, like teaching itself, should be evaluated like other scholarly pursuits. Teaching should be assessed for its congruence with evidence-based pedagogical literature or systematic investigations into effective teaching practices.
One assessment instrument is used for most teaching contexts.	Teaching takes place in the classroom; teaching is didactic.	*How does the context of teaching have an impact on how instructors teach and are assessed?*	Varied contexts for teaching; teaching and learning are integrated (Eyler, 2009; Kuh, 2008).	The contexts for teaching (didactic or experiential) should give rise to diverse, context-specific assessment instruments.

Assessment Implications of Intuitive Teaching

Commonly used assessment tools do not operationally define the standards of good teaching. Although many of these tools use a Likert scale, they do not anchor the scale in effective teaching standards. Instructors can interpret their scores either as norm or criteria referenced depending on which makes them look better unless there are local practices or policies. However, in both cases, we lack comparison standards. I suggest that we do not overtly set these standards because we know that they would be arbitrary standards. This lack of uniform standards is more of a problem for summative evaluation than formative assessments.

If instructors use a norm-referenced approach, who would be the appropriate comparison group: other faculty within a department, a college within a university, or the entire group of faculty members at an institution? Would a good teacher be one whose scores are better than 80 percent of the faculty she or he is compared to? More germane to this book, how do norm-referenced criteria promote better teaching?

Or perhaps if instructors use a criterion-referenced approach, what point on the scale defines good or excellent teaching? How high would the standard have to be? Maybe it might be at least a 3 on a four-point scale or a 5 on a seven-point scale? More relevant to the purposes of this book than what a good score is, what would constitute real improvement?

Can high scores on student evaluations of courses distinguish effective teachers from popular or easy teachers? The answer is not straightforward and may depend on the types of learners who completed these evaluations and the instructional approach. Deep learners rated instructors who pushed them to explore the meaning and implication of what they were learning higher than those instructors who did not do this. However, surface learners (those who learned without understanding) rated these same instructors (who pushed their students) lower. Surface learners rated instructors higher who allowed them to succeed with only recalling the information given to them (Bain & Zimmerman, 2009). Since learning-centered teaching encourages deep learning (Prosser & Trigwell, 1999), I hypothesize that surface learners may not rate learning-centered teachers highly.

Implicit, subjective, and individually defined criteria for good teaching can send a message that most teaching is acceptable without looking at the quality of learning. Such teaching criteria lead to several consequences, including confusion about what good teaching is (McAlpine & Harris, 2002). Inconsistency in the definitions of teaching standards might also reflect the devaluing of teaching compared to research (Weimer, 2006). Because there are no consistently defined standards, instructors may declare their own excellence subjectively, and mostly on the basis of student evaluations. Perhaps because teaching is not as valued as research at many higher education institutions, such ineffective and inappropriate teaching practices continue.

However, these problems can be resolved if educators assume that teaching is not intuitive. All professors can learn effective teaching approaches and techniques. This can lead to clear ideas of what is effective teaching. If teaching is not intuitive, then the criteria for effective teaching should be explicit, objective and uniformly defined, and applied. This might also elevate the importance of teaching in higher education.

Assessment Implications of Teaching Approaches

Good teaching practices should drive assessment tools, but typically that is not what happens. Instead most currently used assessments of teaching instruments assume they reflect good teaching practices. In fact they may not do so because they focus on teacher personality characteristics and teaching styles (Nilson, 2012). However, they should assess how well the instructor creates a successful environment for student learning. Data from these common tools may allow instructors to continue to use teaching methods that are not aligned with or may not help achieve their learning outcomes (Weimer, 2006).

Student evaluation of instructors is the most commonly used method to assess teaching (Theall, 2010). Loeher (2006) found that fifty-nine of sixty-two research universities he surveyed used student evaluation data as the primary method to evaluate teaching. Because the teacher-focused model has been the norm for many years, many commonly used student evaluations of teaching focus on what the instructor does. For example, the SIR II form, developed by ETS and widely used, assesses on eight dimensions of college instruction (Educational Testing Service, 2012). The majority of these dimensions on the SIR II focus on what the instructor does, such as the instructor's way of summarizing or emphasizing important points in class and the instructor's ability to make clear and understandable presentations (Centra & Gaubatz, 2005).

The rationale for the emphasis on teaching performance reflects the older paradigm that good teaching is the desired end product (Barr & Tagg, 1995; Johnson, 2009). For over a dozen years, there has been an increasing focus on learning as the preferred outcome and for teaching to be seen as a means to this end. However, most assessment tools have not made the switch from teaching performance to learning (Johnson, 2009). These tools do not give enough attention to how effectively the instructor fosters student learning. Therefore, we have a disconnect between how instructors are encouraged to teach and how they are evaluated, because assessment instruments often focus on what the instructor does, not on student learning outcomes. Instructors who rarely lecture may even find many of the items on these forms irrelevant to how they teach.

Just like students, instructors attend to what they are evaluated on. Learning-centered assessments of teaching focus on how much the instructor helped students to learn. Current student evaluations of instructors do not foster adoption of these behaviors and do not give professors much encouragement to be more learning centered. If desired outcomes are not linked to performance evaluations, instructors may not use effective teaching behaviors to foster maximum student learning.

Assessment Implications of Evidence–Based Teaching

The consequences discussed in the previous sections reinforce the need for evidence-based assessments of teaching. Most of the commonly used assessments of teaching tools focus on information gathered from student course evaluations and, to a lesser extent peers, to determine the adequacy of the instructor. Students and even faculty peers or chairs may not be aware of best teaching practices or pedagogy; hence, their assessments cannot be depended on to be evidence based.

Educators who have described teaching as a scholarly, evidence-based pursuit do not mention assessing teaching according to these standards (Boyer, 1990; Huber, 2002; Hutchings, 2000; Shulman, 2004a, 2004b; Weimer, 2006). I am extending their idea to assessment of teaching. If teaching is evidence based, it follows logically that assessment of teaching should also be evidence based. The evidence faculty can use to support their assessments of effective teaching should come from the pedagogical literature or on data they have systematically collected.

Perhaps one reason that evidence-based approaches to teaching are not commonly used is there is little pressure to do so. In fact the current models may even perpetuate not using evidence to support teaching. Few of the currently used teaching evaluation systems require or even suggest the use of evidence-based practice as standard criteria for evaluating teaching in higher education. This is a mistake that allows the research-to-practice gap to remain. Therefore, students do not receive the best education because research data are not used. Evidence-based practice has the potential to improve the learning outcomes for all students (Slocum, Spencer, & Detrich, 2012; Spencer, Detrich, & Slocum, 2012).

Since evidence-based teaching implies new standards higher than those currently used, it may make some instructors uncomfortable. Unless it is required, instructors, like all other people, avoid such uncomfortable changes (Blumberg, 2011). If instructors had to describe their own evidence to support their claims about good teaching on teaching assessment tools, more would consider engaging in evidence-based teaching. At the least, if most common assessment tools asked instructors to document the pedagogical literature they use to support their teaching practices, they probably would turn to this literature more often (Blumberg, 2011).

Assessment Instruments Should Reflect Teaching Contexts

Just as most deliberations of teaching focus on didactic instruction, most discussions about evaluating teaching concentrate on traditional, classroom-based education. Many student course evaluations mostly focus on characteristics associated with lectures, such as the appropriate pace of the lecture. Many of the tools used to record observations of teaching also consider what the teacher did, not whether the students were engaged in learning. These tools do not fit the instructional situations where the students are engaged in debates or solving problems in small groups. In fact, instructors perceive the continued use of and importance placed on traditional forms that student complete to evaluate their courses as a barrier to pedagogical innovation (Dewar, 2011).

The situation is even worse for nonclassroom or experiential teaching, such as mentoring students in research or supervising students in clinical, field, or conservatory settings. Here instructors often have few ideas on how to assess the effectiveness of their own teaching, and their peers or chairs rarely offer insights. The standard tools do not fit these situations at all, and many of these experiential teaching experiences are unique. Perhaps because the roles in experiential settings are not traditional teaching and are complex and often context specific, there is a dearth of ways to document and assess experiential teaching. I have not found published student evaluations, teachers' surveys, or peer observation forms that specifically relate to teaching in experiential education. If instructors assess their experiential teaching at all, it is with tools that are not well adapted to these nonclassroom settings and may not elicit meaningful information because the right questions were not asked.

Instructors may identify mostly traditional courses as their formal teaching responsibilities, omitting their experiential teaching on their assessment of their teaching. These experiential teaching roles might not be included on evaluations of teaching because they lack formal mechanisms to evaluate these types of teaching. Documentation and assessment of these experiential teaching roles help to legitimize and improve this teaching.

Processes for Assessing Teaching

Assessment of teaching has additional principles that are intrinsic to the assessment process. Table 7.2 lists common misconceptions about assessing teaching and identifies more accurate alternatives.

TABLE 7.2 Beliefs about Assessing Teaching Inherent to the Assessment Processes

Assessment Belief Stated as a Question	Misconception	Recommended Principle
Can the same tools be used for formative and summative assessments?	Yes; the same assessment tools are often used for formative and summative assessments.	No; use different tools for formative and summative assessments.
Can data from assessments direct improvement efforts?	No; but it is assumed that data from currently used assessment instruments can direct improvement efforts.	No; most currently used assessment tools do not provide these kinds of data. If the instruments are developed to provide constructive feedback data, they can promote improvement efforts.
What sources of data can be used to assess teaching?	The commonly used sources of data about teaching effectiveness mostly come from student perspectives and observations about teaching.	Multiple sources of data about teaching effectiveness exist; documentation of teaching quality should be comprehensive.
What are the instructors' roles in assessing their own teaching?	Generally instructors summarize student and peer perceptions on teaching assessments without critical reflection.	Instructors should critically reflect and integrate what others say in their own teaching assessments.

Use Different Tools for Formative and Summative Assessments

About forty years ago, Michael Scriven distinguished between formative and summative assessments (Madaus, Scriven, & Stufflebeam, 1987). In formative assessments, the evaluator collects and reports data and judgments to assist in the development of programs, people, or processes. The decision-making orientation for formative assessment is proactive. In summative assessments, the evaluator collects data and judgments to make decisions about the continuing status of programs or people. Final grades or promotion and tenure decisions are common summative assessments. The decision-making orientation for summative assessment is retroactive.

Summative assessments are accountability and high-stakes evaluations (Wehlburg, 2010). When instructors compile teaching dossiers for promotion and tenure or for application for academic positions that will be used for summative evaluation purposes, they try to make the case as positive and strong as possible. Formative assessments are different: they are not high-stakes assessments. Instead, they should contain valuable information to identify teaching strengths and weaknesses, which can stimulate investigations about how to teach better. Summative evaluations rarely give the kind of information needed to guide improvement (Weimer, 2010). They tend to be more global or abstract, whereas formative assessments can focus on specific aspects of interest to the instructor.

Each type of assessment has different audiences or stakeholders. The audiences for summative assessments of teaching largely are department chairs, deans, and promotion and tenure committees—those with decision-making power about continuing employment. The primary audience for formative assessment of teaching is the individual instructor. Other audiences in formative assessments include faculty developers, mentors, and department chairs who can help the instructor to grow. Formative assessments are largely intrinsically motivated, whereas summative assessments are often extrinsically driven (Madaus et al., 1987).

For all of these reasons, formative assessments are more effective when they are separate from summative assessments (Weimer, 2010). Because the functions of formative and summative assessments are different, they should ask different types of questions. However, most tools in use currently try to do both, perhaps to the detriment of the quality of the data for both purposes (Weimer, 2010). Many instructors are required to obtain peer observations of their teaching. Instructors can use this observation to improve or change how they teach, but often the same record of observation also goes into dossiers for promotion and tenure. Unless the teaching is truly unacceptable, the observer usually says positive things about the instructor. The record of the observation may not provide enough quality information for instructors to improve their teaching. Furthermore, the instructor may not take the time to debrief with the observer on how to improve his or her teaching.

Foster Improvement Efforts Using Data from Assessment Instruments

The purpose of formative assessment is to give critical feedback while the individual is still in the process of doing the task. This feedback helps to revise or improve what you are doing. Until you retire from teaching totally, you are always in the process of teaching. Therefore, formative feedback serves you at all stages of your career.

If assessments identify instructors who are not teaching effectively, the prospect of a poor summative evaluation can encourage these instructors to make transformative changes in how they teach (Chisholm, Hayes, LaBrecque, & Smith, 2011). Although instructors who are struggling with teaching may benefit the most from helpful feedback, all instructors can improve as a result of receiving insightful critical comments. However, constructive assessments of teaching can motivate most good teachers to strive to become excellent teachers. Receiving practical feedback is often essential to continued professional development and improvement (Smith, 2001). Formative, constructive assessment can provide this feedback to stimulate change because this kind of assessment contains valuable information about one's teaching strengths and weaknesses.

All people benefit from feedback because it helps monitor their progress. Just as many educators are now advocating that students should receive more formative assessments, the same should be true for the instructors. Instructors may rarely receive formative feedback. If higher education were to establish a culture of continuous formative assessment leading to improvement for both students and instructors, teaching would be better and student learning would improve.

One reason that feedback is not more common is the paucity of true formative feedback tools. Currently used student evaluations do not foster better teaching or insights into student learning. Many instructors' ratings remain generally stable over time, an indication that the feedback provided on these evaluations does not lead to real changes. Most assessment tools do not suggest how faculty can improve their teaching because they were not developed for this purpose. Students may not be reflective enough about their own learning to think of ways of changing it. Furthermore, these forms do not even ask the right questions to offer suggestions for improvement. Students might be able to provide helpful feedback when they are asked the right questions, and they have to be taught the principles of constructive feedback.

While instructors need feedback on the quality of their teaching so that they can improve, most tools, especially student evaluations of courses, do not do this. Most tools to assess teaching are still consistent with the traditional teacher-centered model so they focus on the teacher's performance. With the adoption of more learning-centered approaches, instructors would benefit from feedback indicating how effective their teaching is in promoting student learning. Even student evaluation forms that focus more on learning behaviors and student efforts, such as the IDEA Student Evaluation of Instruction Form, do not provide the kind of information helpful for personal faculty development. The IDEA form looks at the relationship of teaching methods to learning objectives (IDEA Center, 2012). In addition, the open-ended comments that some students make can be hurtful, even destructive. Receiving such negative comments can be a real demotivator for better teaching. They end up making faculty think poorly of students and unwilling or very reluctant to spend time working to improve their teaching.

Use Multiple Sources for Data about Teaching Effectiveness

Complex jobs such as teaching require assessments that take into account many perspectives. The use of data from multiple sources of information increases its credibility and validity (Smither, London, & Reilly, 2005). This use of data from many sources leads to a rich evaluation. Multisource feedback assessments, also called 360-degree performance evaluations, use data from self-assessments, as well as peers, subordinates or direct reports, supervisors, and people they interact with, such as clients; these assessments are common in evaluations of managers and executives in business (Smither et al., 2005).

Professors would also benefit from evaluations integrating information from various perspectives, although it is rarely done. As I commented in chapter 4 on critical reflection, most professors use few sources of data about their teaching and assess their teaching by summarizing feedback from peer observations and students' views. These data sources may not provide specific information about instructional practices.

However, there are many additional sources of possible information on teaching effectiveness beyond peers and students. How well the majority of the students did in more advanced courses that build on prerequisite courses indicates how well the students learned and retained the material. Faculty can ask instructors of more advanced courses what elementary concepts the students were able to use and which ones needed further reinforcement. Course artifacts such as syllabi, assignment directions, examinations, and student-generated materials such as essays and projects can reveal much useful information about student learning. Instructors can explain the rationale for inclusion and comment on how effective they were.

Peers or chairs typically observe only a few classes in an evaluation. These observations may focus on specific teaching characteristics such as lecturing skills, ability to interact with the students, student engagement, or classroom management issues. Peer evaluations rarely are comprehensive reviews of a course because they did not participate in all aspects of the course. Peers and chairs should be encouraged to inspect course artifacts. After an observation or a complete evaluation, the instructor and the peer evaluator should engage in a discussion of the effective qualities and those that could be improved. In my experience, however, these debriefing sessions are not as focused on ways to teach better as they could be.

Student feedback often comes from standard end-of-course evaluation forms and may not be specific. Since many institutions are now using online evaluation forms and unless the students are required to complete them, the number of students completing these forms may not be a representative sample of the entire class. At my university, many instructors receive end-of-course evaluations from about one-third of the students, many of whom do not comment on ways to improve teaching.

A review of recent research shows that student evaluations of courses are not as valid as they were twenty years ago (Nilson, 2012). Older research showed a moderately strong positive relationship between student ratings and achievement and thus were linked to learning. Today there is no such relationship, and perhaps even a negative correlation, between instructor ratings and learning. For example, faculty who better prepared students for later courses received lower ratings than those who did not prepare students as well (Nilson, 2012). Whereas in the past, student biases like expected grade, prior interest in subject, or gender of the instructor did not explain much variation in student ratings, this is no longer true. Now student biases have a large impact on ratings: instructor charisma, physical attractiveness and personality, congeniality, confidence, optimism, and enthusiasm can explain up to 50 percent of the variance in ratings. Yet most of these biases are outside the instructor's control or ability to change. They certainly are extraneous to learning. Even students' comments may not help instructors make effective changes in their teaching. In addition, the words students use to describe their teachers mean different things to the students and the instructors. According to students, instructors are rated as not organized if they grade papers slowly or do not follow or change the syllabus (Lauer, 2012). Therefore, unless we ask students to elaborate on what they say, we may misinterpret their comments.

So what do current student end-of-course evaluations really measure? Most likely they rate student satisfaction with the instructor and their course experience. Students want instructors they can relate to, are energetic, care about them, and empathize with them. Many students reward teachers who give them high grades with high ratings. In essence, these evaluations say more about student satisfaction of the teacher as a person than they do about his or her teaching abilities (Nilson, 2012). There are so many differences between the findings of research prior to the 1990s and the more current studies that we need to question the whole idea of student evaluations as a valid measure of good teaching.

Ensure that Teaching Assessments Critically Reflect on Data

While the process of critical self-examination can lead to improved teaching and a more honest assessment of teaching abilities, most instructor assessment forms do not require systematic, ongoing, critical, self-reflection on teaching quality. Coupled with the limited perspectives represented on teaching evaluations, many of these teaching assessment tools focus on the perspectives of others, such as peers, chairs, and students, not on teachers' own critical insights into their teaching. Self-assessments of teaching effectiveness should incorporate the perspectives of peers and students, but they should also include the teachers' critical appraisal of their own teaching quality. While teaching philosophy statements describe what one does in the classroom and why, they do not require reflection on the quality of teaching. I believe that many instructors do not engage in critical self-analysis of their teaching because it is not encouraged enough and they lack easy-to-use tools that facilitate this self-reflection process. Perhaps they may worry about admitting weaknesses or identifying problem areas if they think some administrator will find out and use that information against them.

Although the teaching portfolio structure does not preclude self-assessment, faculty might not examine what they do and why they engage in such practices (Weimer, 2010). Teaching portfolios do not focus on the instructor's own ideas about how well they perceive themselves to be teaching because they largely uncritically reflect what others, especially students, say about the individual teacher. Although Peter Seldin's (2010) popular books offer a format for teaching portfolios and examples, Seldin does not suggest tools to reflect on one's strengths and weaknesses. This analysis is missing because most people develop teaching portfolios for summative evaluation purposes where the admission of weaknesses or areas for improvement can have negative consequences.

As a faculty developer, I often make observations of teaching, review written statements, or listen to instructors describe what they want to achieve or point out to instructors certain behaviors that they are unaware that they are exhibiting. In essence, I am critically reflecting on their teaching. If self-assessment tools were available and easy to use, more instructors might be able to engage in self-analysis of their teaching and discover such incongruities on their own. These tools could help instructors to become aware of their own teaching patterns and practices and prepare for improvement through self-reflection. When professors share their self-assessments with faculty developers, they can gain further insights into how they can improve their teaching.

Summary of the Recommended Principles about Assessing Teaching

In this chapter, I have reviewed the misconceptions and recommended beliefs about teaching discussed in chapter 2 to show their implications for assessing teaching. Furthermore, misconceptions about the assessment processes hinder the use of effective teaching practices that lead to increased student learning. I introduced a more constructive way to think about assessing teaching in an ongoing way in this chapter. Both recommended concepts about teaching and about the assessment process result in a more constructive model of assessing teaching, as summarized in figure 7.1. Figure 7.2 elaborates the details of these ideas. This figure shows each construct as a question and answers the question with the common misconception and the recommended alternative concept. The recommended concepts are in italics. Since figure 7.2 is complex, I simplified it in figure 7.3 to show only the recommended concepts of effective teaching and effective assessment processes intended to foster better teaching. If you employ these principles about assessing teaching, you will gather useful information on how you can teach better.

This chapter lays out a comprehensive plan for teacher development that is a career-long process. It is not something that has to be done all at once. I will integrate all of these recommendations into a model of assessing teaching in the next chapter. The rest of the book uses these recommended concepts of assessing teaching.

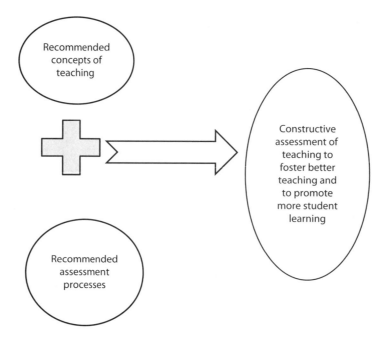

FIGURE 7.1   **The Two Essential Elements of the Constructive Model of Assessing Teaching**

Suggestions for Using Recommended Principles of Assessment to Promote Teaching Growth Coming from This Chapter

- Use different tools for formative and summative assessments.
  - Summative and formative assessment tools should anchor the scale in effective teaching standards.
  - When properly constructed, data from formative assessment instruments should promote improvement efforts.
  - If developed to provide constructive data as formative assessment instruments are intended to do, they can promote improvement efforts.
- Criteria for assessing teaching should be explicit, objective, and uniformly applied to all faculty members.
- Good teaching practices such as learning-centered teaching should drive assessment tools. Assessments of learning-centered teaching include measurements of student learning and teaching strategies to foster learning.
- Desired outcomes, such as increased student learning, should be linked to performance evaluations.

FIGURE 7.2 Assessment of Teaching Based on Beliefs of Teaching and of Beliefs about Assessment

Note: Misconceptions appear in boxes on the left below the question relating to the concept. Recommended concepts are in italics and appear on the right below the question relating to the construct.

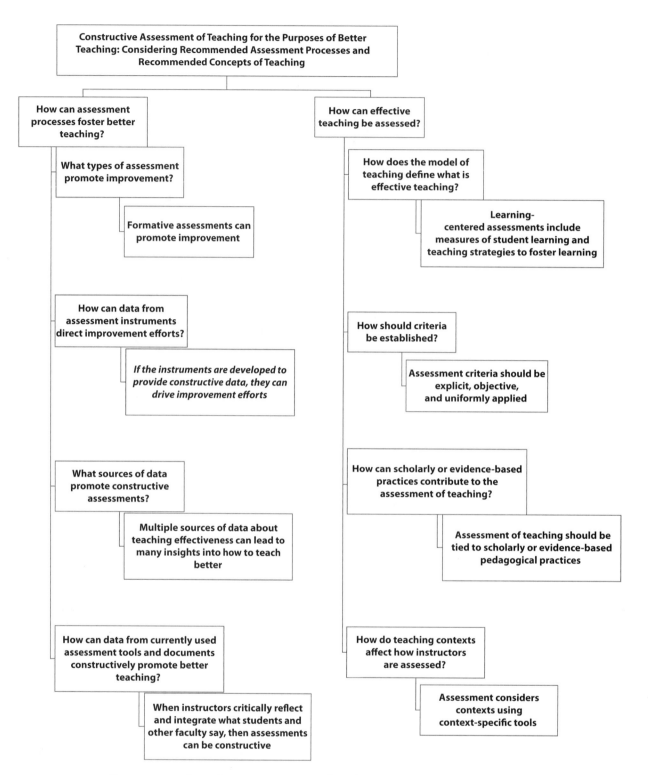

FIGURE 7.3 **Constructive Assessment of Effective Teaching**

- Assessment of teaching, like teaching itself, should be evidence based. It should be tied to scholarly, evidence-based pedagogical best practices.

- The contexts for teaching (classroom, online, or experiential) should give rise to diverse assessment instruments that are context specific.

- Documentation of teaching quality should be comprehensive. Multiple sources of data about teaching effectiveness can lead to more insights into how to teach better than the traditionally used sources, such as end-of-course evaluations.

- When instructors critically reflect and integrate what students, peers, and chairs say, then assessments can constructively provide useful insights as to teaching effectiveness.

- A constructive model of assessing teaching includes recommended beliefs about teaching assessments and assessment processes.

Chapter 8

Model for Assessing Teaching

I ENDED THE PREVIOUS chapter by proposing a set of beliefs about assessing teaching that foster personal growth. These growth-fostering beliefs also promote student learning. Moreover, they correspond to the strategies and assessment tactics that promote better teaching that I discussed in chapter 1, as shown in tables 8.1. I use these more accurate beliefs about assessing teaching to create an informative and constructive model for assessing teaching.

TABLE 8.1 Assessment Strategies and Tactics for Faculty Growth

Assessment Strategies and Tactics	Recommended Beliefs about Assessing Teaching
Assessment Tactic 1: Use the following four strategies to promote better teaching through a self-assessment process	
Strategies • Strategy 1: Define the essential aspects of teaching in classroom, online, and experiential settings to study them.	Good teaching practices such as learning-centered teaching should • Focus on student learning • Drive assessment tools • Assess how well the instructor creates a successful environment for learning. Learning-centered assessments of teaching include • Teaching strategies to foster learning • Measurements of student engagement and learning Desired outcomes such as increased student learning should be linked to performance evaluations.
• Strategy 2: Integrate the study of your teaching with critical self-reflection to determine possible ways to improve teaching.	When instructors critically reflect and integrate what students, peers, and chairs say and document, the results of these reflections can be informative.

(Continued)

TABLE 8.1 Continued

Assessment Strategies and Tactics	Recommended Beliefs about Assessing Teaching
• Strategy 3: Use evidence to support teaching.	Assessment of teaching, like teaching itself, should be evidence based. Teaching should be assessed for its congruence with evidence-based pedagogical literature or systematic investigations into effective teaching practices.
• Strategy 4: Self-assess your teaching as an improvement vehicle.	Criteria for assessing teaching should be explicit, objective, and uniformly applied to all faculty.
Tactics Assessment tactic 2: Separate formative from summative assessments.	Use different tools for formative and summative assessments: • Summative and formative assessment tools should anchor the scale in effective teaching standards. • Formative assessments can promote improvement. • When formative assessment instruments are properly constructed, their data should promote improvement efforts. • If developed to provide informative data as formative assessment instruments are intended to do, they can promote improvement efforts.
Assessment tactic 3: Consider the totality of your teaching and use context-specific assessment tools.	The contexts for teaching (classroom, online, or experiential) should give rise to diverse assessment instruments that are context specific.
Assessment tactic 4: Use data from many sources to inform your self-assessment.	Documentation of teaching quality should be comprehensive. Multiple sources of data about teaching effectiveness can lead to new insights into how to teach better than the traditionally used sources such as end-of-course evaluations.

Assessment Principles

In this chapter I take the concepts discussed in part 1 and integrate them into three types of principles for assessing teaching: (1) the context for assessment, or what to assess; (2) the assessments methods, or how to assess; and (3) the results of this assessment process. Figure 8.1 shows how these principles relate and lists their constituent components. These principles form the basis of this new assessment model to promote faculty growth and increased student learning. I explain how to use this model to assess the effectiveness of teaching and identify ways to teach better.

As chapter 7 made clear, faculty need new models because the current methods do not usually lead to improvement. Professors who serve on promotion and tenure committees have commented how little is actually analyzed or documented about the teaching process or teaching effectiveness (Seldin, 1999). When I presented this model at a national meeting of faculty developers, someone remarked, "There is clearly a need throughout the academy to supplement student course evaluation data with other meaningful and compelling data sets. There is a need for appropriate procedures and tools. This is a very important problem that needs to be attacked in a

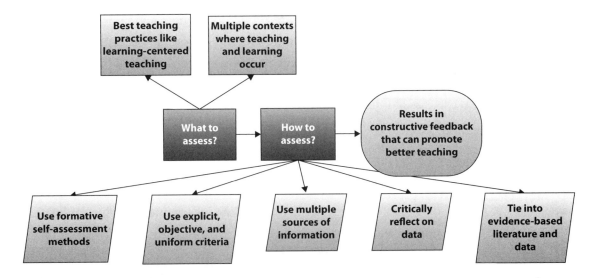

FIGURE 8.1   A Model of Assessment of Effective Teaching to Promote Faculty Growth and Increased Learning

sensible and insightful fashion." I believe this chapter and the rest of the book begin to fill this need for formative assessment. As a result of informative assessments of teaching, instructors can teach more effectively, which will lead to deep and intentional learning for students. Perhaps the model can point the way toward better summative assessments as well.

The Context for Assessment

The context sets the tone for the entire assessment process. Therefore, it needs to be established first as shown on the top row and the first box of the flow diagram in figure 8.1. The context is composed of two essential components: assessing good teaching practices and assessing the multiple contexts in which teaching occurs.

Assessing Good Teaching Practices

Assessments should enable instructors to accurately describe how they teach and reflect best teaching practices. As chapters 2, 3, and 7 discussed, there are various ideas of what constitutes good teaching, which leads to the complex issue of deciding what should be evaluated. An essential aspect of this decision process is to define what criteria to include or what components to assess. Since the purpose of this book is to improve student learning, I chose to apply the currently accepted learning-centered teaching model of pedagogy to define the components upon which to assess teaching.

Barr and Tagg (1995) described a paradigm shift in what we consider effective teaching and began an international movement toward implementing learning-centered teaching. Their article is one of the most cited in higher education since its publication. Their call for a change in how we think about teaching has had a great impact on course design, faculty development, and the direction of professional organizations such as the Association of American Colleges and Universities (Johnson, 2009). Given the enormous influence of Barr and Tagg's classic article and all of the other literature on learning-centered teaching, I have based my assessment of teaching on the way this best practice describes teaching with a focus on the learning process and outcomes.

Good teaching practices should drive assessment tools. I define assessing teaching according to three higher-order guiding principles that reflect the learning-centered approach and define or frame three broad dimensions of teaching that describe characteristics associated with different teaching qualities: the structure for teaching and learning, instructional design responsibilities, and the assessment of learning. Each dimension is well supported in the current literature.

This framework for assessing teaching varies from what is used with teacher-centered approaches (Weimer, 2013). With the older instructor-centered models, the assessment focused on teaching performance or lecturing skills. However, with learning-centered approaches, the instructional design responsibilities emphasize roles other than lecturing skills because they deal with course alignment, organizing educational experiences, and reflecting on instruction. Since the structure for teaching and learning was somewhat unvarying, these aspects were a minor part of assessing teaching. With learning-centered approaches, the structure for teaching and learning takes on a more significant role. The focus on learning outcomes is also new with learning-centered assessments.

Assessing Diverse Teaching Contexts

The contexts for teaching (classroom, online instruction, or experiential) should give rise to diverse assessment instruments that are context specific. Although the teaching processes are quite different in classroom, online, and experiential situations, the desired goals of deep and intentional learning remain constant. Therefore, many of the aspects of teaching that should be assessed are the same. However due to added roles for instructors in experiential environments, such as performing a service in a community agency or directing a student jazz band, these additional components can also be assessed. There are as well some fundamental differences among these varied teaching contexts. When instructors teach classes, they need to focus on the selection of appropriate teaching/learning methods and educational technologies. This is not as important in experiential contexts, where the instructor needs to plan and implement individual experiences to meet the needs of all students. Since some experiential teachers are primarily doing other roles in these environments, teaching may be an added responsibility. Thus, it is important to assess that instructors are available and accessible to ensure that students have successful learning experiences.

Assessment Methods

The bottom row of figure 8.1 shows five assessment methods. From these methods I developed a model and set of processes that identify informative, useful feedback. Since the purpose of these assessments is to offer ways to increase deep and intentional learning through improved teaching, they are formative. Formative feedback assists in this critical self-assessment process (Smith, 2001). The model discussed in the rest of this book addresses only formative assessments because I am committed to helping teachers improve their teaching and student learning.

Criteria for Assessing Teaching

The criteria for assessing teaching should be explicit, objective, and uniformly applied to all faculty members and should be based on pedagogical best practices. Having explicit criteria can lead to a more meaningful self-assessment process as these criteria can guide the instructor to assess more comprehensively. Furthermore, objective criteria can lead to more accurate and consistent assessments. Standards of effective teaching can be established and maintained if the same criteria are applied to all faculty members. These give new professors goals that they can aspire to and can keep experienced professors from getting sloppy in their teaching. When faculty members apply the same criteria to all of their teaching, they can compare their strengths and weaknesses more consistently, a practice that should lead to more informative teaching assessments. Perhaps this will be the first time that instructors who teach in different contexts, including in classroom, online, and experiential settings, will be using the same criteria for all of their varied teaching. (Part 3 is devoted to discussing specific criteria for assessing teaching.)

Critical Reflection

To achieve the dual goals of increasing student learning and faculty growth, instructors need to engage in critical self-reflection and analysis of their teaching (Kreber, 2002). Therefore, critical reflection needs to be incorporated in assessment methods. Brookfield (1995) suggests that instructors use four interconnected perspectives as they critically reflect on their teaching:

instructors' own insights, their students' views, their peers' experiences, and the literature. When instructors assess their engagement in self-reflection, they should critically analyze the data collected from these four sources.

Using self-reflection along with the data gathered from currently used assessment tools is a good first step to improving teaching because this self-assessment process identifies weaknesses (Weimer, 2010). Such assessments help you compare what you are currently doing to what might be possible. You can design feedback mechanisms to give you information to reduce this gap (Smith, 2001). Also, assessments using critical reflections require you to develop a rationale for your teaching, and this leads to informed action. Therefore, assessing your own critical reflections will help you see where and how you can improve your teaching.

Comprehensive Documentation and Multiple Sources of Data

Because teaching is complex, multiple types of data from various sources are necessary to construct a true assessment of teaching quality. Multiple sources of data about teaching effectiveness can lead to more insights into how to teach better than the traditionally used sources such as end-of-course evaluations. Just as qualitative researchers triangulate data from different sources to obtain a fuller and more accurate view of the complex situation they are studying, triangulation of data leads to a richer assessment of teaching.

Documentation of teaching quality should be comprehensive and might include perspectives from stakeholders, a review of materials used in teaching, and those produced by the students. These appropriate stakeholders include current and former students, alumni, peers, and chairs (Berk, 2006). Instead of relying on the common practice of simply summarizing the data from student evaluations of courses and peer observations, instructors should determine the validity of this information and attempt to identify and explain patterns in their self-assessments of their teaching.

Driscoll and Wood (2007) emphasize the essential nature of analyzing student evidence, such as the artifacts they create for a course, as critical to evaluating if learning outcomes have been met. For example, music teachers might review the video of a student performance to assess their own teaching effectiveness. Both the instructor who taught the course and peers can evaluate these instructor- and student-created artifacts as part of a comprehensive assessment of teaching. Comprehensive documentation of teaching quality makes developing a valid plan for improvement easier.

Evidence-Based Assessment of Teaching

Although the concept of evidence-based decision making is consistent with the standards of practice used in other professions and with the accreditation standards used by professional and regional accrediting agencies, it is rarely used to assess teaching. Teaching that is considered adequate or good using current standards frequently does not have evidence-based support. The incorporation of evidence-based decision making into assessments is superior to current standards that rely on perceptions alone because scholarly teaching enhances student learning (Brew & Ginns, 2008).

Since most assessments of teaching do not require evidence-based support, this concept raises the bar from what is used to measure the quality of teaching now (Blumberg, 2011). The teaching assessment model described in this book uses scholarly, evidence-based pedagogical teaching as a standard criterion on which all teaching in higher education can be assessed.

Results of the Assessment Process

As figure 8.1 shows, instructors can improve their teaching if they analyze the information gained from these formative assessment methods. The comprehensive assessment of all essential aspects of teaching can uncover some neglected components. The results of this process can provide new insights and increased value to assessing teaching. Instead of being a busy-work exercise of compiling the student course evaluations that instructors need to do and give to their chair or review committee, this becomes a meaningful exercise for them.

This process should result in revitalized teaching because each aspect describes behaviors that instructors can change (Weimer, 2010). These formative self-assessments of teaching can be seen as a continuous quality improvement vehicle, and it also usually fosters discussions about teaching. Some faculty members seek help on concrete areas where they want to make changes. They may talk to other faculty or staff at centers for excellence in teaching. Finally, instructors can have worthwhile dialogues with department chairs, administrators, and human resource departments on how they can or could be assessed using these principles to determine how much evidence administrators expect or desire. The outcome from these dialogues can lead to improved evaluation of teaching that reflects the local realities (Theall, 2010). For example, some institutions may not expect faculty to conduct research or scholarly work. Therefore, assessments of teaching should not include dissemination of studies on teaching. However, my university values scholarship and considers research on teaching that is published in peer-reviewed journals as a legitimate and valued form of research.

Applying These Principles to Assessing Your Teaching

You may be mostly concerned with the day-to-day aspects of teaching, such as how much content to cover in each class, when to give a test, or what questions will stimulate the best discussion in class. However, to strengthen your teaching, you will need to go beyond the day-to-day concerns (Brookfield, 1995). You need to identify and analyze the assumptions on which you base your teaching processes and use more comprehensive assessment methods. Although the self-assessment methods of critical reflection with documentation and evidence-based decision making are consistent with the standards of practice used in other professions and with accreditation standards, they are not commonly used as teaching improvement tools.

Informative and Constructive Assessment Model for Better Teaching

The guiding principles I have discussed led me to develop a new model for assessing teaching that is grounded in the theory and research literature of higher education. This literature proposes being self-critical, getting formative feedback from many sources, reading pedagogical literature, and conducting scholarship of teaching and learning as ways to improve teaching (Kreber, 2002; Rice & Sorcinelli, 2002; Shulman, 2004a, 2004b; Smith, 2001; Weimer, 2010). I propose an integrated four-level, hierarchical teaching assessment model with increasing layers of support or evidence for the quality of teaching. Each successive level is based on a separate principle, incorporates data and insights from the previous level, and suggests ways professors can improve teaching. I integrate these separate concepts to provide a robust teaching assessment model for better teaching.

Smith (2001) suggests a three-stage transformative process to improve teaching. Gathering feedback and learning through faculty development efforts are at the core of this transformative process. The first stage is when instructors are concerned with the usual aspects of teaching that consume much of their time. Smith (2001), in agreement with others (Shulman, 2004b; Weimer, 2006), says instructors who want to improve their teaching need to engage in scholarly teaching, reading the literature on teaching and learning processes and using best practices based on research evidence to inform their teaching. The transformative change occurs when instructors move from being scholarly teachers to doing the scholarship of teaching and learning (Smith, 2001). It is the most transformative because when the scholarship of teaching and learning is disseminated, it informs others how to teach more effectively and thus has a broader impact. Smith's three-stage transformative model led me to formulate my own model.

Although Smith, Weimer, and Shulman recommend ways to improve teaching, they do not suggest that assessment of the effectiveness of teaching should be based on these transformative processes. Unfortunately few instructors have heeded their advice on how to teach better using the three-stage transformative model, and I think I might know why. The misconceptions about assessing teaching that I have discussed led to commonly used methods and tools for assessing teaching. I gave several examples of the power of assessment in chapter 7. In most cases, the misconceptions about teaching or about assessing teaching did not lead to informative assessments that promote better teaching resulting in increased learning. Yet the same power of assessment can achieve these goals if we change how we assess teaching. Given the clout of assessments, if these recommended beliefs were incorporated into assessment models, they might motivate instructors to use more critical self-analysis and use evidence to support their teaching. I am convinced that when educators use the recommended assessments, they develop new insights that inform how they can improve their teaching and learning. The cases in this book support this assertion.

Hierarchical Model of Assessment of Teaching

Figure 8.2 integrates the assessment principles previously discussed. Each successive layer requires the continued use of the previous layer. You may recall similar pyramids that I used in chapters 4 and 5. I am now spiraling

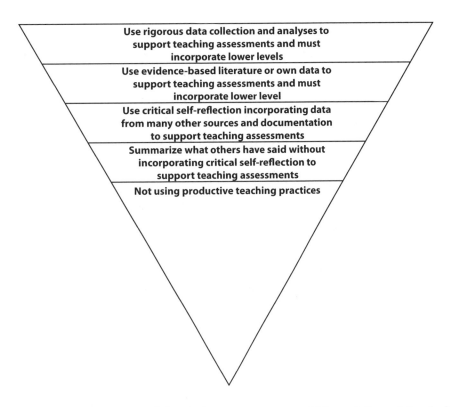

FIGURE 8.2   A Hierarchical Assessment of Teaching Model That Promotes Faculty Growth and Increased Learning

back to the concepts raised in these earlier chapters to show how they are incorporated into the formative assessment of teaching model. Going up the inverted pyramid increases the support for the assessment of teaching.

The common practices of nonreflective assessment are at the next-to-the-bottom level of the pyramid. This layer reflects what happens when instructors summarize in a noncritical way what students write on course evaluations or peers note as a result of observations about their teaching. While neglecting to seriously reflect on all aspects of teaching is acceptable and even the norm at many institutions, it is not helpful for instructors as they strive to improve student learning. Instructors may have a hard time deciding how to improve their teaching from these noncritical notes. However, when they critically reflect on the information provided in these summaries, they can begin to see where they can strengthen their teaching. All of the layers above the bottom two require data from various sources.

The next layer of support requires critical self-reflection of one's teaching, which, with documentation to support these reflections, can show ways to improve teaching. Specific documentation varies by discipline. Some instructors might use quantitative surveys; others may gather qualitative data from focus groups with students to support their claims. Student portfolios or student artifacts can offer evidence that the goals are met. Coupling this self-reflection with data from many sources, and not just from student course evaluations, gives a much richer database on which to analyze what is working and identify areas that instructors could improve. It is important that instructors document these data and their conclusions of this critical self-analysis of teaching.

Evidence-based teaching based on pedagogical literature or data from one's teaching, in addition to critical self-review, forms the fourth layer of support for assessing teaching. When instructors rely on evidence coming from either of these sources, they can explain the rationale for how and why they teach. The use of pedagogical literature or data shows that their teaching is effective or can point to concrete ways to change their teaching. Using evidence to support teaching broadens the support of teaching considerably. If instructors use pedagogical literature to support how and why they teach, they can employ best practices in their teaching. Since they are best practices, they should assist students to learn deeply and with intention.

The final layer with the greatest amount of support requires rigorous evaluations of teaching through systematic data collection and student documentation that they achieved the learning outcomes. This level often involves review of teaching by professional peers or students who reflected on the effectiveness of their instructor's teaching. Peer review of research on teaching through dissemination to professional journals can also be included at this level of support of teaching effectiveness. The use of pedagogical evidence or data can point to concrete ways to change teaching. Once these changes are made and instructors collect appropriate assessment data, they have a great deal of evidence to support that their teaching is effective.

The model discussed in this book uses gathering data from many sources, critical self-assessment, evidence to support teaching, and rigorous data collection and analysis to assess the effectiveness of teaching. These assessment methods can be seen as a hierarchy of increasing support going from the left to the right on the columns labeled "Increasing Standards for Quality of Teaching" on the matrix in table 8.2. I include another, lowest level of teaching, to reflect reality, which I call "not yet using productive teaching practices." This level describes unproductive teaching practices such as not having specified learning goals or using methods that are in conflict with the learning goals. Thus, as the five columns on the right side of table 8.2 show there are five levels or increasing standards to assess the quality of teaching. These increasing standards can be applied to three principles of learning-centered practices listed on the three last rows. Furthermore, this learning-centered assessment model can be used for all teaching contexts as shown in the first cell of table 8.2. To be rated at the next-to-the-highest or the highest levels, the instructor must also meet everything in the third or fourth level as they are cumulative.

TABLE 8.2   An Informative and Constructive Formative Assessment Matrix Model for Teaching

Assess All Essential Aspects of Teaching in All Relevant Teaching Contexts	Increasing Standards for Quality of Teaching				
What should be assessed depends on the definition of teaching used. When a learning-centered approach is used, teaching can be divided into the following higher order guiding principles↓	Not yet using productive teaching practices.	Summarize what others have said without incorporating critical self-reflection to support teaching assessments.	Document critical self-reflection incorporating data from many other sources to support teaching assessments.	Use evidence-based literature or own data to support teaching assessments.	Use rigorous data collection and analyses to support teaching assessments.
1. The structure for teaching and learning					
2. The instructor's design responsibilities					
3. The assessment of learning outcomes					

Summary of the Model

My formative assessment model for all kinds of teaching considers what teaching is and what constitutes increasing support for the assessment of these teaching practices. I defined the essential aspects of teaching that should be assessed through a learning-centered perspective, which led me to three major dimensions of teaching: structures for teaching and learning, instructional design responsibilities, and achievement of learning outcomes. These same dimensions of teaching apply to classroom, online, and experiential settings. They are all equally important and therefore do not represent a hierarchy.

This assessment does employ a layered hierarchy of increasing bases for support of teaching that incorporates assessment methods and principles. Each aspect of teaching can be assessed using a broader base of support: critical assessments of data from many sources with documentation, followed by using evidence-based decision making, and, finally, rigorous data collection and research on teaching. Placing all of the essential aspects of teaching along the horizontal rows of a diagram and the increasing layers of support for assessment along the vertical columns of this diagram result in a matrix for assessing teaching.

Table 8.2 shows this matrix model for formative assessment of classroom, online, and experiential teaching. I modified the inverted pyramid showing the hierarchical layers to support assessments of teaching to be consistent with formative assessment terminology as shown in figure 8.3. Instead of using the typical words such as *not acceptable* or *meets expectations*, which are consistent with summative assessments, I chose more descriptive terminology. The two layers with the least support are described in terms of not yet reaching goals. To be congruent with the model proposed in this chapter, I set the third layer as the lowest satisfactory level, which in fact is a higher standard than commonly used. However, I hope that most faculty members will strive to be above this level. The description of each level includes the terminology to show how one must continue to meet the lower standards at each higher-level of support.

This model suggests an ongoing process with each level leading to growth. It is a comprehensive plan for teacher development but should not be done all at once. It is not even necessary to do all steps because moving up just one level increases teaching effectiveness. Achieving scholarly, evidence-based excellence in teaching is a career-long endeavor. For young faculty or faculty under heavy pressure to do research in their content areas, achieving improvement may be more important than achieving excellence.

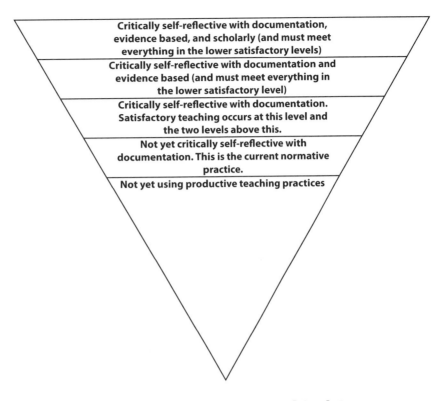

Critically self-reflective with documentation, evidence based, and scholarly (and must meet everything in the lower satisfactory levels)

Critically self-reflective with documentation and evidence based (and must meet everything in the lower satisfactory level)

Critically self-reflective with documentation. Satisfactory teaching occurs at this level and the two levels above this.

Not yet critically self-reflective with documentation. This is the current normative practice.

Not yet using productive teaching practices

FIGURE 8.3 Clarification of the Hierarchical Assessment of Teaching Model That Promotes Faculty Growth and Increased Learning Using Formative Assessment Terminology

Tips to Make This Assessment Process Less Daunting

- To start the process, choose one aspect of your teaching that you want to focus on. Try to choose something that you do consistently in all of your teaching. It could be a policy that you have always had and never questioned its rationale, or an instructional technique you routinely use, or you could assess one aspect of your teaching that you are especially proud of or would like to change.

- List all of the possible sources of data that you currently have or could obtain to assess this aspect of your teaching. Then begin to collect all of this information in one place. Critically reflect on all of the information to make some decisions or develop a better rationale.

- Keep good notes as you teach, and refer to them as you assess yourself.

- Plan to spend a few hours on assessing your teaching periodically throughout each semester.

- Talk to others about your self-assessment process and results. Staff in teaching and learning centers, your mentor, or a very senior professor in your department are good choices to dialogue with.

Suggestions for Self-Assessment to Promote Teaching Growth Coming from This Chapter

- Use the information you have gained from insightful formative assessments to improve your teaching.

- Consider formative self-assessments of teaching as a continuous quality improvement vehicle.

- Critically reflect on data gathered from student course evaluations, peer observations, and reviews of course artifacts.

- Documentation of teaching quality should be comprehensive.

- Assessment of teaching, like teaching itself, should be evidence based.

- Read and incorporate relevant pedagogical literature in higher education to guide your improvement process.

- If you systematically collect and analyze data about aspects of teaching, you will have a broad base of support that your teaching is effective.

SELF-ASSESSMENT RUBRICS

The two chapters in part 3 should be read together as a unit.

Chapter 9

How to Assess Teaching Using Rubrics Based on the Assessment Model

THE LITERATURE ON THE EVALUATION of teaching in higher education contains many assessment forms that others employ to assess teachers, but they do not contain tools that instructors can use for self-reflection and analysis. The model I have developed in previous chapters leads to self-assessment tools that promote critical self-analysis of teaching.

The matrix model for formative assessment in table 8.2 lays the foundation for the development of self-assessment tools that led me to develop a catalogue of rubrics appropriate for self-assessment of teaching in many settings. I chose to develop rubrics since they are commonly used to evaluate student work, and instructors are already familiar with them. Depending on the format, as I show later in this chapter, rubrics can look like matrices. Regardless of their format, they allow evaluators to judge individual behaviors or products on specific criteria according to explicit levels of performance.

What Rubrics Are

Rubrics are easily understood assessment tools. They turn subjective judgments into objective assessments by explicitly defining what is being judged (Walvoord, 1998). Rubrics are objective in the sense that they convey a consensus-based set of values (Arreola, 2006). There are two types of rubrics: rating scales and descriptive rubrics. Rating scales are similar to checklists with quantitative levels and not just yes or no replies. They often employ Likert-type scales going from Strongly Agree to Strongly Disagree or Poor to Excellent performance (Suskie, 2004). Rating scale rubrics are not very helpful for formative feedback because they do not describe explicit intermediate steps. Descriptive rubrics, however, do this well.

Faculty who resist using rubrics to assess their students will probably also be hesitant to use them for self-assessment. Research shows that faculty resistance to rubrics stems from their misconceptions about the potential applications of rubrics. Those who resist do not understand that rubrics can contribute to improved teaching and learning as well as being a summative evaluation tool (Reddy & Andrade, 2010). Embracing the concept of formative feedback should help instructors overcome their reticence to employing these rubrics.

Descriptive Rubric Formats

Descriptive rubrics have three characteristics: the criteria to be assessed, consistent levels of performance, and quality definitions for each level. Assessment criteria are a set of indicators that determine the quality of work. The selection of these indicators signals what is important in the behavior or product being measured. I elaborate on the criteria for assessing teaching in the next chapter. This chapter focuses on the latter two aspects of the self-assessment of teaching rubrics. Instead of a check box in the rating scale rubrics, descriptive rubrics contain a brief description of the expected performance that explicitly states the expectations (Suskie, 2004). Quality definitions explain what a person needs to do to demonstrate a skill or proficiency. They distinguish performance or products into various levels of the criteria. Most rubrics have at least three levels, ranging from Unacceptable to Outstanding (Reddy & Andrade, 2010).

Many rubrics look like matrices as they compare the criteria on the horizontal axis with the levels of the expected performance on the vertical axis. With this format, the descriptions of the quality of the expected performance are briefly listed in the boxes or cells marking the intersection between the criteria and the level. Another format appears like multiple choice questions. In this format, these quality definitions are listed under the headings in the alternatives. The identical rubric component is shown in both formats—the box format in table 9.1 and a multiple choice format in exhibit 9.1 and both are portions of the complete rubric A1, "Develop Learning Outcomes and Use Them to Select Teaching/Learning Methods" in the appendix. I chose the multiple choice format for the self-assessment of teaching rubrics because this format allows more complete descriptions than the boxes. Because teaching is complex, the descriptions of the levels of teaching criteria are also complex. Long or detailed descriptions are also easier to read in the multiple choice format.

Location of Key Aspects on These Rubrics. Guiding principles are listed as the second row in box format, and listed at the top of the page in the multiple choice format. Assessment criteria are listed in the first column on the left in box format and at the top of the page in the multiple choice format. Labels for the consistent levels of performance are listed as the second through six columns on the left in box format and horizontally along the page in the multiple choice format. Quality definitions or descriptions of the expected level of performance for each level are shown in regular font, listed in the boxes under the performance levels in box format and listed horizontally along the page under the performance levels in the multiple choice format.

By inspecting both formats in table 9.1 and exhibit 9.1, you can see the quality definition for the lowest level, or not yet using productive teaching practices for the criterion, described as, "Develop challenging yet reasonable learning outcomes for the acquisition of knowledge, skills, or values and use them to select appropriate teaching/learning methods and educational technologies" is: "I have received feedback that I do not have specified learning goals or do not use appropriate or active learning activities to facilitate learning or use methods that are in conflict with the learning goals." Each quality definition is unique for the criterion and the level on the rubrics.

How These Rubrics Differ from Those That Grade Students

Many instructors employ rubrics to measure behaviors or qualities in others, such as their students, or they ask students to apply them in peer assessments. Sometimes instructors ask students to use rubrics for self-assessment. While many faculty use rubrics to evaluate students, it is less common for them to employ them to assess their own work. Few rubric tools currently exist for these purposes, yet they can be equally as informative. I have previously proposed rubrics to assess learner-centered courses or instructors (Blumberg, 2009a). Those rubrics can be applied for self-assessment or for peer assessment. In this book, the rubrics are intended only for self-assessment. Further differences between faculty self-assessment and student assessment include these:

- Teachers often employ rubrics for formative and summative purposes to assess their students; these rubrics are intended for formative purposes only.

TABLE 9.1 Box Format for a Rubric Component

A1 Develop Learning Outcomes and Use Them to Select Teaching/Learning Methods

GUIDING PRINCIPLE: Structure for Teaching and Learning

Assessment Criteria	Levels of Performance			
	Not Yet Using Productive Teaching Practices (I have received feedback)	**Not Yet Critically Self-Reflective with Documentation (this is the current normative practice)**	**Critically Self-Reflective with Documentation (satisfactory teaching occurs at this level and at the next two levels)**	**Critically Self-Reflective with Documentation, Evidence Based (this must meet everything in the previous level)**	**Critically Self-Reflective with Documentation, Evidence Based, Scholarly (this must meet everything in the previous level)**
Develop challenging yet reasonable learning outcomes for the acquisition of knowledge, skills, or values, and use them to select appropriate teaching/learning methods and educational technologies—An Essential Criterion	• I do not have specified learning goals <u>or</u> • I do not use appropriate or active learning activities to facilitate learning <u>or</u> • I use methods that are in conflict with the learning goals	• I do not critically reflect on the relationship between my learning outcomes or teaching/learning methods and technologies	• I use a variety of teaching/learning methods and technologies that are appropriate for student learning goals <u>and</u> • I create a respectful environment to foster learning (as defined by sensitivity to ethnic and cultural diversity) <u>and</u> • I critically reflect on the relationship between my learning outcomes or teaching/learning methods and technologies	Literature or data from students inform my choice of the selected teaching/learning methods or educational technologies to foster mastery of learning outcomes (cite literature references)	I provide • A clear rationale for my choice of my teaching/learning methods and technologies <u>and</u> • Evidence from student products that my teaching/learning methods facilitate students reaching learning goals

EXHIBIT 9.1   Multiple Choice Format for a Rubric Component

A1   Develop Learning Outcomes and Use Them to Select Teaching/Learning Methods

Guiding Principle: Structure for teaching and learning

Self-Assessment Criterion: Develop challenging yet reasonable learning outcomes for the acquisition of knowledge, skills, or values, and use them to select appropriate teaching/learning methods and educational technologies—An Essential Criterion

Rubric Quality Levels

❏ Not Yet Using Productive Teaching Practices (I have received feedback)

   I do not have specified learning goals <u>or</u>

   I do not use appropriate or active learning activities to facilitate learning <u>or</u>

   I use methods that are in conflict with the learning goals

❏ Not Yet Critically Self-Reflective with Documentation (this is the current normative practice)

   I do not critically reflect on the relationship between my learning outcomes or teaching/learning methods and technologies

❏ Critically Self-Reflective with Documentation (satisfactory teaching occurs at this level and at the next two levels)

   I use a variety of teaching/learning methods and technologies that are appropriate for student learning goals <u>and</u>

   I create a respectful environment to foster learning (as defined by sensitivity to ethnic and cultural diversity) <u>and</u>

   I critically reflect on the relationship between my learning outcomes or teaching/learning methods and technologies

❏ Critically Self-Reflective with Documentation, Evidence Based (this must meet everything in the previous level)

   Literature or data from students inform my choice of the selected teaching/learning methods or educational technologies to foster mastery of learning outcomes (cite literature references)

❏ Critically Self-Reflective with Documentation, Evidence Based, Scholarly (this must meet everything in the previous level)

   I provide

• A clear rationale for my choice of my teaching/learning methods and technologies <u>and</u>

• Evidence from student products that my teaching/learning methods facilitate students reaching learning goals

• Teachers often add the numbers earned on all components to make a final score. Instructors should not add up their individual ratings on these rubrics because there is no minimum good teaching cumulative rating. Instead, the individual ratings point to areas for possible growth and improvement.

- Rubrics that instructors employ to grade students often assign different weights to the criteria. Instead, I divide the criteria into "essential" and "optional." Each essential criterion has the same importance. Some criteria are optional because some instructors may not have the opportunity to engage in this practice.

- Since these rubrics are intended for self-assessment as an improvement tool, there is no need to establish interrater reliability as would be necessary for rubrics used to assess very high stakes decisions such as licensing exams.

Why These Rubrics Are Self-Assessments

Formative self-assessment of teaching is analogous to self-regulated learning because both processes help individuals become more conscious of what they are doing (Pintrich, 2000). In both processes, it is essential to intentionally set goals. Next, the individual identifies strategies that help to achieve these goals. Performance can be compared against these goals. Self-assessment rubrics facilitate each of these self-regulated steps. Because teaching varies by context, I developed separate self-assessment rubric tools reflecting different teaching goals for different environments.

The Rubric Format

The rubric tools describe a list of components or criteria that define excellent and effective teaching. In chapter 3, I discussed the components of essential teaching. These components form the criteria to assess teaching, which I elaborate on in the next chapter. In this section, I walk through the self-assessment rubric template and explain its parts. Each tool is composed of a separate rubrics page for each criterion. I refer to each separate tool as *rubric sets* and each separate criterion as a *rubrics page.* Each rubric page has

- the same five rubric quality levels,
- suggested sources for documentation, and
- a place to indicate the rationale for your rating.

Rubric Template

All of the rubrics follow the same template with this consistent differentiation among the levels This template indicates how you determine which level most accurately reflects your teaching practices. You complete the rubrics by indicating the level you think your teaching represents by checking the box on the left and showing supporting documentation that justifies the level chosen.

Template for All Rubrics

This template illustrates how all of the rubrics are consistently structured:

- *The top of the rubric page identifies the higher-order guiding principle and criterion to be assessed. (These guiding principles are discussed in chapter 3.)*
- *All of the section headings for the various parts of the rubric are in boldface.*
- *The italics explain the headings in all of the rubrics.*

Guiding Principle: Organized according to the three higher-order principles of (1) structure for teaching and learning, (2) instructional design responsibilities, and (3) learning outcomes

Self-Assessment Criterion: Specific to the teaching context

Rubric Quality Levels

❏   Not Yet Using Productive Teaching Practices (I have received feedback)

Check this level if you use unproductive teaching practices associated with this criterion. Since you might not recognize that you engage in these practices, most descriptions of this level include the phrase, "I receive feedback that I engage in these unproductive teaching practices."

❏   Not Yet Critically Self-Reflective with Documentation (this is the current normative practice)

Check this level if you do not reflect on this criterion; you do these productive teaching practices without questioning why or how. This is what most people do today because that is all that is required of them.

❏   Critically Self-Reflective with Documentation (satisfactory teaching occurs at this level and at the next two levels)

Check this level if you use the commonly accepted teaching practices described in the criterion <u>and</u> you critically reflect on data that show how you do use them and you document your use of them

❏   Critically Self-Reflective with Documentation, Evidence Based (this must meet everything in the previous level)

Check this level if you document your justifications and rationale for your teaching practices through evidence. This evidence can come from pedagogical literature or data that you collected to support your teaching practices.

❏   Critically Self-Reflective with Documentation, Evidence Based, Scholarly (this must meet everything in the previous level)

Check this level if you have systematically collected data to support your teaching practices. This level often involves peer review such as through publications or student testimonials that you are successful with this teaching practice.

Further Clarification or Example of Criterion

Optional section: When the component uses educational or psychological concepts that may not be commonly known, they are explained here. There are always further descriptions of this criterion in relevant sections of this book.

Suggested Sources for Documentation

The sources vary depending on the context of the teaching. The lists are long to prompt you to think of many possible sources of support for teaching. The more extensive and the more varied the documentation, the better the support is for teaching practices. Refer to table 9.2 for a further list of possible suggested sources for documentation.

Rationale for Your Rating

Additional sheets can be attached. Please indicate where the evidence can be found on attached syllabi, student products, or your scholarly products or other documents.

Evidence to Support This Rating

Here you write about your rationale for selecting the level above, and include any supporting evidence from many sources. Extra documents can be attached with highlighting to show relevant information.

When appropriate, document literature with citations or data collected at your institution to support decisions or action Cite professional practice guidelines or standards if used.

Here you cite literature or data to support your teaching practices. This is required for the evidence based and scholarly levels. Be comprehensive and honest.

At first glance, these rubrics may appear daunting. That's because teaching is complex. It is impossible to define teaching with a small number of criteria and still do justice to everything teaching entails. Since each rubric page uses the same format and logic, once you understand how to follow them, they will be easier to read. The appendix gives the rubric sets for two common teaching settings. The complete set of rubrics can be accessed by a password-protected website (www.josseybass.com/go /Blumberg). The password is *josseybasshighered*.

Throughout part 1 and in the previous chapter, I showed an inverted pyramid to discuss the hierarchical model of support for teaching. I also incorporated assessment terminology into this inverted pyramid, as displayed in figure 8.3. All of the pyramids used thus far are inverted to reflect that they, like the concepts they represent, do not have a solid base. Now I rotate the pyramid to make it look more stable and demonstrate the correspondence between the pyramid levels and the rubric levels. Rotated pyramids are like the base of a dome of a building: there is much more support at the bottom than at the top. The rows on the pyramid lead to the levels on the rubrics. Figure 9.1 illustrates the hierarchical levels to support the assessment of teaching as expressed in the rotated pyramid, which leads directly to consistent rubric levels. As you read the next sections, refer to the template examples to see how these layers of support become levels on the rubrics.

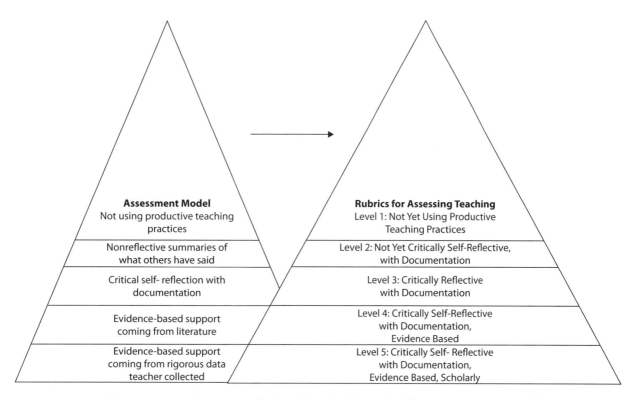

FIGURE 9.1   Correspondence of the Model for Self-Assessment of Teaching to the Rubric Levels

Consistent Levels of Performance on the Rubrics

The following paragraphs describe the rubric levels. The paragraph headings are the labels for the levels on the rubrics. These rubrics provide three levels of acceptable teaching to give professors ways to teach better beyond what they are currently doing. Box 9.1 lists the five levels of performance on all of the rubric pages. To be rated at a higher level, the instructor must also meet everything in previous satisfactory levels because they are cumulative.

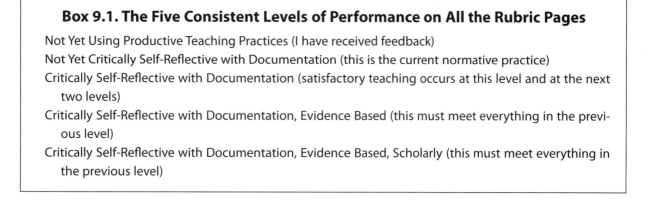

Box 9.1. The Five Consistent Levels of Performance on All the Rubric Pages

Not Yet Using Productive Teaching Practices (I have received feedback)

Not Yet Critically Self-Reflective with Documentation (this is the current normative practice)

Critically Self-Reflective with Documentation (satisfactory teaching occurs at this level and at the next two levels)

Critically Self-Reflective with Documentation, Evidence Based (this must meet everything in the previous level)

Critically Self-Reflective with Documentation, Evidence Based, Scholarly (this must meet everything in the previous level)

Not Yet Using Productive Teaching Practices

I include this lowest level on the rubrics to reflect reality. It describes unproductive teaching practices such as not have specified learning goals or using methods that are in conflict with the learning goals. In some cases, instructors may recognize that they engage in these practices. However, sometimes instructors receive feedback that they are doing this without realizing it themselves. I suspect that few faculty members reading this book engage in these unproductive teaching practices.

Not Yet Critically Self-Reflective with Documentation

Instructors are at this second level if they uncritically summarize what students and peers say about their teaching. Since many academics at all ranks do not critically reflect on their teaching, this is the normative level for most college teachers. As I discussed in chapter 7, most teaching evaluation tools do not prompt faculty members to critically reflect, and as a result many do not engage in this productive exercise. Furthermore, most professors employ assessments of their teaching or develop teaching portfolios for summative evaluation purposes where the admission of weaknesses or areas for improvement can have negative consequences for them. However, when they include only noncritical summaries of what others say without using extensive sources of documentation, they will lack insight into how to improve their teaching. The model described in this book and the rubrics that reflect this model raise the bar for what is a satisfactory teaching assessment to the next level.

Critically Self-Reflective with Documentation

The third level requires that instructors critically reflect on how they use commonly accepted teaching practices. This reflection makes them aware of why they are using specific practices. (I discussed the importance of critical self-reflection in chapter 4.) Instead of just doing these practices, now there is intentionality of purpose.

These accepted teaching practices include using a variety of teaching/learning methods, technologies that are appropriate for student learning goals, and creating a respectful environment to foster learning. Instructors who would rate themselves at this level need to document their intentional use of these teaching practices and reflect on data from many sources as to their effectiveness. Since these rubrics are strictly for the purposes of formative feedback and to offer ways to teach better, instructors should not feel downcast if they are not yet at this level.

Critically Self-Reflective with Documentation, Evidence Based

This level is a much higher standard than the common practice because it requires instructors to use evidence to support their teaching. As I previously discussed, especially in chapter 5, when instructors use evidence to support their teaching, their teaching greatly improves. This evidence can come from pedagogical literature or personal data.

Critically Self-Reflective with Documentation, Evidence Based, Scholarly

The highest level requires that instructors systematically collect and use these data to support teaching practices. For teaching to be assessed at this level, instructors consider teaching like a laboratory for determining how effective they are as teachers. This level often involves peer review such as through publications or student documentation that the instructors are successful with this teaching practice. All teachers should strive for this level; however, the professors most likely to achieve it are experienced faculty. Instructors should not expect to employ rigorous data collection in many aspects of their teaching, but they can aspire to use relevant literature (that is the next-to-the-top level) in as many aspects as they can.

Additional Information on Each Rubric Page

In some cases, the criterion being assessed is an educational concept that may not be familiar or seems abstract. Then the rubric provides further clarification with an example. On the first criterion and the first level shown in table 9.1, instructors may not think that they might be using methods that are in conflict with their learning goals. However, this section (given on the complete rubric in the appendix and the website) states, "Using laboratory activities that require only one correct answer illustrates a conflict with a course goal of inquiry learning," which might help instructors to think about their learning goals and teaching methods.

Sources of Data

In chapter 4, I discussed multiple sources of data to gain insights into teaching and how using data from different data sources yields a more accurate picture of the quality of teaching (Berk, 2006). Student evaluations of courses provide insights into how students perceived the course. Instead of just summarizing these data, teachers should be encouraged to reflect on the accuracy of this information and offer rationales for these evaluations. They can also consider the materials they and their students created for their courses as indicators of opportunities to learn and markers of how well the students met the goals of the course. You will see a good example of using student examination results in the second example I discuss later in this chapter.

When instructors integrate the data from many sources into their critical, reflective, self-assessment ratings, their documentation of the quality of their teaching is stronger. Furthermore, the knowledge achieved by looking at other sources influences what is perceived. When instructors engage in comprehensive, multisource feedback such as would be done as a result of completing these rubrics, they are assessing themselves in a manner similar to the 360-degree feedback used to evaluate executives and managers in corporations (Smither, London, & Reilly, 2005).

Because of this importance of using data from different sources and the fact that most professors currently rely on limited sources of data to validate their teaching effectiveness, each criterion rubric page also lists possible sources of support on which to base the self-assessment rating. Table 9.2 lists a generic inventory of possible data informants grouped by their sources: the person conducting the self-assessment, students, peers, and the literature in higher education. This table is an elaboration of table 4.1.

Inspection of these lists of sources for documentation in the table shows the vast array of useful data for assessment of teaching that instructors and students can provide. End-of-course evaluations might contain questions that ask students to reflect on how much they were challenged in the course. However, many instructors don't realize that student products such as papers, concept maps, and portfolios might also contain reflective information. When instructors ask students to assemble their written assignments from the course into a portfolio, students can be asked to show how their writing improved or to reflect on their best critical thinking. These statements are excellent examples of student reflections.

Although the lists for the peers and the literature are shorter, this does not reduce their importance. To be more explicit, each criterion rubric page lists suggested sources of data that particularly pertain to that criterion. When I pilot-tested these rubrics, instructors told me that these specific lists of possible sources placed alongside the specific rubric prompted them to be more expansive in their critical reflection of all aspects of this criterion.

Documentation

Since documentation is an essential aspect of this self-assessment process, the rubrics remind instructors to document their conclusions. Instructors should add documentation from many sources to give an accurate and complete picture of their teaching. I recommend expansive support for

TABLE 9.2   Sources of Data or Documentation to Use When Assessing Teaching

Self: What the instructor who is doing the self-assessment creates	Student: Any artifacts that the students create	Peer: What other faculty say about your teaching	Literature: Created by others for a larger audience
• Personal reflection such as written in a personal journal • Course materials such as syllabi, assignment directions, examinations • Personal observations about students or personal progress notes on students • Notes from meetings with students, memos sent to students • Documentation from calendar, appointments • Valid and reliable, instructor-created assessments • Documentation using critical incident observations • Self-review of student products • Formative self-assessment tools • Summative assessment instruments • Self-review of assessment plans • Teaching portfolios • Notes after grading projects with notes describing future changes • Concept map on teaching and learning • Description of strategies used to explain ideas to students • Authoring an article on an aspect of teaching for a peer-reviewed publication	• Student-generated evaluations of experiences (i.e., information from standard or course-specific form) • Student assessment data (e.g., pre- and posteducational experience assessment data) • Summary of assessment data such as how students did on tests • Review of student products, performance, on simulations • Review of student progress on drafts, larger projects • Peer review of classmates' papers, projects • Reports, blogs, written reflections of performance from students • Follow-up on student performance in more advanced courses • Follow-up data on where students went after graduation • Student reflections, evaluations, surveys • Reviews of student portfolio/e-portfolios • Teaching award nominations submitted by students • Student-faculty conferences • Student-created concept maps • Student writing an authentic document to be used outside class (e.g., a letter to a newspaper editor or brief for legislators on an issue covered in class) • End-of-semester student reflections on the extent to which they achieved course goals • Feedback from teaching assistants	• Peer assessment data • Chair or unit director report from an annual evaluation, observation, or ongoing discussions • Peer observations—either you being observed or you observing others • Peer coaching • Peer review of student products • Peer review of instructor's materials, assessment plans, or educational products • Teaching awards nominations submitted by peers • Peer review of teaching portfolio • Discussions from faculty learning communities	• Higher education literature, in general or discipline-specific publications • Professional organizations devoted to higher education (AAC&U) or discipline-specific organizations that advance teaching-learning agendas • Regional accreditation, professional or discipline accreditation agencies • ETS, GRE discipline exams • Comparing employer-identified skills and knowledge expectations with course content and assessment strategies

the rating that has been given. This reflective exercise often helps identify existing strengths and areas for future growth. Each criterion asks for the following documentation items and sometimes criterion-specific ones:

- Describe evidence to support this rating, and attach evidence. If this evidence comes from syllabi or other documents, indicate where the evidence can be found on these documents.

- When appropriate, document literature with citations or data collected locally to support decisions or action. Cite professional practice guidelines or standards if used.

Two Examples of Self-Assessments Using the Rubrics

The following examples illustrate how these rubrics can be used for self-assessment. Both instructors in the two examples self-assessed their teaching on the criterion of students demonstrating their ability to apply content or solve problems. For each instructor, only the relevant parts of this rubric page are listed within these examples. The italics in these examples indicate how each professor completed this rubric page. For your reference, the entire rubric page that pertains to these examples follows:

A11 Students Demonstrate Higher-Order Thinking

Rubric Page Corresponding to the Examples in This Chapter

Guiding Principle: Learning outcomes

Self-Assessment Criterion: Students demonstrate the ability to apply the content, use critical thinking, and solve problems related to this discipline at a level that is expected and appropriate for the course—An Essential Criterion

Rubric Quality Levels

❑ Not Yet Using Productive Teaching Practices (I have received feedback)

I use assessments that show that students

- Learn content as isolated facts without meaning and associations <u>or</u>

- Learn content but are unable to apply the content, use critical thinking, or solve problems <u>or</u>

- Fail to learn <u>or</u>

I do not assess the students' understanding, problem solving, or application

❑ Not Yet Critically Self-Reflective with Documentation (this is the current normative practice)

I do not critically reflect on why and how students achieve higher-order learning outcomes

❑ Critically Self-Reflective with Documentation (satisfactory teaching occurs at this level and at the next two levels)

I provide assessment opportunities for students to demonstrate their ability to apply content, think critically, or solve problems <u>and</u>

I document that most students, including low-performing students, acquire some abilities to apply the content, use critical thinking, or solve problems <u>and</u>

I critically reflect on why and how students achieve higher-order learning outcomes

❑ Critically Self-Reflective with Documentation, Evidence Based (this must meet everything in the previous level)

I articulate a clear, explicit, and evidence-based rationale for choice of the application, critical thinking, and problem-solving skills the students demonstrate (cite literature references to support the rationale; if this rationale is based on departmental or college expectations or accreditation agencies, cite these expectations)

❑ Critically Self-Reflective with Documentation, Evidence Based, Scholarly (this must meet everything in the previous level)

I provide evidence through student products that students can apply the content, use critical thinking, and solve problems <u>or</u>

I create a scholarly product based on data showing that students achieved these objectives

Suggested Sources for Documentation

Ones these instructors used are in italics.

- *Self- or peer review of student products (peer reviewed is preferred)*
- Audio or video recording of student performance or explanation of it
- *Higher education literature, either in general or discipline specific (e.g., epistemology of the discipline)*
- Feedback from teaching assistants
- Writing an authentic document to be used outside class, for example, a letter to a newspaper editor or a brief for legislators on an issue covered in class
- Review of how students did on authentic problems
- Student portfolios/e-portfolios
- Follow-up of how students did in more advanced courses that build on what they learned in my course

Rationale for Your Rating

Additional sheets can be attached. Please indicate where the evidence can be found on attached syllabi, student products, or your scholarly products or other documents.

An Example of the Kinds of Problems Students Can Solve

Evidence to Support This Rating

When appropriate, document literature with citations or data collected at your institution to support decisions or action. Cite professional practice guidelines or standards if used.

Example 1 shows a typical professor who is not yet critically reflective of her teaching. This example reflects how professors usually self-assess on this component; this is the current normative level. Example 2 shows more reflection and more evidence. It is well beyond what the vast majority of faculty members do. The professor in this example appropriately rated herself at the critically self-reflective with documentation, evidence based, and scholarly level. When you compare the differences between the first and the second examples, you can see how much insight you can gain into your teaching by using this self-assessment process.

Example 1: A Typical Self-Assessment

Alice Levy had been teaching marketing for three years when she completed these rubrics. She teaches well-organized courses. On her syllabi, she lists five types of assessments, such as tests and individual and group assignments, that allow the students to demonstrate their ability to apply the content. All of the individual and group assignments are clearly described in her syllabi. She is considered a satisfactory teacher by her students. She further reflected on this rubrics page during her fourth year of teaching.

A11   Students Demonstrate Higher-Order Thinking

Guiding Principle: Learning outcomes

Self-Assessment Criterion: Students demonstrate the ability to apply the content, use critical thinking, and solve problems related to this discipline at a level that is expected and appropriate for the course—An Essential Criterion

Rubric Quality Levels

❑ Not Yet Using Productive Teaching Practices (I have received feedback)

I use assessments that show that students

• Learn content as isolated facts without meaning and associations <u>or</u>

• Learn content but are unable to apply the content, use critical thinking, or solve problems <u>or</u>

- Fail to learn <u>or</u>

  I do not assess the students' understanding, problem solving, or application

☑ Not Yet Critically Self-Reflective with Documentation (this is the current normative practice)

Student feedback tells me that students think my assignments help them apply the marketing concepts to real situations of marketing products.

I do not critically reflect why and how students achieve higher-order learning outcomes

While I critically reflect on why and how students achieve higher-order learning outcomes, I did not originally document this, and I do not state it on my syllabus.

❑ Critically Self-Reflective with Documentation (satisfactory teaching occurs at this level and at the next two levels)

I provide assessment opportunities for students to demonstrate their ability to apply content, think critically, or solve problems <u>and</u>

I give tests using different types of questions and assignments. Therefore, my students have opportunities to demonstrate their ability to apply the content using critical thinking and problem solving.

I document that most students, including low-performing students, acquire some abilities to apply the content, use critical thinking, or solve problems <u>and</u>

I could analyze the results of my assessments, but I have not done that yet.

I critically reflect on why and how students achieve higher-order learning outcomes

My assignments follow logically from the content I cover. The assignments reflect the kinds of assignments that entry-level professionals in marketing would get in business. They are very practical and can apply in many business situations.

Rationale for Your Rating

Additional sheets can be attached. Please indicate where the evidence can be found on attached syllabi, student products, or your scholarly products or other documents.

An Example of the Kinds of Problems Students Can Solve

This comes from my syllabus from my undergraduate Introduction to Marketing Class. The class focuses primarily on examples from the pharmaceutical industry. This is a team assignment worth 10 percent of the total grade.

1. *Select a therapeutic category.*
2. *Select an existing product within that category.*
3. *Identify the target segment(s) for this product.*
4. *Identify the product features and benefits for each segment.*
5. *Modify two or three of the product features/benefits so that in essence you are creating a new product.*
6. *Develop a product concept for this new product in the format we discussed in class. Include a photo or drawing of the product as well as a multi-paragraph description.*
7. *Hand in the typed description and the concept board.*

Evidence to Support This Rating

I came to this rating by default. I assumed I was at the third level as I provide assessment opportunities for students to demonstrate their ability to apply content, critical thinking, problem solving, or application. However, when I read all three necessary conditions, I realize that I do not document that most students, including the low-performing students, acquire some abilities to apply the content, use critical thinking, or solve problems. Also while I have a well-thought-out rationale for my assignments, I was not communicating this to others. I did not state it on my original self-assessment last year. Therefore, I rated myself at the lower level. I now know how I can improve my teaching by communicating this to my students.

When appropriate, document literature with citations or data collected at your institution to support decisions or action. Cite professional practice guidelines or standards if used.

None

I agree with Levy's self-assessment. As she points out, she has to do more to be at the critical self-reflective level. First, although she has a rationale for them, she did not explicitly describe it the first time she completed the rubrics. She realizes that she does not explain her reasons to the students. Second, Levy could analyze how her students do on this assignment to be able to show if most students, including the low-performing students, acquire the ability to apply the content. She has the data to be able to do this but never thought to do it. If she finds that most students can apply the content, then Levy will have good evidence to support her claim that she is meeting a stated objective of the course, which is to be able to apply the marketing principles in case studies. If she finds that most students cannot apply the content, she will have data that will motivate her to modify how she teaches, the assignment, or how she grades. However, without using these rubrics and doing this type of analysis, Levy felt comfortable with her teaching effectiveness. After using the rubrics and doing this analysis, Levy and other typical instructors now have new sources for collecting data to support their teaching and have insights into how to teach better.

Example 2: A Professor Whose Self-Assessment Is at the Highest Level

Madhu Mahalingam teaches general chemistry. In chapter 5, I discussed how she teaches problem solving in structured recitations. In this rubric page, she demonstrated her students' problem-solving abilities using examination results. She coded all of her examination questions by level using a published classification scheme and analyzed the results by level. Mahalingam is an exceptionally strong teacher who has focused much of her career on becoming an excellent teacher. I give this example to show the kind of analysis needed to be at the highest level on the rubrics.

A11   Students Demonstrate Higher-Order Thinking

Guiding Principle: Learning outcomes

Self-Assessment Criterion: Students demonstrate the ability to apply the content, use critical thinking, and solve problems related to this discipline at a level that is expected and appropriate for the course—An Essential Criterion

Rubric Quality Levels

☐ Critically Self-Reflective with Documentation (satisfactory teaching occurs at this level and at the next two levels)

I provide assessment opportunities for students to demonstrate their ability to apply content, think critically, or solve problems <u>and</u>

I provide assessment opportunities for students to demonstrate their ability to apply content, critical thinking, problem solving, or application as both formative assessments and summative assessments. I use technology for the formative assessments. These include quizzes on the learning management system I use for the class and online homework. The online homework has tutorials that guide students through the problem solving. These tutorial questions are followed by exercises so that students can build confidence in their ability to solve problems. Often the homework is followed by the online quizzes, which further allow students to build their skills. Students can then practice the skills they acquired in the group problem-solving sessions in recitation described previously.

The summative assessments are three midterm examinations and a final exam. There are problem-solving questions on each one of these evaluations because problem solving is a stated objective of the course. I define what I mean by problem solving using a taxonomy.

I document that most students, including low-performing students, acquire some abilities to apply the content, use critical thinking, or solve problems <u>and</u>

See below

I critically reflect on why and how students achieve higher-order learning outcomes

I explicitly teach the students how to solve these types of problems and give them lots of practice with them. Therefore, it is appropriate that I also test them on their problem-solving skills on the exams. I choose the types of problems intentionally to reflect what students in general chemistry should be able to solve.

☐ Critically Self-Reflective with Documentation, Evidence Based (this must meet everything in the previous level)

I articulate a clear, explicit, and evidence-based rationale for choice of the application, critical thinking, and problem-solving skills the students demonstrate (cite literature references to support the rationale; if this rationale is based on departmental or college expectations or accreditation agencies, cite these expectations)

I use the following classification scheme to determine the level of the questions. The scheme is based on the matrix published by Nygren (2007), which describes learner attributes for various levels of knowledge. I consider level 2 to be appropriate for problem-solving skills in general chemistry, an introductory course. The objective for the course is that students be able to solve problems that require them to make connections between concepts or in other words be able to solve multistep (multiconcept) problems.

	Type of Knowledge	Learner Attributes	Process
Level 0. Pre-Informational (Language)	Terminology	Knows meaning of words	Follows a method
Level 1.0 Informational	Memorizes and repeats information and states facts and definitions	Initiates use of a method—how	
Level 2.0 Comprehension and Understanding: Interpret, summarize, and/or compare information	Is able to make connections between concepts	Rationalizes the use of a method—why; solves single and multistep problems	
Level 3.0 Application	Apply knowledge to a familiar context; is able to use prior knowledge to connect to new knowledge	Explains solution to problem; is able to follow logic of alternate solutions	

Adapted from Nygren (2007)

☒ Critically Self-Reflective with Documentation, Evidence Based, Scholarly (this must meet everything in the previous level)

I provide evidence through student products that students can apply the content, use critical thinking, and solve problems <u>or</u>

See the table below for the exam results.

I create a scholarly product based on data showing that students achieved these objectives

Not done

Rationale for Your Rating

Additional sheets can be attached. Please indicate where the evidence can be found on attached syllabi, student products, or your scholarly products or other documents.

An Example of the Kinds of Problems Students Can Solve

Sample Level 1 question: How many mols of N_2O_4 are contained in 76.3 g N_2O_4? The molar mass of N_2O_4 is 92.02 g/mol.

Single-concept problem that requires knowledge of the relationship of mols and mass.

Sample Level 2 question: Determine the limiting reactant (LR) and the mass (in g) of nitrogen that can be formed from 50.0 g N_2O_4 and 45.0 g N_2H_4. Some possibly useful molar masses are as follows:

$$N_2O_4 = 92.02 \text{ g/mol}, N_2H_4 = 32.05 \text{ g/mol}.$$

$$N_2O_4(l) + 2\,N_2H_4(l) \rightarrow 3\,N_2(g) + 4\,H_2O(g)$$

Evidence to Support This Rating

Exam results by type of question

	Level 1 Percent Correct	*Level 2 Percent Correct*
Exam No. 1	*83.8*	*70.2*
Exam No. 2	*86.9*	*71.4*
Exam No. 3	*71.9*	*58.3*
Final Examination	*73.4*	*77.8*

On 3 out of the 4 examinations, more than 70% of the students got level 2 problem-solving questions correct. The students had a harder time with the content on the third examination, as evidenced by their lower scores on the lower-level questions, as well as the problem-solving questions. The content in exam 1, and to some extent in exam 2, is familiar to students from their high school chemistry. This is reflected in the higher percent correct for level 1 questions for the first two exams. The improvement in problem-solving skills is reflected in the final examination result, as more students get level 2 questions correct. The percentage correct for level 1 questions goes down since the final exam has more content from later chapters, which is mostly new content for a majority of the students. This is evidence that problem solving in a content-rich course like general chemistry requires both foundational knowledge (content) and how the concepts connect to each other (structural knowledge) (Jonassen, 1997).

I did not always get these good results on tests. Several years ago more students did poorly on my exams, and more of my questions were factual. So while the level of my exams has been increasing, the students' abilities to solve problems have also increased over time.

When appropriate, document literature with citations or data collected at your institution to support decisions or action. Cite professional practice guidelines or standards if used.

Nygren, K (2007) Faculty Guidebook, 4th Edition, Beyerlein, Holmes, & Apple, Eds., 2007, Pacific Crest Publications, pp. 165–168

Jonassen D. (1997) Instructional Design Models for Well-Structured and Ill-Structured Problem-Solving Learning Outcomes, ETR&D, Vol 45, No. 1, pp 65–94 ISSN 1042–1629

Mahalingam's example shows how she critically reflected on what higher-order skills she wanted her students to have based on their first-year status in college and her objectives and her teaching practices. She used her exam questions and the student products (their results on these exams) as evidence for this criterion, data that instructors normally obtain. What transformed test results into evidence to show that her students could apply the content, use critical thinking, and solve problems was that Mahalingam systematically analyzed the test results by level of question. To show that her students are successfully solving problems, she coded her examination questions by cognitive level required to answer the question. This is a good practice that all instructors can use by using a common learning taxonomy such as Bloom's (1956) or Anderson's taxonomies (Anderson et al., 2001). (I discussed these taxonomies in chapter 3.) Had Mahalingam just coded her questions according to level and not looked at the test results, she would have been at the Critically Self-Reflective with Documentation, Evidence Based level. Her test results demonstrated that the majority of her students are able to solve problems. This analysis of test questions and student results yields valuable insights into teaching effectiveness. Mahalingam realized that students had more trouble with the content on the third exam and therefore also did worse on the problem-solving questions. It was not poor problem-solving skills but less content mastery. With this information, Mahalingam can review the content on the third exam to see if she can teach these concepts more clearly.

Chapter Summary

I described the rationale for self-assessment of teaching rubrics. This discussion focused on the rubric template and the standards and the desired performance expectations of each standard. In the next chapter, I discuss the different criteria used on the rubrics and the various rubrics for different contexts of teaching.

Rationale for Rubrics for Self-Assessment of Teaching
- These rubrics are a logical extension of the model of assessing excellent and effective teaching I developed in earlier chapters.
  - The constructive and informative model for assessing teaching as expressed in a rotated pyramid leads to rubric levels or consistent standards of expected performance.
  - The combination of the hierarchical model for support for teaching with the aspects of excellent and effective teaching forms rubrics for assessing teaching.
- Rubrics can be used to self-assess your teaching.
- These rubrics foster self-regulation leading to better teaching.
- Each rubric has
  - the same five rubric quality levels,
  - suggested sources for documentation, and
  - a place for you to indicate the rationale for your rating.

All of the rubrics look like this:

Guiding Principle:

Self-Assessment Criterion:

Rubric Quality Levels

❏   Not Yet Using Productive Teaching Practices (I have received feedback)

❏   Not Yet Critically Self-Reflective with Documentation (this is the current normative practice)

❏   Critically Self-Reflective with Documentation (satisfactory teaching occurs at this level and at the next two levels)

❏   Critically Self-Reflective with Documentation, Evidence Based (this must meet everything in the previous level)

❏   Critically Self-Reflective with Documentation, Evidence Based, Scholarly (this must meet everything in the previous level)

Suggested Sources for Documentation

Rationale for Your Rating

Evidence to Support This Rating

Chapter 10

What These Rubrics Assess, and How That Improves Teaching

THIS CHAPTER HAS THREE FOCI: what these rubrics assess, how the context-specific rubrics and rubric sets are similar and different, and how to use the rubrics effectively to teach better. Since teaching takes place in many different situations, including experiential milieus, there are rubrics with context-specific criteria to reflect these diverse settings. Table 10.1 explains how you can decide which rubric sets to use for your teaching contexts. The chapter ends with a discussion of how to use these rubrics effectively to promote better teaching, including tips and advice for personal development. All of the rubrics can be accessed at www.josseybass .com/go/Blumberg. The password is *josseybasshighered.*

TABLE 10.1   Rubrics for Specific Teaching Contexts

Teaching Context	Use Rubric for This Context
Classroom, laboratory	Choose one or both of these two rubrics that corresponds to your teaching situations:
	Rubric A: Rubrics for Improving Face-to-Face, Laboratory, or Online Teaching for Autonomous Instructors:
	• Instructors who control the way the course is taught • Course directors of a multiple instructor course or a multiple section course • Coinstructors with equal responsibility over course
	Rubric B: Rubrics for Improving Face-to-Face, Laboratory, or Online Teaching for Instructors with Limited Autonomy
	• Instructors of multiple section courses with a common syllabus and/or common exams • Instructors within a multiple-instructor course • Graduate instructors who lead a recitation. laboratory, or discussion section of a larger course
Online	Choose one or both of these two rubrics that corresponds to your teaching situation:
	Rubric A: Rubrics for Improving Face-to-Face, Laboratory, or Online Teaching for Autonomous Instructors (see previous examples)
	Rubric B: Rubrics for Improving Face-to-Face, Laboratory, or Online Teaching for Instructors with Limited Autonomy (see previous examples)
Experiential, community, field, or clinical site	Choose one or both of these two rubrics that corresponds to your teaching situation:
	Rubric D: Rubrics for Improving Teaching in Experiential Settings
	• Actually at the experiential site (e.g., clinic or community agency) working with students
	Rubric G: Rubrics for Improving the Direction of Experiential Education
	• Arranges or coordinates experiential learning for students and monitors educational experiences conducted in experiential settings
Research setting or engineering project for undergraduate, graduate, and postdoctoral students or fellows	Rubric C: Rubrics for Improving the Mentoring of Students in Research or Engineering-Type Design Projects
Graphic or fine arts studio settings	Rubric E: Rubrics for Improving Teaching in the Visual or Graphic Arts
Theater, music, or conservatory settings	Rubric F: Rubrics for Improving Teaching in the Performing Arts

Self-Assessment Criteria

This section organizes the self-assessment criteria on the different rubric sets into criteria that are common to all teaching contexts and criteria that are context specific. It also outlines how all of the assessment criteria are arranged on the rubrics.

Criteria Common to All Teaching Contexts

The criteria to be assessed on all of the rubrics correspond to the essential aspects of effective and excellent teaching described in chapter 3. After

---

Box 10.1 Criteria Common on All Rubric Pages

- Plan educational experiences to promote student learning. Table 10.2 shows how this is expressed in many distinctive ways depending on the context. As the table shows, planning education to promote student learning plays a large role in the assessment of teaching.
- Provide frequent and useful formal and informal feedback to students to foster greater learning.
- Provide frequent, well-structured opportunities for students to reflect on their learning.
- Use consistent policies and a process to assess students.
- Ensure students have successful learning experiences by you being available and accessible to them. Online or experiential instructors may receive feedback from students that they were not available to help them or did not spend quality educational time with them.
- Engage in self-analysis and reflection of teaching as part of a review and revision process, including appraisal of content currency and accuracy.
- Assess student mastery of learning outcomes relating to acquisition of knowledge, skills, or values.
- Assess student mastery of higher-order thinking and skills: application, critical thinking, and problem solving related to this discipline at a level that is expected and appropriate. Table 10.3 shows how higher-order thinking is expressed in distinctive ways depending on the context.
- Assess student mastery of learning skills, self-assessment skills that can transcend disciplinary content. Table 10.4 shows how this is expressed in distinctive ways depending on the context.

---

defining essential aspects of effective teaching from the pedagogical literature, I used a consensus model for defining the criteria, a common practice for rubric development that are to be used beyond individual course assessments (Reddy & Andrade, 2010). There are nine teaching constants regardless of setting, expressed as criteria to be assessed on all rubrics as listed in box 10.1. However, three of these constants get expressed in nuanced ways on the various rubric sets. Tables 10.2 through 10.4 explain the nuances of these common criteria.

Criteria Specific to the Teaching Contexts

In addition to these common criteria, there are three context-specific criteria: organizing all educational experiences to facilitate learning and two that relate to serving as a role model. Table 10.5 compares and contrasts these three context-specific criteria on the horizontal rows on the rubric sets.

A Framework for Grouping Criteria on the Rubric Sets

There are two ways the criteria are grouped: by higher-order guiding principles and whether they are essential or optional.

On all of the rubrics, the criteria are organized according to three higher-order guiding principles of effective teaching: structure for teaching and

TABLE 10.2 Rubric-Specific Nuances for the Common Criterion: Plan Educational Experiences to Promote Student Learning

Multiple Ways to Define Students' Expectations as Listed on the Different Rubrics

Autonomous Classroom, Laboratory, Online Instructor	Classroom, Laboratory, Online Instructor with Limited Autonomy	Clinical/Field Teaching for Preceptors or Supervisors	Directors of Experiential/Clinical/Field Experiences	Mentoring Students in Research or Engineering-Type Design Projects	Teaching in the Visual Arts	Teaching in the Performing Arts
Develop challenging yet reasonable learning outcomes for the acquisition of knowledge, skills, or values and use them to select appropriate teaching/learning methods and educational technologies.	Use teaching/learning methods and educational technologies that are consistent with the identified learning outcomes for the acquisition of knowledge, skills, or values.	Institute well-defined expectations and roles for students during experiential learning.	Institute well-defined expectations and roles for students during experiential learning. Plan experiential learning experiences to facilitate learning, and check that learning does occur.	Institute well-defined expectations and roles for students while engaged in a research or project. Plan and implement individualized research or project experiences.	Plan and implement experiences to meet the needs of all students, recognizing that within a class, there may be varying levels of competency; thus, using one type of activity or exercise may not serve the needs of all students equally.	Plan and facilitate experiences to meet the needs of all students, recognizing that within a class, there may be varying levels of competency; thus, using one type of activity or exercise may not serve the needs of all students equally.

Additional Ways to Define Students' Expectations as Listed on the Different Rubrics

Autonomous Classroom, Laboratory, Online Instructor	Classroom, Laboratory, Online Instructor with Limited Autonomy	Clinical/Field Teaching for Preceptors or Supervisors	Directors of Experiential/Clinical/Field Experiences	Mentoring Students in Research or Engineering-Type Design Projects	Teaching in the Visual Arts	Teaching in the Performing Arts
Use teaching/learning methods that promote the achievement of challenging yet reasonable learning outcomes, understanding of content, the ability to apply the content, use critical thinking, and solve problems related to this discipline.			Use teaching/learning methods that promote the achievement of learning outcomes, understanding of content, the ability to apply the content, use critical thinking, and solve problems related to this discipline.	Provide supervised opportunities for students to learn by doing. Specify how to provide supervised opportunities for students to learn by doing and through modeling.	Provide supervised opportunities for students to learn by doing through modeling. Use teaching/learning methods that promote the achievement of artistic skill and expression and visual literacy.	Use teaching/learning methods that promote the achievement of artistic and performance skills and expression.

Learn Setting-Specific Processes as Part of the Definition of Students' Expectations as Listed on the Different Rubrics

0	0	0	Help students understand the research or project design process.	Help students understand the creative/interpretive process or critical thinking/problem solving about art and aesthetic sensibility.	Help students understand the creative process, and encourage critical thinking about art, aesthetic sensibility, and the history of the performing arts discipline.

Align Learning Outcomes

Align learning outcomes: internally with teaching and learning activities and within an educational program. Internal alignment means all three should be the same level on a learning taxonomy (such as Bloom's).	0	Align learning outcomes: internally with teaching and learning activities and assessments and within an educational program. Internal alignment means all three should be the same level on a learning taxonomy (such as Bloom's).	Align learning outcomes: internally with teaching and learning activities and assessments and within an educational program. Internal alignment means all three should be the same level on a learning taxonomy (such as Bloom's).	0	Alignment may occur more naturally. For example, students may be assessed as they engage in the usual authentic activities of the site.

Development or Revision of Course

Development or revision of course is an optional criterion.	Development or revision of course is an optional criterion.	Development or revision of experiential learning is an optional criterion.	Development of experiential offerings or revision of existing ones is an essential criterion.	Design of research experiences is an optional criterion.	Development or revision of courses/experiences is an optional criterion.

0 = not present on that rubric.

TABLE 10.3 Rubric-Specific Nuances for the Common Criterion: Higher-Order Thinking Skills

Classroom, Laboratory, Online Autonomous Instructor or Instructor with Limited Autonomy	Clinical/Field Teaching for Preceptors or Supervisors	Directors of Experiential/Clinical/ Field Experiences	Mentoring Students in Research or Engineering-Type Design Projects	Teaching in the Visual Arts	Teaching in the Performing Arts
Apply the content, use critical thinking, and solve problems related to this discipline at a level that is expected and appropriate for course.	Apply the content, use critical thinking, and solve problems related to this discipline.	Apply the content, use critical thinking, and solve problems related to this discipline.	Apply the content, use critical thinking, and solve problems related to this research or project design.	Apply the content, think critically about art and aesthetic sensibility, and solve problems related to this discipline.	Engage in critical thinking about art, aesthetic sensibility, and the history of the performing arts discipline.
0	Clinical/professional reasoning process and clinical/professional judgment using evidence-based decision making.	Clinical/professional reasoning process and clinical/professional judgment using evidence-based decision making.	0	Creative/interpretive process in the visual arts.	Creative process in the performing arts.

Engage in craft and artistic expression. |
| 0 | 0 | 0 | Results or products of research or design experience. | Creative outcomes/ products, craft, and expression, visual literacy and aesthetic sensibility. | Artistic and performance skills in academic and performance situations. |

0 = not present on that rubric.

TABLE 10.4 Rubric-Specific Nuances for the Common Criterion: Learning Skills

Classroom, Laboratory, Online Autonomous Instructor or Instructor with Limited Autonomy	Clinical/Field Teaching for Preceptors or Supervisors	Directors of Experiential/Clinical/ Field Experiences	Mentoring Students in Research or Engineering-Type Design Projects	Teaching in the Visual Arts	Teaching in the Performing Arts
Learning skills that can transcend disciplinary content (time management, organization of data, or knowing where to look for information) and self-assessment skills (assessment of strengths/weaknesses, or of own learning abilities).	Learning skills that can transcend disciplinary content (time management, organization of data, or knowing where to look for evidence-based information) and self-assessment skills (assessment of strengths/ weaknesses, or of own learning abilities).	Learning skills that can transcend disciplinary content (time management, organization of data, or knowing where to look for evidence-based information) and self-assessment skills (assessment of strengths/ weaknesses, or of own learning abilities).	Ability to continue to do research or design projects or ability to develop further relevant skills and to self-assess research or design skills and self-assessment of strengths/weaknesses.	Students demonstrate continued growth as artists by • Finding one's own style • Developing skills and craft • Developing artistic impulse or intuition • Critically engaging in the history of the visual arts • Carry these artistic traditions forward.	Students demonstrate continued growth as artists and performers by • Finding one's own voice or style • Developing skills and craft • Developing artistic impulse or intuition • Critically engaging in the history of the performing arts discipline • Carrying these performing traditions forward

TABLE 10.5 Distinctive Criteria Associated with Specific Teaching Contexts Foster Learning Experiences

Assessment Criteria as Listed on the Different Rubrics	Classroom, Laboratory, Online Autonomous Instructor, or Instructor with Limited Autonomy	Clinical/Field Teaching for Preceptors or Supervisors	Directors of Experiential/ Clinical/Field Experiences	Mentoring Students in Research or Engineering-Type Design Projects	Teaching in the Visual Arts	Teaching in the Performing Arts
Organize educational experiences to foster learning. In experiential settings, instructors need to be very conscious of providing a range of experiences that allow students to grow.	This criterion occurs by design in learning-centered classrooms or online settings. It does not occur automatically in traditional or instructor-centered classrooms or online settings	This activity needs to be planned intentionally so that students are not just doing routine or clerical jobs repeatedly. Instructors need to take time to explain how to do more complex jobs and then to closely monitor students as they begin to perform them.		While research often involves routine tasks, such as washing glassware in a lab or data entry in a policy research study, instructors need to plan more appropriate educational experiences to foster learning.	Instructors in the performing and visual arts need to be concerned with the development of the students' artistic growth and aesthetic sensibility, as well as achievement of artistic skill and expression and not just performing or creating art.	

Serve as a Role Model

Distinctive Criteria within Specific Rubrics↓	Classroom, Laboratory, Online Autonomous Instructor, or Instructor with Limited Autonomy	Clinical/Field Teaching for Preceptors or Supervisors	Directors of Experiential/ Clinical/Field Experiences	Mentoring Students in Research or Engineering-Type Design Projects	Teaching in the Visual Arts	Teaching in the Performing Arts
Model ethical behavior; serve as a role model doing actual work of site.	0	Serve as a role model by adhering to current professional and ethical standards of discipline and provide optimal services or care to be a role model practitioner according to professional standards.	Adhere to current professional and ethical standards of this profession or discipline.	Adhere to current professional and ethical standards in research or project design; insist that the student avoid plagiarism and fabrication of data.	Serve as a role model by adhering to current artistic and ethical standards in the instructor's discipline, and avoid visual plagiarism.	Serve as a role model by adhering to current artistic and ethical standards in the instructor's discipline.
Model distinctive site-specific processes.	0	Use evidence-based decision making.	0	Use a research process like the scientific method.	Model creative process, create art.	Model creative process, performance skills.

Note: 0 = not present on that rubric. [comment]

learning, instructional design responsibilities, and learning outcomes, as discussed in chapter 8. Providing feedback to students is an example of a criterion for the structure for the teaching and learning guiding principle. The instructor reflecting on the effectiveness of his or her teaching is an example of instructional design responsibilities, and the third guiding principle consists of all the components involved with assessing students.

The rubrics contain essential and optional criteria to assess teaching. The essential criteria characterize the vital aspects of all teaching, such as planning for student learning and assessing students. The optional criteria, such as using creativity in teaching, may not apply to every teaching situation. Yet some instructors may feel the optional components, such as developing new courses, are what distinguishes their teaching. The optional criteria also contain hard-to-measure aspects, such as helping students acquire intrinsic motivation to learn.

The list of criteria may include components that instructors do not commonly think of as part of their teaching. I provide the list of the criteria for the rubric set for autonomous classroom, online, or laboratory teachers in box 10.2.

Box 10.2. Criteria for Assessment of Autonomous Classroom, Online, and Laboratory Teachers

The rubric set for autonomous classroom, online, and laboratory teaching asks instructors to assess themselves on the following criteria.

Essential Criteria for Excellent, Effective Classroom, Laboratory, or Online Teaching

Guiding Principle of Structure for Teaching and Learning

- Develop challenging yet reasonable learning outcomes for the acquisition of knowledge, skills, or values, and use them to select appropriate teaching/learning methods and educational technologies.
- Use teaching/learning methods that promote the achievement of challenging yet reasonable learning outcomes, understanding of content, the ability to apply the content, use critical thinking, and solve problems related to this discipline.
- Provide frequent and useful formal and informal feedback to students to foster greater learning.
- Provide frequent, well-structured opportunities for students to reflect on their learning.
- Use consistent policies and a process to assess students.
- Ensure students have successful learning experiences through your availability and accessibility.

Guiding Principle of Instructional Design Responsibilities

- Align learning outcomes internally with teaching and learning activities and assessments and within an educational program.
- Organize all educational experiences to facilitate learning.
- Engage in self-analysis and reflection of teaching as part of a review and revision process, including appraisal of content currency and accuracy.

(Continued)

Guiding Principle of Learning Outcomes

- Students achieve challenging yet reasonable learning outcomes of acquisition of knowledge, skills, or values.
- Students demonstrate the ability to apply the content, use critical thinking, and solve problems related to this discipline at a level that is expected and appropriate for the course.
- Students demonstrate learning skills that can transcend disciplinary content (time management or knowing where to look for information) and self-assessment skills (assessment of strengths and weaknesses or of own learning abilities).

Optional Criteria for Excellent, Effective Teaching

Guiding Principle of Structure for Teaching and Learning

- Help students to acquire or use intrinsic motivation to learn.

Guiding Principle of Instructional Design Responsibilities

- Creativity in teaching.
- Development of new or unique courses or revision of existing ones.
- Contribute to the enhancement of instructional programs or accreditation process.

Rubric Sets Are Teaching Context Specific

Teaching varies by its context. However, most teaching assessment tools ignore the differences and assume that teaching is a one-size-fits-all situation. Therefore, it is not surprising that these assessments have marginal value when it comes to suggesting ways to teach better. My goal in providing different sets of self-assessment rubrics is to show how assessing teaching differs by teaching context. The most common teaching situation occurs in classrooms or online in courses. Yet even here, there are differences in how teaching occurs. Assessing teaching that occurs in all kinds of settings, not just looking at teaching in classrooms or online, should help elevate these other types of teaching. Finally, I discuss a unique teaching situation to illustrate this point.

Degree of Teaching Autonomy

The autonomy instructors have in their traditional classroom, laboratory, and online courses varies. At one end on this continuum is the common situation where the instructor is entirely responsible for the course: the instructor designs the course, selects the textbook, determines assignments and how students will be assessed, and decides on the teaching methods that will be used. These instructors have a lot of leeway in how they teach the course.

At the other end of this continuum are four possible teaching scenarios. First are instructors who teach a class (or several) in a multiple-instructor course. Here a course director makes the major instructional decisions, and the individual instructors need to follow the overall plan for the course. This kind of teaching model is common in the health professions education, especially in the preclinical years of medical school.

The second and third scenarios involve multiple instructor courses where a course director or planner has a great deal of oversight about the course. In the second scenario, each instructor teaches the course alone, but each section has the same syllabus, learning objectives, content, and assessments. This type of course is common in general education courses such as English composition or mathematics. In the third scenario, teachers are given a course to teach where everything from the content, calendar, assignments, and assessments is decided. It is a prepackaged course, and the instructor has no instructional decision-making autonomy. This teaching scenario is common in large, online courses taught by for-profit colleges and in military training.

Fourth, graduate students or instructors may teach a recitation section as part of a large enrollment course taught by another professor.

In all of these situations, the instructor might want to teach better. Those who teach in any of these reduced-autonomy situations may find that the traditional teaching assessment tools do not serve them well because they ask questions over which the instructor has no control. Since these teaching situations require different types of assessment tools, I created a rubric set for teachers who have autonomy in how they teach their courses and a rubric set for instructors who are part of a multiple instructor course or a common course with many identical sections.

Directors of Experiential, Clinical, and Field Education

These directors coordinate clinical, field, community, or service-learning experiences for students. These are educational responsibilities and are distinct from the actual supervisors or clinicians at these sites. Since this work has a direct impact on student learning, it is education, not service. My work with these types of instructors indicates that they have no guidance in how to assess their work. They often have unique positions within departments and cannot ask peers to observe their work. Because they often have reduced teaching loads to allow time for coordinating students in experiential settings, they often base their assessments on their educational work on a small fraction of their responsibilities. The director's educational role is often indirect in that they plan experiences and evaluate the quality of the sites and the students' learning but do not actually teach the students at these sites. They have great problem-solving skills and behind-the-scenes responsibilities of making decisions that allow the students to learn in many different experiential settings. A comparison of the criteria for directors of experiential learning with the criteria for other types of teaching shows how the teaching responsibilities are quite different. Tables 10.2 through 10.5 illustrate these differences.

Rubrics for Experiential Settings

As you might have realized from inspecting the tables, rubric sets for experiential teaching are longer than for classroom teaching. The added criteria relate to the complex relationship between the instructor and the learner in experiential contexts. Individuals in these experiential settings have dual responsibilities: teaching and working in the authentic setting such as attending to clinical care responsibilities or providing professional expertise to a community agency.

The experiential rubric sets list aspects that experiential instructors may not have considered. Perhaps just by reading them, such instructors will become more aware of their complex roles in experiential settings. Most instructors do not reflect on their professional roles or what they do in authentic situations as part of their teaching. However, if students are present, they are always teaching. Therefore, these professional roles need to be assessed also.

Several researchers have told me that completing the mentoring rubrics was a meaningful experience for them. Completing this exercise was the first time they really considered the many ways they try to foster student learning in their laboratories. Professors who mentor students in research that is not laboratory based remarked that they might not have much interaction with their students, so they might not be as mindful of their teaching responsibilities with their students. For example, one social scientist said that he never thought to ask his doctoral students to reflect on their learning, yet he used reflection often in his classroom teaching with undergraduate and graduate students.

Using the Self-Assessment Rubrics Effectively

This section discusses how to use these rubrics to promote personal growth.

Tips for Completing These Rubrics
- Do not attempt to complete the rubrics all at once. It is best to work on them a little bit at a time but on an ongoing basis.
  - Expect to invest time when you complete the rubrics.
  - Reflecting on your teaching requires effort.
  - This investment is worth it as you can gain real insights into your teaching.

- List all of the contexts in which you teach, especially your nonclassroom teaching. To do a full assessment of your teaching, complete the rubric set for each teaching context.

- Consider your teaching across all the courses and settings in which you currently teach, not just on the basis of one or two courses.

- Refer to the suggested sources for documentation and further clarification to help you complete the rubrics and see what sources of documentation might help.

- To complete these rubrics accurately, integrate information from other sources into your self-assessment. Using data from various sources leads to a richer assessment.

- Each successive level expects you to meet everything in the previous level and below. Therefore, rate yourself at the highest level at which you meet all of the criteria.

- Many levels include multiple aspects connected by *and* and *or*. For aspects connected by *and*, you should do all of them to check this level. For aspects connected by *or*, you need to do only one of them.

- Indicate your overall rating on each criterion by checking the appropriate level for your teaching. It is possible that you may meet some of the elements on a level but not all of them. Remember that this is a self-assessment, so documentation is more important than the actual level you rate yourself.

  - If you meet all but one aspect of a level, consider yourself at this level while you identify that aspect for immediate improvement.

  - If you meet only one aspect of a higher level, rate yourself at the lower level but also indicate which aspect you are on at the higher level. Recognizing that you did not meet the other aspects gives you a direction for change.

  - You will see an example of a self-assessment that straddles two levels in case 4.

- Provide the supporting evidence to show why the ratings are accurate. This documentation is essential to validate your ratings. If you are using another document, such as syllabi or student artifacts, indicate on these documents what you are referring to on the rubrics by including the name of the form, the principle, the criterion, and your rating close to the evidence that supports this rating. The same evidence can support several criteria. You can see how other instructors provided supporting evidence in the two examples given in the previous chapter and the cases that follow.

- Use the information you gain from the self-assessment to make incremental changes to your teaching:
  - Choose a few components to work on rather than trying to change everything at once.
  - Each level on the rubric suggests concrete behaviors that you can incorporate.
  - Try to read the literature in a few areas that you wish to improve.
  - Focus on one aspect of your teaching or one context at a time.

How to Manage the Growth Process without Feeling Overwhelmed

- Develop a plan for how and when you will focus on your teaching improvement.

- Complete a few rubric pages at a time, perhaps starting with one from each guiding principle.

- Focus on improving your teaching in one or two components at a time.

- Work with a professional colleague.

- Seek help from staff in a teaching and learning center or senior faculty.

- Periodically review the progress you have made and your overall plan.

Expected Level of Performance:

- While the criteria remain the same for all types of instructors or faculty, the level of expectations may change. For example, beginning faculty, adjunct faculty, or professors who have heavy research or service responsibilities should strive to be at the critically self-reflective with documentation level for most, if not all, of their teaching. Faculty who are striving to be excellent teachers might aim for the levels that include evidence based or scholarly.

- Few faculty members will rate themselves as meeting the higher or highest level on many components, or even any of them. In fact, the current normative practice is the second level: "Not yet critically self-reflective with documentation."

- The level you strive for should be consistent with your roles and responsibilities. In consultation with your chair, pick which components you will aim to be evidence based or scholarly. For example, the second professor described in chapter 9 is an experienced senior-level teacher at a university that values teaching, evidence-based practices, and scholarship of teaching and learning. Her chair fully supports and values the evidence-based scholarly work Mahalingam does to show that first-year students are learning in her gateway chemistry courses.

- Achieving improvement may be more important than achieving the highest level.

The Rubrics as Faculty Improvement Tools

Assessment works best when it is ongoing, and this is even truer of formative feedback. Assessment is not end in itself; rather, it is a process and a means for self-improvement and learning (Maki, 2004). The process of engaging in ongoing, critical self-reflection done to teach better has much more power than when it is done once every five years, such as when professors are going up for promotion. Completing these rubrics places the locus of control with you because you want to improve rather than with external audiences who judge your performance. The hierarchical strategies as reflected on the levels on the rubrics are based on essential faculty development principles discussed in the literature. You can benefit from trying any one of the strategies even if you did not follow through with the rest. Once you see how you can teach better, you should have revitalized your teaching.

The use of these self-assessment rubrics can begin a continuous learning and improvement process for you. When you use the rubrics, you will

- have opportunities to go beyond what is currently practiced to what is more desirable,

- clarify what good performance is through concrete and objective examples of excellent, effective teaching,

- receive diagnostic feedback that identifies areas for possible incremental improvement,

- have different aspirations for your teaching as reflected by the three acceptable levels,

- identify best teaching practices,

- integrate your teaching as a body of work and not just individual courses, and

- have data that can be placed in dossiers for promotion and tenure or when you apply for another academic position.

Completing the rubrics provides data about what you do in your teaching compared to what you think you do or what students say about you. Armed with these data, you should be motivated to make significant changes. But feedback is of no use unless it results in action. Research shows that professors report using active learning, inquiry-based instruction, or educational technologies more than they actually do (Ebert-May et al., 2011; Palsole & Brunk-Chavez, 2011). If you have a learning or improving orientation or attitude, you are likely to make significant changes (Smither, London, & Reilly, 2005). With this improving orientation, you can be motivated to learn new skills or seek help from others or the literature.

Here are a few ways to use the rubrics to plan how to teach better:

- As a self-directed way to identify ways to grow your teaching. You would be working alone here.

- As a shared investigation of effective teaching in a faculty learning community. Here you and your peers might decide to change your teaching based on the same criteria. Together you could read and discuss the relevant literature on this concept.

- As a structure for systematically gathering evidence of effective teaching in preparation of a tenure and promotion dossier. In addition to identifying strengths, you might find areas you want to improve before you submit your dossier.

- As part of a peer consulting relationship focused on what you would like to improve about your teaching.

- As part of a formal process working with a faculty developer or a mentor.

- As a springboard to beginning a useful dialogue with your chair about your varied teaching roles and responsibilities. Together you can plan your future direction, such as engaging in scholarly work on teaching.

Since this book describes a new model for assessing teaching and also uses a much higher standard, your self-assessment of your teaching may appear quite different from what is currently used. It might be a good idea to discuss these ideas at your institution to obtain greater understanding and acceptance of these principles. They might have to be adapted to your local culture. For example, it is important to determine if your chair or dean will value rigorous data collection or scholarly work on teaching before you seek to do this.

I emphasize again that this book proposes a career-long growth process. The rubrics indicate you can engage in this process at different levels and to different degrees. The model and the rubrics lay out a comprehensive plan for ongoing teacher development. It is not something that should be done all at once or all at the highest level.

Chapter Summary

- Since instructors teach in very different types of settings, different self-reflective rubrics mirror these varied teaching roles including

  - teaching a course face-to-face or online where the instructor has autonomy,
  - teaching a course face-to-face or online where the instructor has limited autonomy,
  - mentoring undergraduate, graduate students, or postdoctoral fellows in research, or an engineering type research project,
  - precepting or supervising students in clinical, field, or community settings,
  - teaching in studio settings in the visual or graphic arts,
  - teaching in theater or music or conservatory settings in the performing arts, and
  - directing clinical, experiential education or service-learning.

- These rubrics contain nine criteria that are common to all teaching situations. The essential aspects of excellent and effective teaching define these common criteria. There also are context-specific criteria.

- Each rubric set contains at least twelve essential criteria that are both common to all rubric sets and context specific and several optional criteria to use for self-assessment of teaching.

How to Use the Rubrics Effectively

- Beginning instructors can use these self-assessment rubrics to identify their teaching strengths and areas that they will want to improve.

- At all levels of experience, instructors can use these rubrics when they want to change how they teach or they discover issues or concerns about their teaching.

- These rubrics can be used throughout an entire career as part of a continuous improvement process, as the cases show.

- Faculty developers can use these rubrics when they work with individual instructors.

- Ongoing self-assessment of teaching can lead to excellent, effective and inspired teaching.

CASES SHOWING EFFECTIVE USES FOR THE RUBRICS

Introduction

I describe five cases reflecting very different contexts of teaching and faculty members with different amounts of experience teaching. In the first three cases, the professors assessed their classroom teaching. Elizabeth Amy Janke used these rubrics in her first year as an assistant professor to plan her future growth as an effective teacher and then reviewed her progress in her third year. After Janke learned about the rubrics, she did all of the work reported here on her own. Then she shared her self-assessments with me. Stu Proff was a pretenure professor who was worrying that his teaching evaluations might prevent him getting promoted and tenured. He sought my help prior to his pretenure review. I worked with Proff throughout this process. Susan Wainwright is an experienced, tenured associate professor who used the rubrics to document her scholarship of teaching and learning. She embraced the rubrics and completed them on her own to support her claim that she is an excellent teacher for her promotion. In the last two cases, the professors assessed their teaching in experiential settings. Nathan West is a pretenure assistant professor of chemistry who supervises undergraduate and graduate students in laboratory research. He used the rubrics as a way to check his progress toward effective teaching; he did all of the work on his own. Michael Cawley is a full professor who precepts professional pharmacy students on their clinical rotations. He did all of his personal development on his own. Because I respected Cawley as a senior clinician-preceptor, I asked him if he would use the rubrics to assess his precepting. With the exception of Stu Proff, all of these cases are real professors, and I used their names and actual examples. Because Stu Proff represents a struggling professor, he is not a real person but reflects several faculty I have worked with.

Each case shows how the professor completed the rubric pages for several criteria. Italics on the rubrics indicate how the instructor self-assessed his or her teaching. Only the selected rubric pages and the relevant parts of these rubric pages are given here. The table here lists the criteria that I discuss in these cases as well a brief sketch of the professors. While you may be inclined to read only the case or cases that seem to be the most congruent with your level of experience or teaching context, I hope you will read all of them. There are different lessons about growth and improvement to be learned in each.

Guide to the Cases

Guiding Principle and Self-Assessment Criteria	Case Name and Rubric Criteria Pages Displayed for Each Instructor						
	Elizabeth Amy Janke: assistant professor used rubrics to plan for and show growth over time	Stu Proff: fictional pretenured, assistant professor used rubrics to help him to teach better	Susan Wainwright: senior professor used rubrics to document her scholarship of teaching and learning	Nathan West: pretenure assistant professor used rubrics to assess how he mentors students in research	Michael Cawley: senior professor used rubrics to assess the effectiveness of a new model of precepting	Alice Levy: Example 1 given in chapter 9, used rubrics in a typical self-assessment way	Madhu Mahalingam: Example 2, given in chapter 9, used rubrics to show a scholarly approach to her teaching
Guiding principles: Structure for teaching and learning							
Develop learning outcomes and use them to select teaching/learning methods.			X				
Institute well-defined expectations and roles for the student while engaged in research or project.				X			
Provide feedback to students.		X					
Provide opportunities for students to reflect on their learning.	X						
Use consistent policies and a process to assess students.		X					
Help students understand the research or project design process and decision-making criteria.				X			
Optional criterion: Help students to acquire or use intrinsic motivation to learn.					X		

Guide to the Cases (*Continued*)

Guiding principles: Instructional design responsibilities						
Conduct reviews and revisions of teaching.			X		X	
Align learning outcomes.		X	X			
Organize all educational experiences to facilitate learning.	X					
Guiding principles: Learning outcomes						
Students acquire knowledge, skills, or values.	X					
Students demonstrate higher-order thinking.				X		X
Students demonstrate learning skills and self-assessment skills.			X			
Students demonstrate an ability to continue to do research or design projects or ability to develop further relevant skills.		X				

How a Beginning Assistant Professor Used Rubrics to Plan and Track Her Personal Faculty Development

Elizabeth Amy Janke is an assistant professor of psychology. Prior to securing this full-time, tenure track faculty position, Janke served as an adjunct professor at different institutions teaching different courses while working as a researcher. She anticipated that in her tenure track position, she would have the opportunity to teach the same courses repeatedly so that she could spend time developing these courses and reflecting on her teaching.

She completed the rubrics in her first year in a pretenure position at this university. Janke saw the rubrics as a personal faculty development tool as she assessed where she was currently and helped her plan how she wanted to improve her teaching. At the end of the following year, Janke displayed her self-assessment and her personal plans for success at a poster session at the 2011 Lilly-East Conference on College and University Teaching. The faculty members who attended the poster session rated her poster the best at that conference. This conference also provided Janke with many good ideas to help her improve her teaching. Since it has been a few years since she completed the rubrics, Janke thought it would be a good idea to track her progress toward meeting her development goals by revisiting the rubrics.

Janke's desire to be intentional about her teaching and her serious reflection on how and why she was teaching led her to require all of her students the first year she taught here to do weekly reflections on their learning and on the class. She read each of them very carefully and gave the students detailed feedback. In retrospect, she realized that she couldn't continue providing that much feedback and has changed what she now does. Given her emphasis on reflection, I am including her rubric page, "Provide opportunities for students to reflect on their learning." Perhaps because she is a research-oriented psychologist, Janke wanted every aspect of her courses to be positive learning experiences, and she wanted to be able to assess that her students achieved the goals of the courses. Therefore, I am including her rubric pages, "Organizing all educational experiences to facilitate learning" and "Determining if the student achieved the knowledge and skills learning outcomes."

The rubrics for selected aspects of Elizabeth Amy Janke's self-assessment of her teaching follow. Janke's responses are in italics. Only the sources of documentation Janke used are listed. For a complete list of the possible sources of documentation, see the actual rubrics in the appendix or online.

A4   Provide Opportunities for Students to Reflect on Their Learning

---

Guiding Principle: Structure for teaching and learning

Self-Assessment Criterion: Provide frequent, well-structured opportunities for students to reflect on their learning—An Essential Criterion

Rubric Quality Levels

❏ Not Yet Using Productive Teaching Practices (I have received feedback)

I provide infrequent limited opportunities for student reflection <u>or</u>

My reflection requirements are too unstructured to foster learning

❏ Not Yet Critically Self-Reflective with Documentation (this is the current normative practice)

I do not think about why students need opportunities to reflect

❏ Critically Self-Reflective with Documentation (satisfactory teaching occurs at this level and at the next two levels)

Year 1 Status

I document that I provide

- Appropriate, frequent opportunities for student reflection <u>and</u>
- Reflection that is structured and specific to allow students to learn from reflections <u>and</u>
- Documentation that students did the reflections <u>and</u>

I critically think about why and how students need opportunities to reflect <u>and</u>

I assess the quality of the reflections and the types of reflection opportunities I provide

In my first year here, I required all of my students to do a 2-page weekly reflection on their learning and on the class. The reflections were well structured and focused to help me understand how the students were processing the material, where they were having difficulties, and how they felt about the material. I had three goals for these reflections:

- *Provide a good learning opportunity for the students*
- *Give the students formative feedback on a regular basis*
- *Because I believed that reflections were so important, I wanted the students to learn the value of them also*

I read each of them very carefully, graded them, and gave the students detailed feedback, and I wrote lots of reflective comments on each of them. In retrospect, I realized that I went overboard with reflections because it left me little time to devote to the other aspects of teaching such as preparing for class or course management. My enthusiasm for reflection left me exhausted, but still convinced that reflections were important. I just knew I had to change my approach.

Students also had to stretch to write these reflections weekly, so some of them wrote on tangential questions that were not really part of the learning outcomes for the class.

☒ Critically Self-Reflective with Documentation, Evidence Based (this must meet everything in the previous level)

Goal for Years 2 to 3; Current Status Met by Year 3

I document that the reflection methods I ask the students to complete are

- Valid and reliable reflection methods; the choice of these methods comes from the literature on student reflection, standard reflection methods developed by the program, or the professional associations if available <u>or</u>
- Informed by a clear and explicit rationale for the choice of reflection methods and approaches (cite supporting evidence on the validity, reliability, and effectiveness of methods and supporting pedagogical literature)

See my evolution of my reflections below.

I collect lots of data about these reflections. Students now are doing a pre- and postsurvey using SALG assessing the aspects of the course and their reflections as blogs. I think it is working well now.

I took a course on online teaching from Magna Publishers that helped me to think more about student reflections. When I attended the Lily conference, I went to several sessions on reflection. I read a few articles and parts of a book on reflection. I consulted with the Teaching and Learning Center and spoke to senior professors in my department. When I integrated all of this into a new way to conduct reflections, I think I have a valid and reliable method to conduct student reflections.

❑ Critically Self-Reflective with Documentation, Evidence Based, Scholarly (this must meet everything in the previous level)

Goals for the Future

I provide

- A clear rationale for the choice of reflection methods and approaches <u>and</u>
- Evidence from student products that they learned as a result of these reflections

I have the data to be able to show that students learned from these reflections. I just need to analyze these data. I want to do this in the next few years.

I already have a clear rationale for the choice of the reflection methods and approaches that is based on what others recommend.

Suggested Sources for Documentation

- *Copies of reflection assignments given to the students and their answers*
- *Student-generated evaluations of experiences (i.e., information from standard or course-specific form)*
- *Notes of meetings, conferences with students, memos sent to students*
- *Student reflections, evaluations, blogs, surveys*
- *Review of student products*

- *Reports from students*
- *Documented use of standardized reflection tools SALG*
- *Valid and reliable assessments that the instructor creates*
- *End-of-semester student reflections on whether they achieved the goals or outcomes of the course and how they achieved them, reflections on learning*
- *Provide opportunities for students to reflect on their learning.*

Rationale for Your Rating

Additional sheets can be attached. Please indicate where the evidence can be found on attached syllabi, student products, or your scholarly products or other documents.

Evidence to Support This Rating

Evolution of student reflections:

Year 1: Each student wrote weekly 2-page reflections on their learning and on the content. I provided detailed reflective comments individually. It was too much work, but it was also very much 1:1 and not creating a sense of a community of learners.

Year 2: Instead of individual reflections, students blogged and had to respond to each other's blogs. There was more interaction among the students about their learning. However, the blogs took on a life of their own and were not connected with class.

Year 3: I continued the blogs, but I structured them differently. But now I use the student comments to organize and stimulate class discussions. This is working well. I fixed my earlier problems while still meeting my three reflection goals.

In the future I want to systematically analyze the blogs and really determine how effective they are.
    When appropriate, document literature with citations or data collected at your institution to support decisions or action. Cite professional practice guidelines or standards if used.
Lilly conference presentations on reflections, blogging
Magna online course on online teaching

A8   Organize All Educational Experiences to Facilitate Learning

Guiding Principle: Instructional design responsibilities

Self-Assessment Criterion: Organize all educational experiences to facilitate learning—An Essential Criterion

Rubric Quality Levels

☒ Critically Self-Reflective with Documentation (satisfactory teaching occurs at this level and the next two levels)

Year 1 Status

I document that as perceived by students or peers and my own review of the syllabus and other course material that

- All course materials and course delivery are organized <u>and</u>
- I meet deadlines <u>and</u>
- I return student work in a timely way with feedback provided <u>and</u>
- Students have opportunities to learn from graded work <u>and</u>

I critically reflect on the organization of the educational experiences

I do all of the above. Given that I value reflections so much, I critically reflect on how the educational experiences should be organized. I want everything to be a worthwhile learning experience.

However, in year 1, I did not really have a rationale for what I was doing based on student achievement, feedback, or organizing themes of the discipline. I aspired to do this over the next couple of years.

☒ Critically Self-Reflective with Documentation, Evidence Based (this must meet everything in the previous level)

Goal for Years 2 to 3; Current Status Met by Year 3

I provide a rationale to support organization and delivery. Course organization is informed by

- Student achievement or feedback <u>or</u>
- Evidence-based understanding of the content such as using overarching, organizing themes of the discipline

After year 1, I have been collecting data based on student feedback provided to me in my course evaluations, especially coming from the SALG data. I collect a pre- and postcourse assessment in every course I teach. For example, I always ask specific questions that give me insights into how well the students learned. I ask if specific course assignments and activities fostered meeting the learning outcomes, how I can improve my syllabus to convey information about the course, etc. The feedback I receive from students has informed how I teach. For example, the majority of the students in my health psychology course wanted more tests so that they would have less content to study for each test. So I changed from a midterm and final exam to three exams in addition to a large service-learning component that I consider to be the heart of the course.

Recently, I organize my courses around themes that relate to the discipline. For example, my abnormal psychology course is organized around six themes such as diagnosis and, treatment. I focus on these themes for every psychological abnormality we discuss. Since I have many second-year students who are not psychology majors but largely future health professionals, these themes make sense to them and this structure helps them to learn the content.

☐ Critically Self-Reflective with Documentation, Evidence Based, Scholarly (this must meet everything in the previous level)

Not Planning to Move to This Level

I provide evidence from student products that students understand content well because

- Students have integrated into their thinking the organizing themes of the discipline <u>or</u>
- Students use the organizing themes as scaffolds on which they built further learning <u>or</u>

I create a scholarly product based on data about organization of teaching

I have the data to be able to move to this level, but I do not plan to do so now. For example, I could analyze if the students really integrate the themes of the course into their thinking. I choose not to take the time to engage in this data analysis. It is not really my teaching interest; I just use them because I think they work with the students.

Further Clarification or Example of Criterion

An overarching, organizing theme is a discipline-specific conceptual framework that helps experts integrate much of the material. Experts use these themes to learn new material: for example, the relationship of structure and function is an organizing theme of biology, homeostasis is an organizing theme in physiology, and the drive to modernity is an organizing theme in history.

Suggested Sources for Documentation

- *Higher education literature, either in general or discipline specific (e.g., epistemology of the discipline)*
- *Self-review of course materials that includes a summary statement illustrating the overall organization and organizing themes; course materials may include course syllabi, assignments, teaching/learning activities, assessment activities. I use my teaching notes.*
- *Student course evaluations (i.e., information from standard or course-specific form)*
- *Reflections from students*
- *Review of how I explain to students how entire course (in-class work, assignments, assessments) is integrated*

Rationale for Your Rating

Additional sheets can be attached. Please indicate where the evidence can be found on attached syllabi, student products, or your scholarly products or other documents.

Evidence to Support This Rating

List the organizing schemes you used, if any.

Abnormal psychology: diagnosis, treatment, etiology

That is what I do in my research; why shouldn't I do that in my teaching. These concepts make sense to me. See attached summary of feedback from students [not attached here].

When appropriate, document literature with citations or data collected at your institution to support decisions or action. Cite professional practice guidelines or standards if used.

American Psychiatric Association (2000) DSM manual.

National Institute on the Teaching of Psychology (NIToP) presentations on best practices

A10   Students Achieve Learning Outcomes of Acquisition of Knowledge, Skills, or Values

Guiding Principle: Learning outcomes

Self-Assessment Criterion: Students achieve challenging yet reasonable learning outcomes of acquisition of knowledge, skills, or values—An Essential Criterion

Rubric Quality Levels

☒ Critically Self-Reflective with Documentation (satisfactory teaching occurs at this level and at the next two levels)

Year 1 Status

I provide assessment opportunities for students to demonstrate their acquisition of knowledge, skills, or values <u>and</u>

I document that most students, including low-performing students, acquire knowledge <u>or</u> skills <u>or</u> values <u>and</u>

See grade distribution table for Abnormal Psychology below.

I critically reflect on why and how students achieve learning outcomes of knowledge, skills, or values; the choice of the knowledge, these skills, or the values might be based on departmental or college expectations or accreditation agencies

Throughout my teaching career, I have written weekly reflections of how my teaching is going. I have always paid special attention to the top- and bottom-performing students. I think about how I should assess students. While I use mostly multiple choice and short answer questions, I develop scenarios for the questions.

50% of the student's grade in Health Psychology involves development of a health program for students at a neighborhood private school. This grade is composed of smaller subprojects that the students complete and I grade throughout the semester.

See grade distribution table for this service-learning project for Health Psychology below.

☒ Critically Self-Reflective with Documentation, Evidence Based (this must meet everything in the previous level)

Goal for Years 2 to 3; Current Status Met by Year 3

I articulate a clear, explicit, and rationale for choice of the specific knowledge, skills, and values the students demonstrate (cite literature references to support the rationale; if this rationale is based on departmental or college expectations or accreditation agencies, cite these expectations)

The knowledge, skills, and values that I expect my students to be able to demonstrate are based on the literature of these disciplines, especially literature on evidence-based decision making in psychology.

The literature on evidence-based practice in psychology focuses strongly in three areas: clinical expertise, the client values, and the extant literature. Decision making takes place at the nexus of these three, with an understanding of the environmental contingencies that may necessarily influence this decision making. Thus, these areas are reflected in my choice of knowledge (e.g., knowing the evidence-based paradigm, recent research in an area), skills (e.g., being able to apply an evidence-based approach in the case of a particular "client"), and values (e.g., incorporating the "client" values as part of decision making) focused around evidence based practice and decision making.

See reference list below.

❑ Critically Self-Reflective with Documentation, Evidence Based, Scholarly (this must meet everything in the previous level)

Not Planning to Move to This Level

I provide

- Evidence from student products that students have gained competence in this knowledge, these skills, or these values and have mastered relevant learning outcomes <u>or</u>
- Create a scholarly product (i.e., peer-reviewed publication) that demonstrates students acquired the knowledge, developed skills, and values

Suggested Sources for Documentation

- *Self-review of student products*
- Higher education literature, either in general or discipline specific (e.g., *epistemology of the discipline*)

Rationale for Your Rating

Additional sheets can be attached. Please indicate where the evidence can be found on attached syllabi, student products, or your scholarly products or other documents.

What Knowledge, Skills, or Values Were Achieved?

For Abnormal Psychology:

- *Knowledge and comprehension of modern, empirically based approaches to normal versus abnormal behavior and the most prevalent disorders according to the following primary course themes: Defining Characteristics; Diagnostic Features; Etiology; Course, Onset, and Prognosis; Prevalence and Impact; and Treatment.*
- *Critical evaluation and application of this knowledge to clinical case material within group case discussions.*
- *Knowledge and comprehension of the psychological theories proposed to explain health behaviors, the role of health psychology/behavioral medicine in the management of chronic medical conditions and the promotion of healthful living, and the current understanding of factors promoting engagement in health behaviors.*
- *Critical evaluation and application of relevant evidence and theories of health behavior in the creation of health promotion materials and dissemination of these materials through a health promotion campaign to meet the needs of a community organization in a culturally relevant manner.*

Evidence to Support This Rating

Grade distributions comparing the first time I taught the course and the most recent times I taught it. My grading standards have gotten harder and more objective, but the students still achieve these learning outcomes.

Abnormal Psychology

Grade	Number of Students Earning This Grade in 2010	Number of Students Earning This Grade in 2012
A	9	6
A-	5	18
B+	4	8
B	5	6
B-	4	0
C+	6	1
C	3	1
C-	2	0
D	0	0
F	0	0

Health Psychology: Grade on service-learning project

Grade	Number of Students Earning This Grade in 2009	Number of Students Earning This Grade in 2011
A+	5	0
A	7	6
A-	0	1
B+	0	4
B	0	3
B-	0	0
C+	0	0
C	0	0
C-	0	0
D	0	0
F	0	0

When appropriate, document literature with citations or data collected at your institution to support decisions or action. Cite professional practice guidelines or standards if used.

American Psychological Association. (2005) Policy Statement on Evidence-Based Practice in Psychology.

Spring B. Evidence-based practice in clinical psychology: what it is, why it matters; what you need to know. J Clin Psychol. 2007 Jul;63(7):611–31

Trierweiler, S. J. (2006). Training the next generation of psychologist clinicians: Good judgment and methodological realism at the interface between science and practice. In C. D. Goodheart, A. F. Kazdin & R. J. Sternberg (Eds.), Evidence-Based Psychotherapy: Where Practice and Research Meet (pp. 211–238). Washington, DC: American Psychological Association.

These rubric pages offer a prospective and a retrospective view of Janke's teaching and her personal development. She has added further support for her teaching by using more evidence since the first time she completed the rubrics. Janke feels that she should teach using evidence-based approaches. She wrote on one of the rubric pages not included here, "Evidence-based approaches are what I do in my research. Why shouldn't I also use the same thought process in my teaching? This approach of reflection and evidence-based teaching makes sense to me, and I strive to use it consistently in everything I do." While she realizes that she could be doing scholarship on all aspects of her teaching and knows that she has the data to be able to do this, she is truthful that she is not going to do this. Of the three components I profiled, Janke plans to conduct a systematic data analysis of only one of them: "Provide opportunities for students to reflect on their learning." She is pleased with where she is on the other two criteria and does not want to spend the time to analyze the data she has to reach the highest level on the others. This was a priority decision based on her teaching interests and her other research demands. Table C1.1 tracks her plans and progress.

TABLE C1.1 Janke's Plans and Progress on Her Teaching Development

	Rubric Criteria Ratings over Time			
Rubric Levels	**First-Year Status**	**Second- and Third-Year Goal**	**Third-Year, Current Status**	**Future Directions**
Not yet using productive teaching practices				
Not yet critically self-reflective with documentation				
Critically self-reflective with documentation	Opportunities for student reflection Organize all educational experiences to facilitate learning Students achieve acquisition of knowledge, skills, or values			
Critically self-reflective with documentation, evidence based		Opportunities for student reflection Organize all educational experiences to facilitate learning Students achieve acquisition of knowledge, skills, or values	Opportunities for student reflection Organize all educational experiences to facilitate learning Students achieve acquisition of knowledge, skills, or values	Organize all educational experiences to facilitate learning Students achieve acquisition of knowledge, skills, or values
Critically self-reflective with documentation, evidence based, scholarly				Opportunities for student reflection

Case 2

How a Faculty Developer Used the Rubrics with a Pretenure Instructor to Facilitate Improvement

Stu Proff is a fictional assistant professor, an amalgam of many faculty members I have worked with over the years. Proff teaches accounting in a university where few students major in accounting or business. Thus, enrollments in his classes are low. He has been teaching for a couple of years and faces his pretenure review soon. He came to me concerned that his teaching evaluations from his students are not as good as his departmental average scores.

To begin this improvement process, I asked him to complete the rubrics for an autonomous classroom teacher. Table C2.1 summarizes his self-assessment ratings on the twelve essential criteria. Proff is doing some things in a satisfactory manner; his teaching is not unacceptable in every category.

TABLE C2.1   Summary of Stu Proff's Self-Assessment Ratings

Criteria	Level 1: Not Yet Using Productive Teaching Practices	Level 2: Not Yet Critically Self-Reflective with Documentation	Level 3: Critically Self-Reflective with Documentation	Level 4: Critically Self-Reflective with Documentation, Evidence Based	Level 5: Critically Self-Reflective with Documentation, Evidence Based, Scholarly
Total number assessed this way	6	3	3	0	0

Here is how Proff rated himself on each of the criteria (the asterisks identify the rubrics that follow):

Level 1: Not Yet Using Productive Teaching Practices

A1   Develop Learning Outcomes and Use Them to Select Teaching/Learning Methods

A2   Promote Higher-Order Thinking

A4   Provide Opportunities for Students to Reflect on Their Learning

A7   Align Learning Outcomes*

A11 Students Demonstrate Higher-Order Thinking

A12 Students Demonstrate Learning Skills and Self-Assessment Skills

Level 2: Not Yet Critically Self-Reflective with Documentation

A3   Provide Feedback to Students to Foster Greater Learning*

A9   Conduct Reviews and Revisions of Teaching

A10 Students Achieve Learning Outcomes of Acquisition of Knowledge, Skills, or Values

Level 3: Critically Self-Reflective with Documentation

A5   Use Consistent Policies and Processes to Assess Students*

A6   Ensure Students Have Successful Learning Experiences through My Availability and Accessibility

A8   Organize All Educational Experiences to Facilitate Learning*

I chose to show a rubric for each of the three levels that Proff's self-assessment revealed. The rubrics for these selected aspects of Stu Proff's self-assessment of his teaching follow.

A3   Provide Feedback to Students to Foster Greater Learning

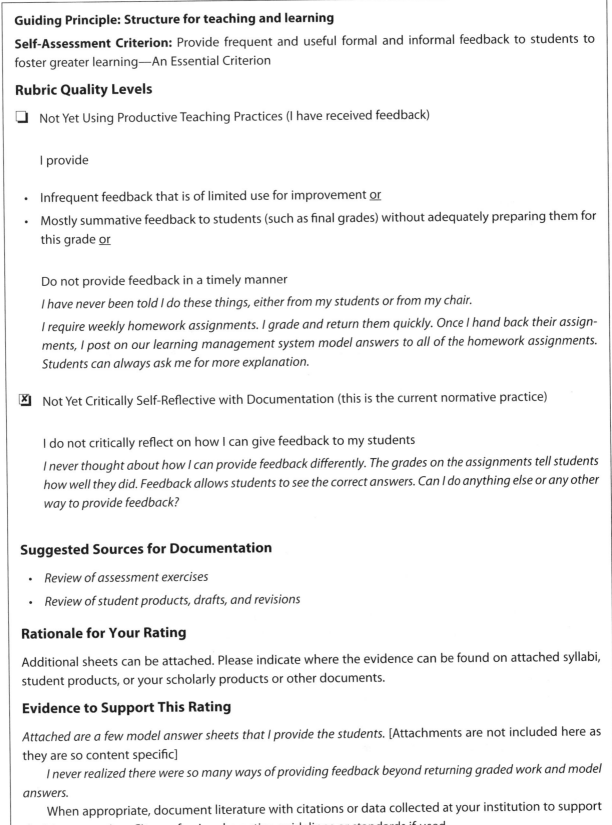

Guiding Principle: Structure for teaching and learning

Self-Assessment Criterion: Provide frequent and useful formal and informal feedback to students to foster greater learning—An Essential Criterion

Rubric Quality Levels

☐   Not Yet Using Productive Teaching Practices (I have received feedback)

I provide

- Infrequent feedback that is of limited use for improvement <u>or</u>
- Mostly summative feedback to students (such as final grades) without adequately preparing them for this grade <u>or</u>

Do not provide feedback in a timely manner

I have never been told I do these things, either from my students or from my chair.

I require weekly homework assignments. I grade and return them quickly. Once I hand back their assignments, I post on our learning management system model answers to all of the homework assignments. Students can always ask me for more explanation.

☒   Not Yet Critically Self-Reflective with Documentation (this is the current normative practice)

I do not critically reflect on how I can give feedback to my students

I never thought about how I can provide feedback differently. The grades on the assignments tell students how well they did. Feedback allows students to see the correct answers. Can I do anything else or any other way to provide feedback?

Suggested Sources for Documentation

- *Review of assessment exercises*
- *Review of student products, drafts, and revisions*

Rationale for Your Rating

Additional sheets can be attached. Please indicate where the evidence can be found on attached syllabi, student products, or your scholarly products or other documents.

Evidence to Support This Rating

Attached are a few model answer sheets that I provide the students. [Attachments are not included here as they are so content specific]

I never realized there were so many ways of providing feedback beyond returning graded work and model answers.

When appropriate, document literature with citations or data collected at your institution to support decisions or action. Cite professional practice guidelines or standards if used.

I do not read the educational literature.

A5   Use Consistent Policies and Processes to Assess Students

Guiding Principle: Structure for teaching and learning

Self-Assessment Criterion: Use consistent policies and processes to assess students—An Essential Criterion

Rubric Quality Levels

❏   Not Yet Using Productive Teaching Practices (I have received feedback)

I assign final grades without providing student with a rationale for the grades <u>or</u>

I do not grade and return student work in a timely way with feedback provided <u>or</u>

I use inconsistent or unexplained methods to assess students

I have not received feedback that I do these things, either from my students or from my chair.

❏   Not Yet Critically Self-Reflective with Documentation (this is the current normative practice)

I do not critically reflect on my selection of policies and processes on assessment

The basis for all of my assessments policies are the university's and the department's policies.

I try to be consistent with these policies. I think about assessment processes and try to be fair and objective.

☒   Critically Self-Reflective with Documentation (satisfactory teaching occurs at this level and at the next two levels)

I document that I consistently

- Use specified grading standards, such as grading rubric, and predetermined weights of projects or assignments to assign grades <u>and</u>
- Maintain fair and consistent standards of grading <u>and</u>
- Grade and return student work in a timely way with feedback provided <u>and</u>
- Critically think about my policies and process to assess students

I provide grading rubrics for all assignments before the assignments are due. I have developed several drafts of these rubrics and modify them as a result of how students do.

I provide grades with model answers throughout the semester.

I grade and return all assignments within a week of being handed in.

My syllabi state how students will be graded and the weights for every assignment and test.

Suggested Sources for Documentation

- *Review of assessment plans*
- *Review of assessment tools*

Rationale for Your Rating

Additional sheets can be attached. Please indicate where the evidence can be found on attached syllabi, student products, or your scholarly products or other documents.

Evidence to Support This Rating

Attached are the grading policies from my syllabi, the departmental grading policies, and the university grading standards (what percentage is required to earn an A, B, C, D or F) [not attached here].

    Attached are sample grading rubrics for assignments in different courses [not attached here].

When appropriate, document literature with citations or data collected at your institution to support decisions or action. Cite professional practice guidelines or standards if used.

    Student end-of-course evaluations indicate my grading policies are fair (average scores range from 4.3–4.5, with 5 the highest possible score). Comments include, "I knew how I was going to be graded." "He is objective in grading."

    Teaching is like accounting: It is important to follow policies and processes in a consistent way. Accounting has right or wrong answers.

A7   Align Learning Outcomes

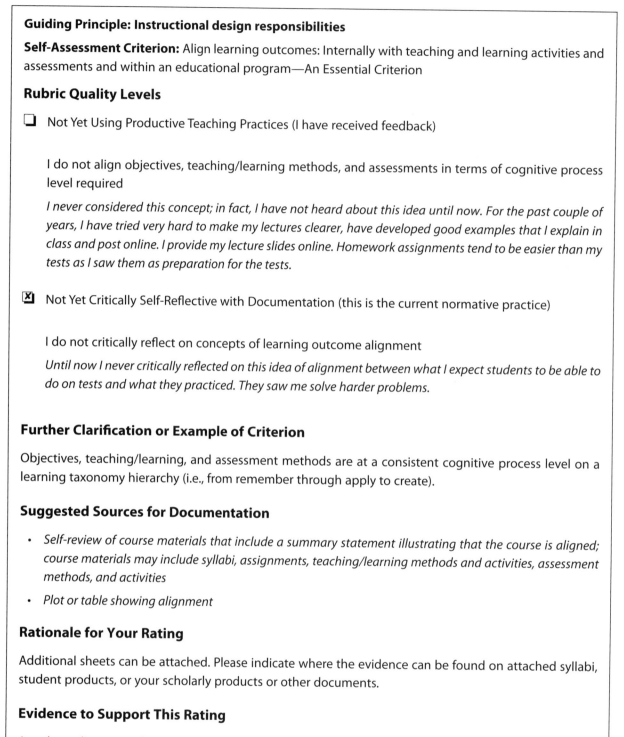

Guiding Principle: Instructional design responsibilities

Self-Assessment Criterion: Align learning outcomes: Internally with teaching and learning activities and assessments and within an educational program—An Essential Criterion

Rubric Quality Levels

❑ Not Yet Using Productive Teaching Practices (I have received feedback)

I do not align objectives, teaching/learning methods, and assessments in terms of cognitive process level required

I never considered this concept; in fact, I have not heard about this idea until now. For the past couple of years, I have tried very hard to make my lectures clearer, have developed good examples that I explain in class and post online. I provide my lecture slides online. Homework assignments tend to be easier than my tests as I saw them as preparation for the tests.

☒ Not Yet Critically Self-Reflective with Documentation (this is the current normative practice)

I do not critically reflect on concepts of learning outcome alignment

Until now I never critically reflected on this idea of alignment between what I expect students to be able to do on tests and what they practiced. They saw me solve harder problems.

Further Clarification or Example of Criterion

Objectives, teaching/learning, and assessment methods are at a consistent cognitive process level on a learning taxonomy hierarchy (i.e., from remember through apply to create).

Suggested Sources for Documentation

- *Self-review of course materials that include a summary statement illustrating that the course is aligned; course materials may include syllabi, assignments, teaching/learning methods and activities, assessment methods, and activities*
- *Plot or table showing alignment*

Rationale for Your Rating

Additional sheets can be attached. Please indicate where the evidence can be found on attached syllabi, student products, or your scholarly products or other documents.

Evidence to Support This Rating

Attach an alignment plot or figure, if used, such as given at the end of the rubrics set.

1. *Students do not do well on my tests; students have commented on end-of-course evaluations that my tests are more difficult than homework (hw). I thought that was appropriate since hw is a way to see if students understand the basic concepts.*

2. *Upon inspection of my plot, shown in table C2.2, it appears that my learning outcomes are not aligned with how students learn. I routinely lecture in class and give students homework assignments. Perhaps students need to practice solving problems in class before doing their hw so I can guide them, offer immediate assistance when needed, and give them more practice. Also the hw problems need to be at a higher level on the taxonomy.*

Always thought that if I taught more clearly, students would be able to learn material.

When appropriate, document literature with citations or data collected at your institution to support decisions or action. Cite professional practice guidelines or standards if used.

I do not read educational literature.

TABLE C2.2   Alignment Table for Stu Proff's Courses

	Aspect Not Included in Course	Low Level (recognize, recall knowledge)	Medium Level (apply, organize, or analyze)	High Level (synthesize, critique, or evaluate)
Learning outcome: Students will be able to solve real-world accounting problems using standard accounting rules and conventions				X
Teaching/learning methods: Students study from my lectures and complete homework assignments, which are straightforward problems			X	
Assessment task requirements: Students need to solve real-world accounting problems using standard accounting rules and conventions				X

Directions for use of course alignment table: Alignment of level of learning outcome, teaching, or learning methods, and assessment methods

1. Use a separate table for each major course learning outcome.

2. Along the learning outcome row, briefly list one learning outcome in the correct cells according to the level of cognitive process or verb listed.

3. Along the teaching/learning methods row, briefly list the teaching and learning methods in the correct cells by determining what level of cognitive process the students need to use during the teaching and learning activities.

4. Along the assessment row, briefly list the assessment task requirements in the correct cells by determining what level of cognitive process the students need to use during the assessment tasks.

5. Draw a line or lines connecting the cells marked in these three columns.

   - A straight, vertical line connecting all rows means this is aligned.
   - One or more diagonal lines, without a corresponding vertical line connecting the learning outcome, illustrates that the course is misaligned.

Next, I asked him to group the criteria from the rubrics considering his rating on them into three categories: what he did that he was pleased with, what he did that he now sees as problematic, and what areas he had not considered before completing the rubric. I then asked him to create a concept map of his teaching according to these categories. His grouping, shown in the concept map in figure C2.1, helped determine which criteria to focus on.

The process of completing and talking about the rubrics and the concept map led Proff to insights into his own teaching practices. His alignment plot of the cognitive demand required of his students showed that the learning outcomes and assessments were at a consistently high level, but what he required of the students in terms of homework practice was at a lower level (table C2.2). He never considered that lecturing and providing students with problems that he solved and clearly explained was not the best way to teach. Proff realized that course misalignment might be the key to his problems: "Perhaps I am not allowing the students enough opportunity to think at a high level."

Once he decided he needed to align his learning outcomes with his teaching and learning activities and assessment, he realized that he needed to change how he taught. Instead of lecturing routinely in class, he decided to give students more opportunities to solve harder accounting problems in class under his guidance. He hopes that once students practice solving such problems in a low-stakes classroom environment, they might do better on his tests. Proff feels that if students do better on his tests, they will give him higher ratings on the end-of-course evaluations. He now has a plan for how he will improve his teaching based on the rubrics and the subsequent work we did together.

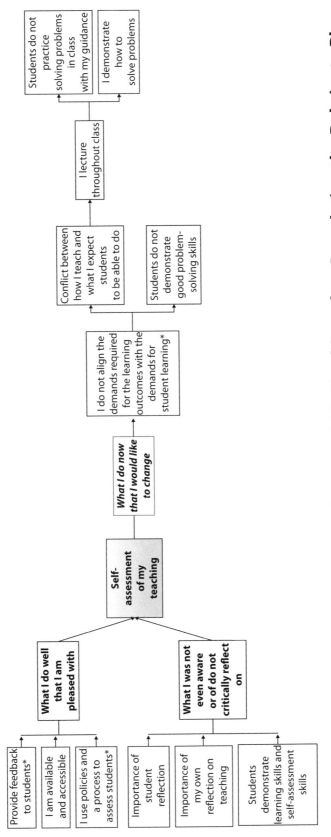

FIGURE C2.1   Concept Map of How Stu Proff Grouped His Teaching after Completing the Rubrics to Plan for Change

*Rubrics attached.

Case 3

How an Experienced Professor Used the Rubrics to Document Her Scholarship of Teaching and Learning

Susan Wainwright was an associate professor of physical therapy when she completed the rubrics. You were introduced to her in box 5.5 to describe how she used naturalistic observations to improve her teaching. That box describes how she changed her teaching to meet her learning outcomes.

Several years have passed since Wainwright changed her teaching to require more classroom discussions of clinical cases, and she has continued to conduct research on the effectiveness of her teaching. Wainwright wanted to assess how much impact her scholarship about her teaching had on what she actually did and if the students benefited from her work. Wainwright describes her teaching as, "entirely intentional and explicit." She reflects continuously on her teaching, uses many assessment tools, and explains her rationale to her students. When Wainwright first heard of the self-assessment rubrics, she felt they fit her teaching philosophy and practices. Therefore, it is not surprising that she scored herself at least at the satisfactory level on every criterion and at the highest level (critical reflective, evidence based and scholarly) on 45 percent of the twelve essential criteria. I chose to show the rubrics for three of these criteria scored at the highest level: "Teaching/learning methods to promote acquisition of knowledge, skills, values," "Align learning outcomes," and "Conduct self-analysis and reflection."

A1   Develop Learning Outcomes and Use Them to Select Teaching/Learning Methods

Guiding Principle: Structure for teaching and learning

Self-assessment Criterion: Develop challenging yet reasonable learning outcomes for the acquisition of knowledge, skills, or values, and use them to select appropriate teaching/learning methods and educational technologies—An Essential Criterion

Rubric Quality Levels

❑   Critically Self-Reflective with Documentation (satisfactory teaching occurs at this level and at the next two levels)

I use a variety of teaching/learning methods and technologies that are appropriate for student learning goals <u>and</u>

I create a respectful environment to foster learning (as defined by sensitivity to ethnic and cultural diversity) <u>and</u>

I critically reflect on the relationship between my learning outcomes or teaching/learning methods and technologies

See below for the different techniques I use:

I had the goal of implementing learning-centered teaching. I wanted the students to assume greater responsibility for their own learning. I intentionally used three indicators of greater responsibility for learning: students coming to class more prepared, students participating more in class activities in appropriate ways, and students would be able to carry on extended conversations using the content with each other and not talking directly to me.

I audiotaped several classes so I could reflect on how effective these various teaching/learning methods were. As a result of my analyses of these tapes, I realized that unless I changed the way I taught, including greater expectations for students to come prepared and the structure of the class itself, I was doing too much direct teacher talk and the students were not engaging in meaningful discussions among themselves.

❑   Critically Self-Reflective with Documentation, Evidence Based (this must meet everything in the previous level)

Literature or data from students inform my choice of the selected teaching/learning methods or educational technologies to foster mastery of learning outcomes (cite literature references).

Evidence to support what I am doing that comes from the literature on learner-centered teaching, action theory learning processes

This literature motivated my selection of the following class activities:

- *Sustained student discussion in small and large groups*
- *Discussion of clinical cases in small groups in class*

This literature also recommends that instructors help students to learn on their own by guiding their learning. To help students prepare for class, I gave them case studies with guided questions that they did before class.

Evidence to support what I am doing that comes from data I collected:

I used interaction analysis to quantify the nature of verbal interactions in my classes. Interaction analysis uses ten categories of teacher or student talk. I analyzed the tapes of my classes to determine who was talking and the purpose of the speech. At baseline, I did 78% of the talking, with the great majority of that direct teacher talk (instructing). Once I totally reformed how my classes were run, I was talking less than half of the time, with direct teacher talk only 20%. Student talk (either initiated by them or sustained conversation) rose from 16% at baseline to 55%.

☒ Critically Self-Reflective with Documentation, Evidence Based, Scholarly (this must meet everything in the previous level)

I provide

- A clear rationale for my choice of my teaching/learning methods and technologies <u>and</u>
- Evidence from student products that my teaching/learning methods facilitate students reaching learning goals

I explained my rationale for these teaching methods and the research on classroom interactions in an article I published: Using self-assessment to assess the effectiveness of learner centered instructional design and delivery (Wainwright, S. (2009). Journal of Faculty Development 2009, 23(3)22-28.) This is the main thesis of this paper.

The article shows through ratios of student and teacher talk and quotes from a sustained student discussion that the students were taking responsibility for their learning and contributing to class discussions.

I achieved my benchmark goal of increasing student interactions and decreasing direct teacher instructional talk. I also achieved the goal that students were taking more responsibility for their learning.

Suggested Sources for Documentation

- *Higher education literature, either in general or discipline specific (e.g., epistemology of the discipline)*
- *Self-review of course materials that include a summary statement illustrating that the teaching/ learning methods are appropriate for the student learning goals*
- *Reports from students, audio or video recording of student performance, or explanation of it*
- *Student course evaluations*

Rationale for Your Rating

Additional sheets can be attached. Please indicate where the evidence can be found on attached syllabi, student products, or your scholarly products or other documents.

Specify Student Learning Goals

Analyze the neurophysiological mechanisms involved with cognition, sensation (including pain) and perception, and selected voluntary motor tasks and automatic and involuntary motor behaviors.

Specify Learning Methods Used

Teaching and learning methods used:

- *Direct teacher talk—informative, instructional talk*
- *Indirect teacher talk—supportive, facilitative, affirmative comments*
- *Sustained student discussion in small and large groups*
- *Students prepare for class by completing case studies with guided questions*
- *Discussion of clinical cases in small groups in class*

At the baseline, I was using far more teacher talk. After I changed how I handled class, majority of the time in class was spent in discussion of clinical cases in small groups. This was a deliberate and intentional shift in what we do in class as a result of reflecting on how students learn.

Once I changed how I teach, I asked the students if the prior-to-class preparation helped them to function better in class. The majority of them saw it was very helpful.

Evidence to Support This Rating

If this evidence comes from syllabi or other documents, please indicate where the evidence can be found on these documents.

I developed instructional objectives in cognition, the afferent systems and the efferent systems to match the learning outcomes. See Table T.2 [not included in this book].

When appropriate, document literature with citations or data collected at your institution to support decisions or action. Cite professional practice guidelines or standards if used.

Amidon, Hough (1967) Interaction Analysis. Addison-Wesley.

Argyris and Schön (1974) Theory in practice. Jossey-Bass

Blumberg (2009) Developing Learner-Centered Teaching. Jossey-Bass.

Weimer (2013) Learner-Centered Teaching 2nd ed. Jossey-Bass.

A7　Align Learning Outcomes

Guiding Principle: Instructional design responsibilities

Self-Assessment Criterion: Align learning outcomes: Internally with teaching and learning activities and assessments and within an educational program—An Essential Criterion

Rubric Quality Levels

❏ Critically Self-Reflective with Documentation (satisfactory teaching occurs at this level and at the next two levels)

I show (on a table or figure) how planned objectives, teaching/learning methods, and assessment methods both within a course and across the educational program are aligned or misaligned <u>and</u>

I have a plan to make them aligned if misalignment occurs <u>and</u>

I critically reflect on concepts of learning outcome alignment

See table C3.1.

In order to make this table and show that my course is aligned, I had to critically reflect on what I need to do to ensure course alignment. When I first started teaching this course, I did most of the talking and did not provide adequate opportunities for students to analyze the mechanisms. Now I explicitly give students compare-and-contrast situations and scenarios. Exam questions and assignments are consciously selected to be aligned with the learning outcomes.

❏ Critically Self-Reflective with Documentation, Evidence Based (this must meet everything in the previous level)

Literature or data inform my choice of consistent cognitive process level for the objectives, teaching/learning methods, and assessment methods (cite literature references) <u>and</u>

I provide evidence that objectives, teaching/learning methods, and assessment are explicitly, coherently, and consistently aligned in my syllabus and delivery

Anderson's (Anderson et al., 2001) modification of Bloom's taxonomy.

The attached table appears in the student syllabus, and I post it on the course learning management system.

☒ Critically Self-Reflective with Documentation, Evidence Based, Scholarly (this must meet everything in the previous level)

I have data to show that the course is aligned between and across courses in the curriculum in terms of prerequisites or more advanced courses <u>and</u>

I provide an evidence-based rationale supported by student learning for my choice of consistent levels of cognitive process for the objectives, teaching/learning, and assessment

Six peers have analyzed my course and found it to be aligned internally and externally within the PT curriculum. For example, they indicated that there was a match between objectives and my teaching

approaches. We have an annual curriculum review, and the entire department has examined my course and found it aligned.

I also ask students if they perceive that my objectives, what they are required to do, and how I assess them are consistent. The students report consistency.

Further Clarification or Example of Criterion

Objectives, teaching/learning, and assessment methods are at a consistent cognitive process level on a learning taxonomy hierarchy (i.e., from remember through apply to create).

Suggested Sources for Documentation

- *Self-review of course materials that include a summary statement illustrating that the course is aligned; course materials may include syllabi*
- *Plot or table showing alignment*
- *Peer or self-review of alignment data*

Rationale for Your Rating

Additional sheets can be attached. Please indicate where the evidence can be found on attached syllabi, student products, or your scholarly products or other documents.

Evidence to Support This Rating

Attach an alignment plot or figure, if used.

See table C3.1.

When appropriate, document literature with citations or data collected at your institution to support decisions or action. Cite professional practice guidelines or standards if used.

Anderson's (Anderson et al., 2001) modification of Bloom's taxonomy

Shepard KF, Jensen GM. Handbook of Teaching for Physical Therapists, 2nd Edition, 2002, Butterworth Heinemann, Woburn MA. This text was required for a graduate-level education course that I took. I found the teaching grid especially useful in preparing instructional activities within the context of learning objectives. This set the stage for me to slip easily into use of the course alignment table.

What overarching organizing theme of your discipline does this objective relate to? *The answer is integration of foundational science and theory with clinical reasoning in patient/client management.*

TABLE C3.1 Course Alignment Table Supporting Wainwright's Contention That Her Course Is Aligned

What level is each of the following?	Aspect is not included in the course	1. Remember (recognize, recall)	2. Understand (interpret, exemplify, classify, summarize, infer, compare, explain)	3. Apply (execute, implement)	4. Analyze (differentiate, organize, attribute)	5. Evaluate (check, critique)	6. Create (generate, plan, produce)
Course objective					*Analyze the neurophysiological mechanisms involved with cognition, sensation (including pain), and perception, and selected voluntary motor tasks and automatic and involuntary motor behaviors.*	*These levels are not assessed within this course objective.*	
Teaching/learning methods		*Subsumed in the higher-level dimensions.*	*Class discussion of terminology.*	*Use provided templates to observe/document movement in children and adults.*	*Compare and contrast novice vs. expert motor behavior.* *Compare infant movement from zero to 24 months.*		
Assessment task requirements			Examination Assignment #3 Assignment #5	Examination Assignment #4	Examination Assignment #3 Assignment #6		

Source: The cognitive process dimension is based on Anderson and Krathwohl (2001).

A9   Conduct Reviews and Revisions of Teaching

Guiding Principle: Instructional design responsibilities

Self-Assessment Criterion: Engage in self-analysis and reflection of teaching as part of a review and revision process including appraisal of content currency and accuracy—An Essential Criterion

Rubric Quality Levels

❑ Critically Self-Reflective with Documentation (satisfactory teaching occurs at this level and at the next two levels)

I collect assessment data or feedback data from the students <u>and</u>

I conduct self-analysis or reflections on my teaching as part of a review and revision process to

- Identify areas for improvement <u>and</u>
- Change experience or expectations as a result of consistent feedback or reviews or changes in content <u>and</u>
- Share these reflections or other assessments as necessary <u>and</u>

I recognize when students have not met learning outcomes <u>and</u>

I have adequate knowledge and I use accurate and current content

Several years ago I participated in a faculty learning community on learning-centered teaching and attended workshops on the topic. The ideas we discussed and the material we read persuaded me that I wanted to use this approach in all of my teaching. I learned different techniques through these discussions. These workshops and the faculty learning community were a huge catalyst for change for me.

I constantly reflect on the quality of my teaching through analyzing data. I try to improve my teaching to increase the student learning.

❑ Critically Self-Reflective with Documentation, Evidence Based (this must meet everything in the previous level)

I use assessment data, self-analysis, reflection, or pedagogical literature to

- Propose or implement significant changes to courses if necessary <u>or</u>
- Show why the contents should be kept the same <u>or</u>
- Offer a rationale for not incorporating suggested changes

Schön's ideas about reflection on action greatly influenced why I reflect on my teaching and how I constantly collect data to inform my teaching.

I realized that I need to be effective about my teaching, responsive to what students say about my teaching. I looked at how well they achieve the learning outcomes at least five years ago:

- *I audiotaped many of my classes to determine who was talking and the quality of the interactions.*
- *Routinely I give students surveys to gather more insights into how they are learning. See tables T3 and T7 for the scores and comments students made* [not included in this book].
- *Periodically I ask peers to observe my class and offer me feedback so I can improve. See table T8 for written feedback I receive from these observations* [not included in this book].

I reflect on all of this data and make appropriate changes.

☒ Critically Self-Reflective with Documentation, Evidence Based, Scholarly (this must meet everything in the previous level)

I provide evidence to show how teaching has changed and improved as a result of assessment or self-analysis

At baseline, I was far too directive and gave the students all of the content they needed to learn. I wanted to engage in more learning-centered approaches, so I changed how I teach. Unfortunately the students did not come prepared to do the work I expected, and while I talked less, I still was lecturing and answering questions too often. Then I required the students to read the material and answer questions that relate to case studies prior to class. Since I have implemented this practice, the students are coming to class prepared, and they are more engaged in discussions. They demonstrated that they could apply the material better on assessments and their feedback was positive that these changes really improved their mastery of the learning outcomes.

I create a scholarly product (i.e., peer-reviewed publication) that demonstrates student learning using course assessment data, reflection, revisions of teaching, course planning, and reflection on teaching

Wainwright (2009)

Suggested Sources for Documentation

- *Personal reflections*
- *Student course evaluations*
- *Course assessment data*
- *Higher education literature, either in general or discipline specific*
- *Video recording of student performance*
- *Peer assessment data, discussions with peers or debriefings after assessment, peer coaching*
- *Peer-reviewed presentation or publication*
- *Teaching portfolios*
- *Discussions from faculty learning communities*

Rationale for Your Rating

Additional sheets can be attached. Please indicate where the evidence can be found on attached syllabi, student products, or your scholarly products or other documents.

Evidence to Support This Rating

See above and my article.

Cite pedagogical literature, professional practice guidelines, or standards if used to support your rationale.

Schön (1987) Educating the Reflective Practitioner. Jossey-Bass

Wainwright, S. (2009). Using self-assessment to assess the effectiveness of learner-centered instructional design and delivery. Journal of Faculty Development. 23(3) 22-28.

When appropriate, provide data collected by you or your department to support decisions or action.

See above and my article.

I surveyed the students with the purpose of trying to get students to be reflective about their class preparation and their level of active learning in class. Results showed that 57% of the students stated that they spent time reviewing their notes prior to class to prepare for the class activity.

Wainwright's self-assessment rubrics show a consistent pattern of critically reflecting on all aspects of her teaching, using evidence from the literature and data that she collected and making changes as a result of her reflections and the evidence. She achieves her goal of being intentional in her teaching. The supporting documents (I have not attached but refer to them) show that she is also explicit and documents the evidence extensively. In fact, Wainwright had more supporting tables attached to her rubrics than any other professor who completed the rubrics. When a senior-level peer saw how she assessed her teaching using these rubrics and their supporting tables, the peer remarked this was the most organized approach to assessing teaching she had ever seen. Wainwright is an exceptionally strong teacher with many years of experience. She says that her evidence-based profession of physical therapy, as well as her systematic research perspective, fosters her approach to teaching.

How a Pretenured Professor Used the Rubrics to Assess His Mentoring Undergraduate and Graduate Students in Research

Nathan West just completed his second year as an assistant professor of chemistry after his postdoctoral work. He takes mentoring students in research very seriously and wants to do an effective job with students in his lab. West observed that he was not taught how to mentor students to do research. He thinks this is a shortcoming of his graduate and postdoctoral education. This has been a challenge for him, so he is critically reflecting on the components of the rubric page, "Help student(s) understand the research or project design process and decision-making criteria."

All of his life he has been fascinated by chemical reactions, especially making fires. He wants to instill this same love of discovery in his students. West judges his success as a research mentor by the number of students who continue doing research in his field. Therefore, I show his rubric for, "Students demonstrate an ability to continue to do research or design projects or ability to develop further relevant skills and to self-assess research or design skills and self-assessment of strengths/weaknesses." Like most other researchers, West is concerned that his students develop skills so that they can do meaningful research that leads to presentations and publications. Since his field is inorganic chemistry, where he works with highly flammable substances and reactions, he stresses safety as a primary concern for his students. Because of these safety concerns, West is especially concerned with the rubric page, "Institute well-defined expectations and roles for the student while engaged in research or project." These rubric pages are shown next.

C1   Institute Well-Defined Expectations and Roles for Students

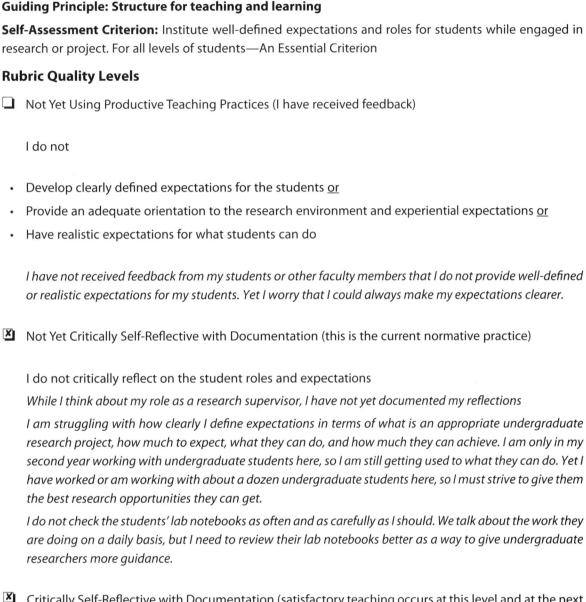

Guiding Principle: Structure for teaching and learning

Self-Assessment Criterion: Institute well-defined expectations and roles for students while engaged in research or project. For all levels of students—An Essential Criterion

Rubric Quality Levels

❏ Not Yet Using Productive Teaching Practices (I have received feedback)

I do not

- Develop clearly defined expectations for the students <u>or</u>
- Provide an adequate orientation to the research environment and experiential expectations <u>or</u>
- Have realistic expectations for what students can do

I have not received feedback from my students or other faculty members that I do not provide well-defined or realistic expectations for my students. Yet I worry that I could always make my expectations clearer.

☒ Not Yet Critically Self-Reflective with Documentation (this is the current normative practice)

I do not critically reflect on the student roles and expectations

While I think about my role as a research supervisor, I have not yet documented my reflections

I am struggling with how clearly I define expectations in terms of what is an appropriate undergraduate research project, how much to expect, what they can do, and how much they can achieve. I am only in my second year working with undergraduate students here, so I am still getting used to what they can do. Yet I have worked or am working with about a dozen undergraduate students here, so I must strive to give them the best research opportunities they can get.

I do not check the students' lab notebooks as often and as carefully as I should. We talk about the work they are doing on a daily basis, but I need to review their lab notebooks better as a way to give undergraduate researchers more guidance.

☒ Critically Self-Reflective with Documentation (satisfactory teaching occurs at this level and at the next two levels)

I provide an adequate orientation to the environment and research or project expectation <u>and</u>

I have developed extensive safety practices guidelines. I looked at web pages from researchers in my field from other universities for guidance and then modified them to fit my lab. All students receive extensive training in the use of these chemicals before they can begin working in the lab.

I use insight into the research or project to inform my choices in the development of clearly defined expectations for students in different situations <u>and</u>

I have clearly defined expectations for when students can be in the lab, but these relate to safety.

I have realistic expectations for what students can do based on level of student and previous research experiences <u>and</u>

I do not feel that I have fully reached this level yet because I do not provide adequate documentation. I would like to develop a written document to give the students as an orientation, but I have not done this yet.

I critically reflect on the student roles and expectations

I constantly reflect on the student roles and expectations in the lab.

Suggested Sources for Documentation

- *Personal reflection*
- Student assessment data (e.g., pre- and postassessment data) *I would like to do this, but am not yet doing this*
- *Lab notebooks*
- *Higher education literature, discipline specific*

Rationale for Your Rating

Additional sheets can be attached. Please indicate where the evidence can be found on attached syllabi, student products, or your scholarly products or other documents.

Evidence to Support This Rating

1. *Safety expectations. See attached Specific Laboratory Safety Issues manual.* [He attached a seventeen-page safety manual that he gives to his students.] *The manual covers specific laboratory safety issues such as handling acids, specific volatile substances, solutions and elements that react violently with water, acids, and oxygenated compounds that can ignite spontaneously. The manual also describes some actual laboratory accidents and how they should be prevented and handled and standard operating procedure for various pyrophoric (igniting spontaneously) chemicals.* [It is not included in this book.]

2. *Expectations in terms of research. All students are expected to maintain a lab notebook detailing what they have done. I do not spell out project expectations for students; I would like to do this better.*

When appropriate, document literature with citations or data collected at your institution to support decisions or action. Cite professional practice guidelines or standards if used.

See attached document Standard Operating Procedure: The Safe Use of Pyrophoric Chemicals in the Laboratory developed by the university's Department of Environmental Health & Radiation Safety. [It is not included in this book.]

C5   Help Undergraduate Students Understand the Research or Project Design Process and the Decision-Making Criteria

Guiding Principle: Structure for teaching and learning

Self-Assessment Criterion: Help students understand the research or project design process and decision-making criteria. For mentoring undergraduate students—An Essential Criterion

Rubric Quality Levels

☒ Critically Self-Reflective with Documentation (satisfactory teaching occurs at this level and at the next two levels)

I critically reflect on how I help students identify and suggest ways to test appropriate hypotheses or problems in the research or design project <u>and</u>

I reflect on how I explain the purpose and desired outcomes resulting from activities

I constantly think about I help students understand the research process. For example, I help students identify and test hypotheses. I grill students by making them tell me what they think what is going on here, what could go wrong. If the experiment does not come out the way the student predicted, I make the student try to explain a few ways why did it go wrong, what they can think they can do to fix it. Often with undergraduates, I have to really ask them lots of questions and help them to think more about the research process and how they make decisions. I need to tease it out of them. I am sure it drives them crazy with all of my questioning, but it is the way they learn how to conduct research.

In the beginning, I explain the purpose of desired activities, but then I try to get them to reason it out themselves.

I have the students generate these research report documents (see below) on their own first, and then I give them some suggestions and allow them to make changes, and we go back and forth so that we end up with a quality product and they gain experience in thinking and writing about science and drawing conclusions from their results.

☐ Critically Self-Reflective with Documentation, Evidence Based (this must meet everything in the previous level)

I document how I help students identify possible solutions to authentic research or design problems; the literature helps to identify these authentic problems <u>and</u>

I use evidence-based literature and guidelines to explain decision making (cite references for literature) <u>and</u>

I discuss implementation of decisions and policies developed

We do not formally test students on their understanding of the research process or decision making. I think that would be a good idea for graduate students.

Suggested Sources for Documentation

- *Personal reflection*
- *Review of student products, including lab notebook, reports*

- *Reports from students*
- *Follow-up data on where student went after graduation, type of job, graduate school or postdoctoral fellowship, publications when no longer working with mentor, continuation of research on his or her own*

Rationale for Your Rating

Additional sheets can be attached. Please indicate where the evidence can be found on attached syllabi, student products, or your scholarly products or other documents.

Evidence to Support This Rating

See the attached laboratory research reports from four undergraduate research students and my comments that I made on their reports [not included in this book].

See attached two posters presented at the ACS meeting where the students and I coauthored the posters [not included in this book].

When appropriate, document literature citation or data collected at this institution to support decisions or action. Cite professional practice guidelines or standards if used.

While I don't have a ton of written documents to support my research methods, I always try to tell my students how I think about problems and how I come up with experiments to do. Also, while they are each given a project to work on, they have a lot of leeway to do the individual experiments that they want to do for the most part. I have them present their work at group meetings weekly and explain why they are doing what they are doing. The goal of all of this is for them to learn how to carry out a research project independently and learn critical thinking skills.

C15   Students Demonstrate Learning Skills and Continue to Do Research or Design Projects

Guiding Principle: Learning outcomes

Self-Assessment Criterion: Students demonstrate an ability to continue to do research or design projects or ability to develop further relevant skills and to self-assess research or design skills and self-assessment of strengths/weaknesses. For mentoring all levels—An Essential Criterion

Rubric Quality Levels

❏ Critically Self-Reflective with Documentation (satisfactory teaching occurs at this level and at the next two levels)

I provide assessment opportunities for students to demonstrate some further research or project design skills learning and self-assessment skills <u>and</u>

On a regular basis I informally assess the students' research skills as they learn more advanced lab techniques.

I provide opportunities for students to learn and demonstrate some further research or project design skills <u>or</u> self-assessment of their ability to do research or design projects <u>or</u> of their strengths and weaknesses; the choice of these skills might be based on departmental or college expectations or accreditation agencies <u>and</u>

I provide opportunities for students to succeed by minimizing risk in the research or design process <u>and</u>

I critically reflect on how and why students develop the ability to continue to do research or to develop further skills

I regularly ask the students to self-assess if they are comfortable with the lab skills. I watch students as they begin to perform lab skills. Because of the flammable nature of the lab, I never let undergraduate students work alone. As they work in the lab, I monitor their skill level and offer suggestions for improvement.

☒ Critically Self-Reflective with Documentation, Evidence Based (this must meet everything in the previous level)

Most students, including lower-performing students, demonstrate their mastery of research and learning to learn skills and self-assessment skills <u>and</u>

I am only in my second year here, yet 3/5 of my undergraduate students who worked with me and have graduated are now in doctoral programs in a similar field to the research they did with me. My first undergraduate student wanted to take a different career path and go into industry and not research. After working with me, he changed his mind and is now in a PhD program in my field.

I have had two students who have gone on to grad school independently come back and tell me that my teaching methods have really helped them succeed thus far in graduate school, so that makes me feel like I am doing something right.

I articulate a clear, explicit, and evidence-based rationale for choice of the specific skills the students demonstrate (cite references for literature to support the rationale; if this rationale is based on departmental or college expectations or accreditation agencies, cite these expectations)

The specific skills are laboratory skills with pyrophoric chemicals as required for work in this field. See an earlier rubric about my rationale.

Students need to learn the scientific method—how to identify and test hypotheses, understand the relationship between data and supporting or rejecting hypotheses, how to report data. These are standard skills in chemistry as specified in the ACS guidelines for chemistry majors.

Suggested Sources for Documentation

- *Personal reflections, evaluations*
- *Review of student products, recording of student products, or explanation of products*
- *Peer review of student research*
- *Follow-up of how students did in further research*
- *Follow-up data on where student went after graduation*

Rationale for Your Rating

Additional sheets can be attached. Please indicate where the evidence can be found on attached syllabi, student products, or your scholarly products or other documents.

What Learning-to-Learn Skills Were Developed?

- *Research skills, ability to develop and test hypotheses*
- *Desire to continue to do research*
- *Logical, scientific thinking*
- *Ability to develop a poster for presentation at a professional meeting*
- *Ability to write an acceptable submission to be judged for a conference or publication*
- *Beginning to learn how to write an article to be published in a scientific journal*

Evidence to Support This Rating

My students have presented at the university's annual research poster day.

Both undergraduate and graduate students of mine are presenting at this year's American Chemical Society conference.

I will soon be sending out an article that is coauthored with an undergraduate student for publication consideration in a peer-reviewed journal.

When appropriate, document literature citation or data collected at this institution to support decisions or action. Cite professional practice guidelines or standards if used.

ACS guide for educational programs (American Chemical Society, 2008)

You will notice that West indicated that he is at two levels on the first rubric given. For safety considerations, he developed very explicit expectations, but he has not yet done this for other student expectations. He wants to develop similar detailed expectations for all aspects of student research. Thus, he considered himself at two levels on that rubrics page.

Case 5

How an Experienced Clinical Professor Used the Rubrics to Assess His Changed Roles While Precepting or Supervising Students in Hospital Settings

Michael Cawley is a full professor of pharmacy practice and has been providing patient care and supervising student pharmacists for more than fifteen years. When he started working in the intensive care unit (ICU) of a large teaching hospital, he was the only clinical pharmacist assigned to this unit. Partially due to his ability to have a positive impact on patient care and with the assistance of other staff pharmacists, the hospital system added two full-time clinical pharmacists to the ICUs. Cawley developed a new model for precepting students that also benefits the pharmacists employed at these intensive care units. Table C5.1 summarizes the differences between his old, traditional precepting model and the new model. His old model is used by many health professionals and involved direct supervision of students as they and he provided patient care.

Now he is the secondary preceptor and focuses more time on education. He precepts up to six pharmacy students who are on five-week rotations at ICUs at several hospital sites associated with one larger health care system. The time that he spends with the students now focuses on

TABLE C5.1   Comparison of Cawley's Old Traditional Precepting Model with His New Precepting Model

Component	Characteristics of Traditional Precepting Model Cawley Used	Characteristics of Cawley's New Precepting Model	Comments
Clinical site	1 ICU	Up to four intensive care units, some of them specialized units such as medical/surgical or trauma ICU.	Through student discussions, students now learn about other types of critically ill patients even though they may not be assigned to those units.
Number of students per rotation	Two	Up to six.	
Direct supervision of student's patient care	Worked with students directly in hospital.	Does not work directly with students in hospital.	With the old model, Cawley was the only pharmacist on the unit. A pharmacist employed at the hospital now directly supervises students.
Number of hours per week exclusively dedicated to student education	3	6	Cawley now meets the students away from the patients' beds so they can focus on education.
Role of instructor	Ensure student provides good clinical care, provide educational opportunities.	Focus on providing excellent educational opportunities.	Cawley is now a secondary preceptor, with the ICU pharmacists as the primary preceptors. He used to be the only preceptor.
How students are assessed	Direct observation by preceptor.	Pharmacists on the ICU directly observe students on the unit. Cawley provides his insights to the preceptors, but he does not grade the students because he does not observe them interacting with patients or other health professionals on the unit.	
Exposure to different ways of collecting and organizing data	Students were exposed only to Cawley's data collection and organizing systems.	Students are now exposed to several ways to collect and organize data since they now have two preceptors and hear from their peers about other preceptors.	

education, including the proper use of medications for patients in the ICU and the students' interactions with other medical professionals as a member of the ICU team. Cawley also serves as a consulting senior pharmacist to the pharmacists at these ICUs, provides them with evidence-based articles, and is assisting them in conducting research or quality assessment projects at these units.

Cawley used the rubrics to assess the effectiveness of his precepting with this new model. Therefore, one of the rubric pages I show is, "Engage in Self-Analysis and Reflection of Teaching as Part of a Review and Revision Process."

He summarizes his main motivation as, "I just want to help every student to succeed as a professional pharmacist regardless of their setting." Thus, he values developing students' intrinsic motivation to learn and succeed. For this reason, I include his assessment from the rubric page, "Help students to acquire or use intrinsic motivation to learn." This criterion is quite abstract and may be hard to document that an instructor has done this. Yet Cawley did a nice job of quantifying what he does to motivate students. He sees four essential aspects contributing to success: using evidence-based medical decision making routinely, developing self-directed learning skills so they will stay current in this rapidly changing field, being professional in everything they do, and developing confidence to work as part of a health care team. Thus, I included his rubric page for "Students demonstrate learning skills that can transcend disciplinary content and self-assessment skills." The learning skills Cawley chose are common ones for professional students.

The rubric pages follow.

D16   Help Students to Acquire or Use Intrinsic Motivation to Learn

Guiding principle: Structure for teaching and learning

Self-Assessment Criterion: Help students to acquire or use intrinsic motivation to learn (i.e., personal desire to learn, seeing relevancy for individual student goals) while recognizing their extrinsic reasons to earn grades—An Optional Criterion. *Note:* May not be appropriate in all types of settings.

Rubric Quality Levels

❏ Critically Self-Reflective with Documentation (satisfactory teaching occurs at this level and at the next two levels)

I provide some opportunities for students to become intrinsically motivated to learn by connecting student goals with educational outcomes, nurturing a personal desire to achieve, and using some extrinsic motivators to get students to engage in experiential activities <u>and</u>

I critically reflect on why and how students should acquire intrinsic motivation to learn
My office is filled with inspirational posters and sayings that I constantly share with students. I show students motivational videos.

I discuss the concept of pharmacy professionalism with students and ask them to read the literature on it.

❏ Critically Self-Reflective with Documentation, Evidence Based (this must meet everything in the previous level)

I articulate how my enthusiasm, abilities, teaching style, or methods provide many opportunities for students to become intrinsically motivated to learn even when the experience appears not to fit their personal goals <u>or</u>

I realize that most students taking a rotation in intensive care are not going to work in intensive care settings. I want them to see the relevance of understanding intensive care to inpatient and outpatient pharmacists. Even more important to me is that students learn to be intrinsically motivated to act professionally.

I constantly tell students that we are a team, we are in this together. My goal is their success.

I share many personal motivating stories that emphasize the importance of accuracy and precision in calculations that may be required in dispensing patients prescriptions. These stories can be scary while they are motivating. For example, I talk about a pharmacist who went to prison because of a medication error. The pharmacist was responsible for dispensing the dose that resulted in a drug overdose that ultimately caused the death of a child. Pharmacy is a field where clinicians need to be internally motivated to always be accurate, precise, and up-to-date. The stakes are very high, and we ultimately are responsible for the medicines our patients receive and take. I am well known for my motivating stories.

I am nominated by students for a teaching award

I have been nominated for 5 awards.

☒ Critically Self-Reflective with Documentation, Evidence Based, Scholarly (this must meet everything in the previous level)

I provide evidence through student comments or evaluations that my efforts to motivate, inspire, and encourage students have led students to become intrinsically motivated and confident to learn even when the experience appears not to fit the students' original goals <u>or</u>

I win a teaching award that used student nominations or input

My nickname given to me by some students is "Coach Cawley" because they say I act like a coach to them and not just an instructor. Just two months ago, the students who were about to graduate picked me to speak to them about motivation, personal growth, and development.

My peers in my department have told me that they have heard that the students like me because I try so hard to get them to succeed.

I am very proud of this reputation, as I want to intrinsically motivate the students. When I reflect and look back on my career, I know I made a difference in student's lives.

I have won 5 awards: Lindback Award for Distinguished Teaching, Educational Bright Idea Award, Eagle Award for Outstanding Performance and Contribution to a Team, One of the Outstanding Academic Advisors of the Year, and Principles of Human Disorders and Pharmacotherapeutics Teacher of the Year Award.

Suggested Sources for Documentation

- *Reports from students*
- *Student course evaluations (i.e., information from standard or course-specific form)*
- *Personal reflection*
- *Higher education literature, either in general or discipline specific*

Rationale for Your Rating

Additional sheets can be attached. Please indicate where the evidence can be found on attached syllabi, student products, or your scholarly products or other documents.

Evidence to Support This Rating

The aspects of pharmacist professionalism that I use to relate to intrinsic motivation are altruism, honesty, integrity, respect for others, professional presence, professional stewardship, dedication, and commitment to excellence (as discussed in the literature).

I help students to find their passion and pursue it. A few years ago I had a first-generation-American student who was doing well and set to graduate soon. Discussions with her showed that she had no interest in becoming a pharmacist. Her parents forced her to do it because it is a high-status field that pays well. She really wanted to go into fashion design. I convinced her to graduate, and together we talked to her parents about allowing her to pursue her dreams. She applied to a prestigious fashion design college in New York and matriculated there. Since then, I have gotten notes from her thanking me for empowering her to change fields and helping her to convince her parents she should be allowed to do so. She is doing well in her fashion design career and is very happy.

When appropriate, document literature with citations or data collected at your institution to support decisions or action. Cite professional practice guidelines or standards if used.

American College of Clinical Pharmacy. Tenets of Professionalism for Pharmacy Students. Pharmacotherapy. 2009:29 (6) 757–759.

Roth, MT, Zlactic, TD. Development of Student Professionalism. Pharmacotherapy. 2009:29 (6) 749–756.

D11   Conduct Reviews/Revision of Teaching

Guiding Principle: Instructional design responsibilities

Self-Assessment Criterion: Engage in self-analysis and reflection of teaching as part of a review and revision process including appraisal of content currency and accuracy—An Essential Criterion

Rubric Quality Levels

☒ Critically Self-Reflective with Documentation (satisfactory teaching occurs at this level and at the next two levels)

I collect assessment data or feedback data from the students <u>and</u>

I conduct self-analysis or reflections on my teaching to identify areas for improvement <u>and</u>

I change the experiences I provide students or expectations as a result of consistent feedback or reviews or changes in content <u>and</u>

I share these reflections or other assessments of me <u>and</u>

I recognize when students have not met learning outcomes or lack knowledge <u>and</u>

I use accurate and current content <u>and</u>

I critically analyze or reflect on my experiential teaching as part of a review and revision process
I have done a lot of reflecting on my precepting and especially on the differences between the old, traditional model and the new one. I think this is a more efficient model for the primary preceptors and for educating the students. Because I meet with all of the students assigned to the hospital system's ICUs together for 6 hours a week, the preceptors have 6 hours to do other things without supervising students. It is a more efficient way to educate students because I am working with more students at once and the time I spend with them is totally focused on educational issues.

I think this model could work with other students in other types of practices. I realize this model could only work with an experienced preceptor-clinician. However, most clinical departments have both senior- and junior-level preceptors. When students go to rotations in big cities, there are multiple sites that offer similar types of experiences, such as multiple ICU sites or multiple surgery sites. This model would work well with the balance of junior preceptors at these sites and senior professors serving as secondary preceptors.

❑ Critically Self-Reflective with Documentation, Evidence Based (this must meet everything in the previous level)
I use assessment data, self-analysis, reflection, or pedagogical literature to

- Identify areas that I could improve <u>or</u>
- Propose or implement significant changes to experiences if necessary <u>or</u>
- Show why the experiences should be kept the same <u>or</u>
- Offer a rationale for not incorporating suggested changes

I have not seen any literature on this model of precepting students.
I have not formally collected data to compare the two models of educating. However, I think I could do such a study by comparing my model with how other preceptors function.

Suggested Sources for Documentation

- *Personal reflection*

Rationale for Your Rating

Additional sheets can be attached. Please indicate where the evidence can be found on attached syllabi, student products, or your scholarly products or other documents.

Evidence to Support This Rating

I have many insights into how this model works compared to the traditional model that I and most of my peers have used for years. However, I have not done any formal data collection. I have not analyzed the student rotation evaluations to see if they like this model compared to what they are used to.

See attached table [table C5.2] for a summary of my reflections of the important differences between the old and new models. (Refer to table C5.1 for more information on the contrasts mentioned in table C5.2.)

When appropriate, document literature with citations or data collected at your institution to support decisions or action. Cite professional practice guidelines or standards if used.

None

D15 Students Demonstrate Learning and Self-Assessment Skills

Guiding Principle: Learning outcomes

Self-Assessment Criterion: Students demonstrate learning skills that can transcend disciplinary content (time management, organization of data, or knowing where to look for evidence-based information, professional behavior skills, self-directed learning skills) and self-assessment skills (assessment of strengths/weaknesses or of own learning abilities)—An Essential Criterion

Rubric Quality Levels

❏ Critically Self-Reflective with Documentation (satisfactory teaching occurs at this level and at the next two levels)

I provide assessment opportunities for students to demonstrate learning and self-assessment skills <u>and</u>

I assess students when they hand in their care plans and formally at the middle and end points of the rotation

I document that most students, including the low-performing students, acquire some learning and self-assessment skills

The choice of these skills might be based on departmental or college expectations or accreditation agencies <u>and</u>

I critically reflect on why and how students can demonstrate learning skills.

These skills (listed below) are required for all competent pharmacists and generally accepted by my profession.

❏ Critically Self-Reflective with Documentation, Evidence Based (this must meet everything in the previous level)

I document that most students, including the low-performing students, demonstrate their mastery of continuing learning skills and self-assessment skills <u>and</u>

Only once in the past years, a student did not meet the expected levels of professionalism and demonstration of evidence-based decision making. I determined the need to develop a competency-based rubric that required the student to complete 5 basic objectives. These 5 basic objectives were considered absolutely necessary to demonstrate minimal acceptable competency as a sixth-year doctor of pharmacy candidate. These objectives were presented to the student in the presence of another clinical pharmacy practitioner as a witness. The student agreed to sign the rubric and understood the consequences if he was not successful in achieving the objectives.

I articulate a clear, explicit, and evidence-based rationale for the choice of the specific skills the students demonstrate (cite references for literature to support the rationale; if this rationale is based on departmental or college expectations or accreditation agencies, cite these expectations)

At the beginning of every rotation, the students and I discuss goals and expectations of the clinical rotation. All students understand their expectations.

By the third week of the rotation (midpoint evaluation), I provide feedback to the students assessing their strengths and limitations. The students have another two weeks to improve upon the skills that require improvement. If the student is identified early in the clinical rotation (first one-two weeks) in demonstrating unprofessional behavior or significant limitations in therapeutic decision making, a competency-based rubric would then be developed to demonstrate minimal competency required to pass the clinical rotation.

Because different types of specialists are working in the ICUs, student may be confused which professional evidence-based guidelines to use. I discuss how they should decide which guideline or what professional association's guidelines to use.

☒ Critically Self-Reflective with Documentation, Evidence Based, Scholarly (this must meet everything in the previous level)

I provide evidence from student products that students have gained competence in these skills <u>or</u>

I provide evidence through required care plans that the students know evidence-based clinical/professional reasoning processes tailored to individual patient/client variables. I constantly ask students: what information did you find, where did you find this information, why did you choose that source specifically, and give me brief summary of the research, guideline, or article. Majority of the students successfully met the expectations.

I create a scholarly product (i.e., peer-reviewed publication) that demonstrates students developed learning skills

> *Not done*

Further Clarification or Example of Criterion

These skills are also called process outcomes or metacognitive skills. Learning skills include time management, self-monitoring, goal setting, determining a personal need to know more, knowing how to get information, determining when need is met, and development of self-awareness of own learning abilities. Development of self-assessment skills includes assessment of learning abilities and of their abilities in general.

Suggested Sources for Documentation

- *Personal progress notes on students, notes of meetings with students, memos sent to students*
- *Student assessment data, reports from students, student portfolios/e-portfolios*
- *Authentic assessments where the students need to use these learning skills*
- Higher education literature, either in general or *discipline specific*

Rationale for Your Rating

Additional sheets can be attached. Please indicate where the evidence can be found on attached syllabi, student products, or your scholarly products or other documents.

What Learning Skills Were Developed?

- *Evidence-based decision making as a routine way of thinking about patient care*
- *Developing self-directed learning skills so students will stay current in this rapidly changing field*
- *Developing professional behaviors*

Rationale for This Rating

These are the essential characteristics of a competent pharmacist regardless of practice site. I realize that the majority of the students I train will not work in ICU settings. Therefore, it is much more important for them to learn these three skills that transcend the practice setting rather than focus on ICU-specific pharmacy skills.

If they do a residency in intensive care or most hospital-based residency programs, they will learn these ICU-specific skills.

I assume that if students develop the evidence-based habit and function as professionals, they will know how to continue to learn after graduation. I do not formally assess students on this skill and do not follow up after this rotation. Pharmacists are required to engage in continuing education activities to maintain their license.

Evidence to Support This Rating

Attached contract that students sign at the beginning of the rotation [not attached in this book]. *Among the relevant requirements, the contract requires students to*

Find and be able to discuss more than 3 evidence-based articles relating to specific patient drug treatment regiments

Develop more than 3 evidence-based pharmaceutical care plans for patients

Attached is the grading rubric I use to assess students on these skills [not included in this book]. *The rubric assesses students on professional behavior, knowledge, and therapeutic judgments based on evidence-based decisions.*

When appropriate, document literature citation or data collected at this institution to support decisions or action. Cite professional practice guidelines or standards if used.

American College of Clinical Pharmacy. Tenets of Professionalism for Pharmacy Students. Pharmacotherapy. 2009:29 (6) 757–759. (American College of Clinical Pharmacy, 2009)

Roth, MT, Zlactic, TD. Development of Student Professionalism. Pharmacotherapy. 2009:29 (6)749–756. (Roth, MT, Zlactic, TD., 2009)

www.hsl.unc.edu/Services/Tutorials/EBM/welcome.htm

Through the rubric process, Cawley gained insights into the advantages and disadvantages of the two precepting models that are summarized in Table Case 5.2.

TABLE C5.2 Cawley's Reflections on Important Differences between the Old Model and His New Model of Precepting

Category	Old Model	New Model	Implications or Conclusions
Depth versus breadth of discussion about patients	*Because I had two students who were each assigned two patients, the students and I went into more detail on each patient. There was depth but not much breadth. This may have given the students unrealistic expectations about patient load in reality.*	*Now that I have up to six students at a time, and therefore the group needs to talk about more patients, there is greater breadth and less depth.*	*I think greater breadth is preferred over depth because of the high expectations in real practice. I recognize the loss of depth may also be a disadvantage for the students.*

Assessment process	I was the only person to assess the students.	Now I offer my thoughts about how a student is functioning, but I do not grade them myself.	With the new model, a few students have not taken my educational sessions seriously because they feel they are not being graded on this work. These tend to be the less motivated or immature students. Most students value the educational sessions.
Exposure to data collection and organization systems	Exposure to only one system (mine). This system did not work well with every student.	Since students are now exposed to several data collection and organization systems, they can pick what works for them or modify the system they learned when they see how others organize data.	With the new model, students realize there are several correct data collection and organizational systems. It is not the system that is end product, but how well the student can present the data and manage the patient care.
Amount of direct supervision of patient care the student received	When I was on the unit, I supervised the students closely.	Since I am not on the unit, I do not supervise the students in their patient care. The primary preceptors have other responsibilities, so they probably are not supervising as much.	The old system was better because students were supervised more. However, given the current realities of patient care, there probably would be less supervision even with the old model today.
Students meeting the expectations of the rotation	Majority of the students meet the expectations of the rotation.	Majority of the students meet the expectations of the rotation.	I have not observed any differences in the quality of the student performance or in the number of students not meeting the expectations of the rotation that is a function of the models.

Comparisons among the Cases

These professors vary in terms of years of experience teaching, and their self-assessments reflect these differences. For the most part, the two senior professors were at a higher level than the three junior professors. This may not always be the case since I selected two outstanding senior professors who critically reflect on their teaching and strive to improve. I suspect Nathan West will become an outstanding teacher who will rate himself on the higher or highest levels on these self-assessments in a few years. It does take time to use evidence-based teaching and to collect systematic data or write scholarly articles on one's teaching. Elizabeth Amy Janke showed that she became an evidence-based teacher in a few years. She attributes this growth to hearing good ideas at higher education conferences, consulting with the Teaching and Learning Center and senior faculty in her department, and her bias toward critical reflection and evidence-based approaches that led her to collect data about teaching.

The vocabularies these professors use to assess themselves reflect their disciplines and their experiences. The disciplines help determine their worldview and partly justify why they teach the way they do. These disciplinary approaches may help some faculty to use critical reflection and evidence-based approaches to their teaching. I think artists have to reflect on their products and performances regularly; therefore, what they learn as a result can easily transfer to their teaching. I suspect that faculty who are in any of the sciences, health sciences, or engineering will be more naturally inclined to accept evidence-based teaching as it is consistent with what they do in research. Alberts (2012) refers to this kind of teaching as "scientific teaching" as a way to foster the scientists' adoption of evidence-based approaches to teaching. I hope that as a result of reading these cases, faculty in other disciplines can now see the value in this assessment model and in using the rubrics.

Mentors of research, especially laboratory research, and preceptors have intensive relationships with few students. Therefore, their expectations and outcomes are different from those of classroom teachers. Undergraduate research is not required in West's chemistry department; students take a research elective, so he gets only students who are interested in the course. Thus, it is appropriate that West would like his students to want to continue doing research in his field. Probably most scientists who mentor students' research want their students to continue their research in this field; this becomes a desired outcome. In contrast, all pharmacy students must take a year of clinical rotations, some of which will not be in their particular area of interest. Some clinicians may list as a desired outcome that they motivate more students to go into their specialty. However, mature clinicians realize that they are training many students who may not continue working in their specialty but the students need to learn something about it. Therefore, Michael Cawley's desired outcomes are broader than learning the skills associated with his specialty. Since he states that he wants to increase intrinsic motivation and wants all students to succeed, he is proud that he helped a student to get out of pharmacy when he realized this was not the right career for her. Again this takes maturity and confidence to help a student in this way.

There are other possible comparisons that you might see. I encourage you to consider how your teaching experience and context compare with these cases.

Comparison of Impact of Completing the Rubrics on These Cases

Janke planned her own improvement path as a result of completing the rubrics; Stu Proff worked with me to develop ways to improve.

Janke is very reflective and self-motivated. In her first year of teaching, she started a website to document her progress toward promotion and tenure and posted her rubrics on that site.

Proff was motivated to improve his teaching evaluations because they are important at my university to get tenure and a promotion. He is not normally very reflective about his teaching, and the process of completing the rubrics was quite insightful for him. On several rubrics he noted, "I never thought about this before" or, "I do not read educational literature." I think he will change his teaching on the basis of what he learned in our interactions.

Because West is so reflective of what he is doing while mentoring students in research, I suspect the exercise of completing the rubrics did not lead to many new insights. I think it helped him to articulate his ideas about mentoring. Furthermore, they are a good record of where he is at this stage in his career now, and he will be able to compare this to where he is in the future. The rubrics make it explicit for West what he still wants to do.

Both Susan Wainwright and Cawley are experienced professors who want to continue to improve their teaching. Wainwright may not have gained many insights into how she can improve, as she rated herself at the highest level on almost half of the criteria. However, this exercise was reinforcing for her that she was on the right track. She commented that completing the rubrics helped her to pull all of her work on her teaching together and allowed her to see how much she had improved her teaching over the years.

Cawley used the rubrics to assess if he was still an effective preceptor since he is using a nontraditional precepting model. Given the results of his self-assessment, he may develop an article about this precepting model to share with other preceptors.

Summary of the Cases

The cases contain descriptions of how five professors used the rubrics to assess their teaching. These self-assessments reflect the differences in faculty roles between researchers and clinicians and classroom teachers, as I discussed in earlier chapters. These cases should give you a good idea of how to use these rubrics, what kinds of data to provide, and how each criterion asks about different aspects teaching.

The cases illustrated all but two essential criteria on rubrics for instructor with autonomy: they did not show an example of the criteria "Ensure students have successful learning experiences through availability and accessibility" and "Promote higher-order thinking." These cases also described an example of all but one criterion (about availability and accessibility) that is common to all rubric sets.

In each case, the process of completing the rubrics led to the professors' meeting the dual goals of fostering better teaching to lead to increased student learning and invigorated teaching. The cases showed how these professors adapted the rubrics to fit their own teaching. As a result of reading these cases, you should be able to complete the rubrics to better assess your own teaching, and I hope that you will be able to apply some of the suggestions made by these professors to your own teaching.

References

Alberts, B. (2012, February 22). *Urgently need: A redefinition of science education.* Paper presented at Temple University Stem Education Lecture Series, Philadelphia.

Alexander, P., & Murphy, P. (1998). The research base for APA's learner-centered psychological principles. In N. Lambert & B. Mccombs (Eds.), *How students learn* (pp. 25–60). Washington, DC: American Psychological Association.

Allen, D. E., Donham, R. S., & Bernhardt, S. A. (2010). Problem-based learning. In W. Buskist & J. E. Groccia (Eds.), *Evidence-based teaching* (pp. 21–30). New Directions for Teaching and Learning, no. 128. San Francisco: Jossey-Bass.

Ambrose, S., Bridges, M., DiPietro, M., Lovett, M., & Norman, M. (2010). *How learning works.* San Francisco: Jossey-Bass.

American Chemical Society. (2008). *ACS Undergraduate Professional Education in Chemistry.* Retrieved from http://portal.acs.org/portal/PublicWebSite/about/governance/committees/training/acsapproved/degreeprogram/WPCP_008491

American Psychiatric Association. (2000). *Diagnostic and statistical manual of mental disorders* (4th ed.). Washington, DC: American Psychiatric Association.

American Psychological Association. (2005). *American Psychology Association Policy Statement on Evidence-Based Practice in Psychology.* Retrieved from www.Apapracticecentral.Org/Ce/Courses/Ebpstatement.Pdf

Amidon, E. J., & Hough, J. E. (1967). *Interaction analysis: Theory, research and practice.* Reading, MA: Addison-Wesley.

Anderson, L., & Krathwohl, D. (Eds.). (2001). *A taxonomy for learning, teaching, and assessing.* New York: Longman.

Angelo, T. A., & Cross, K. P. (1993). *Classroom assessment techniques* (2nd ed.). San Francisco: Jossey-Bass.

Argyris, C., & Schön, D. A. (1974). *Teaching in practice: Increasing professional effectiveness.* San Francisco: Jossey-Bass.

Arreola, R. A. (2006). *Developing a comprehensive faculty evaluation system* (3rd ed.). Bolton, MA: Anker.

Association of American Colleges and Universities. (2002, July). *Greater expectations for undergraduate education: Report on a national task force.* Retrieved from Www.Greaterexpectations.Org/Pdf/Gex .Final.Pdf

Astin, A. W., & Vogelgesang, L. J. (2006). *Understanding the effects of service-learning: A study of students and faculty.* Los Angeles: Graduate School of Education and Information Studies University of California, Los Angeles.

Austin, A., Sorcinelli, M., & McDaniels, M. (2007). Understanding new faculty: Background, aspirations, challenges, and growth. In R. Perry & J. Smart (Eds.), *The scholarship of teaching and learning in higher education: An evidence-based perspective* (pp. 39–89). Dordrecht, Netherlands: Springer.

Bain, K., & Zimmerman, J. (2009). Understanding great teaching. *Peer Review, 11*(1), 9–12.

Baron, J. B. (1998). Using learner-centered assessment on a large scale. In N. M. Lambert & B. L. McCombs (Eds.), *How students learn* (pp. 211–249). Washington, DC: American Psychological Association.

Barr, R. B., & Tagg, J. (1995, November/December). From teaching to learning: A new paradigm for undergraduate education. *Change, 27*, 12–25.

Bereiter, C., & Scardamalia, M. (1989). Intentional learning as a goal of instruction. In L. Resnick (Ed.), *Knowing, learning and instruction* (pp. 361–392). Hillsdale, NJ: Erlbaum.

Bergmann, J., & Sams, A. (2012). *Flip your classroom: Reach every student in every class every day.* Washington, DC: International Society for Technology in Education.

Berk, R. A. (2006). *Thirteen strategies to measure college teaching.* Sterling, VA: Stylus.

Biggs, J. (1999). *Teaching for quality learning at university.* Buckingham, England: Open University Press.

Bishop-Clark, C., & Dietz-Uhler, B. (2012). *Engaging in the scholarship of teaching and learning.* Sterling, VA: Stylus.

Blackburn, R., & Lawrence, J. (1995). *Faculty at work: Motivation, expectation and satisfaction.* Baltimore, MD: Johns Hopkins University Press.

Bloom, B. S. (Ed.). (1956). *Taxonomy of educational objectives. The classification of educational goals. Handbook I. Cognitive domain.* New York: Mckay.

Blumberg, P. (2000). Evaluating the evidence that problem-based learners are self-directed learners: A review of the literature. In D. H. Evensen & C. E. Hmelo (Eds.), *Problem-based learning: A research perspective on learning interactions* (pp. 199–226). Mahwah, NJ: Erlbaum.

Blumberg, P. (2007). Problem-based learning: A prototypical example of learning-centered teaching. *Journal of Student Centered Learning, 3*(2), 111–125.

Blumberg, P. (2009a). *Developing learner-centered teaching: A practical guide for faculty.* San Francisco: Jossey-Bass.

Blumberg, P. (2009b). Maximizing learning through course alignment and using different types of knowledge. *Innovative Higher Education, 34*(2), 93–103.

Blumberg, P. (2011). Making evidence-based practice an essential aspect of teaching. *Journal of Faculty Development, 26*(1), 1–6.

Bonwell, C., & Eison, J. (1991). *Active learning: Creating excitement in the classroom.* Washington, DC: George Washington University, School of Education and Human Development.

Boye, A. P. (2011). Effecting change in limited-control classroom environments: A case study. In J. E. Miller & J. E. Groccia (Eds.), *To improve the academy, vol. 30: Resources for faculty, instruction, and organizational development* (pp. 85–98). San Francisco: Jossey-Bass.

Boyer, E. L. (1990). *Scholarship reconsidered: Priorities of the professoriate.* Princeton, NJ: Carnegie Foundation for the Advancement of Teaching.

Bransford, J., Brown, A., & Cocking, R. (Eds.). (2000). *How people learn: Brain, mind, experiences and school.* Washington, DC: National Academies Press.

Brew, A., & Ginns, P. (2008). The relationship between engagement in scholarship of teaching and learning and students' course experiences. *Assessment and Evaluation in Higher Education, 33*(5), 535–545.

Brookfield, S. (1995). *Becoming a critically reflective teacher.* San Francisco: Jossey-Bass.

Brookfield, S. D., & Preskill, S. (1999). *Discussion as a way of teaching.* San Francisco: Jossey-Bass.

Buskist, W., & Groccia, J. E. (Eds.). (2011). *Evidence-based teaching* (pp. 21–30). New Directions for Teaching and Learning, no. 128. San Francisco: Jossey-Bass.

Candy, P. (1991). *Self-direction for lifelong learning.* San Francisco: Jossey-Bass.

Carey, S. (2009). From the editor. *Peer Review, 11*(2), 3.

Centra, J., & Gaubatz, N. (2005). *Students' perceptions of learning and instructional effectiveness in college courses.* Retrieved from www.ets.org/Media/Products/perceptions.pdf

Chisholm, M., Hayes, E., LaBrecque, S., & Smith, D. (2011). The role of faculty evaluation in transformative change. *Journal of Faculty Development, 25*(1), 36–42.

Cross, K., & Steadman, M. (1996). *Classroom research: Implementing the scholarship of teaching.* San Francisco: Jossey-Bass.

Dewar, J. (2011). Helping stakeholders understand the limitations of SRT (student ratings of teaching) data: Are we doing enough. *Journal of Faculty Development, 25*(3), 40–44.

Dewey, J. (1933). *How we think: A restatement of reflective thinking to the educational process.* Boston: Heath. (Original work published 1910.)

Diamond, R. M. (2008). *Designing and assessing courses and curricula* (3rd ed.). San Francisco: Jossey-Bass.

DiPietro, M. (2012). Millennial students: insights from generational theory and learning science. In J. E. Groccia (Ed.), *To improve the academy, vol. 32: Resources for faculty, instructional, and organizational development* (pp. 161–176). San Francisco: Jossey-Bass.

Dolan, E. (2007). Grappling with the literature of educational research and practice. *CBE-Life Sciences Education, 6*, 289–296.

Doyle, T. (2011). *Learner-centered teaching: Putting the research on learning into practice.* Sterling, VA: Stylus.

Driscoll, A., & Wood, S. (2007). *Outcomes-based assessment for learner-centered education.* Sterling, VA: Stylus.

Ebert-May, D., Derting, T. L., Hodder, J., Momsen, J. L., Long, T. M., & Jardelza, S. E. (2011). What we say is not what we do: Effective evaluation of faculty professional development programs. *Bioscience, 61*(7), 550–558.

EBSCO Academic Databases for Academic Institutions. (2013). *Professional development.* Retrieved from www.ebscohost/academicdatabases

Edgerton, R. (2004). Introduction. In L. S. Shulman, *Teaching as community property* (pp. 1–8). San Francisco: Jossey-Bass.

Educational Testing Service. (2012). *About the SIR II Student Instructional Report.* Retrieved from www.ets.org/sir_ii/about

Epstein, M. L., Lazarus, A. D., Calvano, T. B., Matthews, K. A., Hendel, R. A., Epstein, B. B., et al. (2002). Immediate feedback assessment technique promotes learning and corrects inaccurate first responses. *Psychological Record, 52*(2), 187–201.

Eyler, J. (2009). The power of experiential education. *Liberal Education, 95*(4), 24–31.

Felton, P., & Clayton, P. H. (2011). Service-learning. In W. Buskist & J. E. Groccia (Eds.), *Evidence-based teaching* (pp. 75–84). New Directions for Teaching and Learning, no. 128. San Francisco: Jossey-Bass.

Fink, L. D. (2003). *Creating significant learning experiences.* San Francisco: Jossey-Bass.

Freeland, R. M. (2009). The Clark/AAC&U Conference on Liberal Education and Effective Practice. *Liberal Education, 95*(4), 6–9.

Fox, M. A., & Hackerman, N. (Ed.). (2003). *Evaluating and improving undergraduate teaching in sciences, technology, engineering and mathematics.* Washington, DC: National Academies Press.

Guyatt, G., Haynes, B., Jaeschle, R., Cook, D., & Green, L. (2000). Users' guide to medical literature XXV. Evidence-based medicine: Principles for applying the users' guides to patient care. *Journal of the American Medical Association, 284*(10), 1290–1296.

Handelsman, J., Ebert-May, D., Beichner, R. B., Bruns, P., Chang, A., DeHaan, R., Gentile, J., Lauffler, S., Stewart, J., Tilghman, S., & Wood, W. (2004). Scientific teaching. *Science, 304*, 521–522.

Higher Education Research Institute at UCLA. (2009). *The American College Teacher National Norms 2007–2008.* Los Angeles: Graduate School of Education and Information Studies University of California, Los Angeles.

Howe, N., & Strauss, W. (2007). *Millennials go to college* (2nd ed.). Washington, DC: American Association of Collegiate Registrars and Admissions Offices (AACRAO) and Life Course Associates.

Huber, M. T. (2002). Disciplinary styles in the scholarship of teaching and learning: Reflections on the Carnegie Academy for the scholarship of teaching and learning. In M. T. Huber & S. P. Morreale (Eds.), *Disciplinary styles in the scholarship of teaching and learning: Exploring common ground* (pp. 25–44). Washington, DC: American Association for Higher Education and Carnegie Foundation for the Advancement of Teaching.

Huber, M. T., & Hutchings, P. (2005). *The advancement of learning: Building the teaching commons.* San Francisco: Jossey-Bass.

Hutchings, P. (2000). *Opening lines: Approaches to the scholarship of teaching and learning.* Menlo Park, CA: Carnegie Foundation for the Advancement of Teaching.

Hutchings, P., Huber, M. T., & Ciccone, A. (2011). *The scholarship of teaching and learning reconsidered.* San Francisco: Jossey-Bass.

Hutchings, P., & Shulman, L. S. (1999). The scholarship of teaching in higher education: New elaborations, new developments. *Change, 31*(5), 10–15.

IDEA Center. *Student ratings of instruction.* Retrieved from www.theideacenter.org/services/student-ratings/sample-forms-student-ratings-instruction

Ideishi, R. (2009). Occupational therapy service-learning and early childhood education. In K. Flecky & L. Gitlow (Eds.), *Service-learning in occupational therapy education* (pp. 237–251). Sudbury, MA: Jones and Bartlett.

Jacobs, D. (2000). A chemical mixture of methods. In P. Hutchings (Ed.), *Opening lines: Approaches to the scholarship of teaching and learning* (pp. 41–52). Menlo Park, CA: Carnegie Foundation for the Advancement of Teaching.

Johnson, T. (2009). Learning-centered evaluation of teaching. *To improve the academy, vol. 27: Resources for faculty, instructional and organizational development* (pp. 332–348). San Francisco: Jossey-Bass.

Johnston, T. (2012). *Physical therapy examination simulation as a diagnostic tool to assess student learning and teaching needs.* Retrieved from www.Usciences.Edu/Teaching/Innovations/Innovations%202012.Pdf

Jonassen, D. (1997). Instructional design model for well-structured and ill-structured problem-solving outcomes. *Educational Technology Research and Development, 45*(1), 65–94.

Jones, R. (2005). Liberal education for the twenty-first century: Business expectations. *Liberal Education, 91*(2), 32–37.

Kegan, R. (1994). *In over our heads: The mental demands of modern life.* Cambridge, MA: Harvard University Press.

Knowles, M. (1984). *Andragogy in action: Applying modern principles of adult education.* San Francisco: Jossey-Bass.

Kolb, D. A. (1984). *Experiential learning: Experience as a source of learning and development.* Englewood Cliffs, NJ: Prentice Hall.

Kramer, P., Ideishi, R., Kearney, P., Cohen, M., Ames, J., Shea, G., Schemm, R., & Blumberg, P. (2007). Achieving curricular themes through learner-centered teaching. *Occupational Therapy in Health Care, 21*(1), 185–198.

Kreber, C. (2002). Teaching excellence, teaching expertise, and the scholarship of teaching. *Innovative Higher Education, 27*(1), 5–23.

Kuh, G. D. (2008). *High-impact educational practices.* Washington, DC: Association of American Colleges and Universities.

Kuh, G. D., Kinzie, J., Schuh, J. H., & Whitt, W. (2005). *Student success in college creating conditions that matter.* San Francisco: Jossey-Bass.

Lambert, N., & McCombs, B. (1998). Introduction: Learner-centered schools and classrooms as a direction for school reform. In N. Lambert & B. Mccombs (Eds.), *How students learn* (pp. 1–15). Washington, DC: American Psychological Association.

Lauer, C. (2012). A comparison of faculty and student perspectives on course evaluation terminology. In J. Groccia & L. Cruz (Ed.), *To improve the academy, vol. 31: Resources for faculty, instructional, and organizational development* (pp. 195–212). San Francisco: Jossey-Bass.

Loeher, L. (2006). *An examination of research university faculty evaluation policies and practices.* Unpublished manuscript.

Madaus, G .F., Scriven, M. S., & Stufflebeam, D. L. (Eds.). (1987). *Evaluation models: Viewpoints on education and human service evaluation* (6th ed.). Norwell, MA: Kluwer.

Mahalingam, M., Schaefer, F., & Morlino, E. (2008). Promoting student learning through group problem solving in general chemistry recitations. *Journal of Chemical Education, 85*(11), 1577–1581.

Maki, P. (2004). *Assessing for learning.* Sterling, VA: Stylus.

Marzano, R. (1998). Cognitive, metacognitive, and conative considerations in classroom assessment. In N. M. Lambert & B. L. McCombs (Eds.), *How students learn* (pp. 241–266). Washington, DC: American Psychological Association.

Mayer, R. (1998). Cognitive theory for education: What teachers need to know. In N. M. Lambert & B. L. McCombs (Eds.), *How students learn* (pp. 353–377). Washington, DC: American Psychological Association.

Mazur, E. (1997). *Peer instruction: A user's manual.* Upper Saddle River, NJ: Prentice Hall.

McAlpine, L., & Harris, R. (2002). Evaluating teaching effectiveness and teaching improvement: A language for institutional policies and academic development practices. *International Journal for Academic Development, 7*(1), 7–17.

McKeachie, W. (2007). Good teaching makes a difference—and we know what it is. In R. Perry & J. Smart (Eds.), *The scholarship of teaching and learning in higher education: An evidence-based perspective* (pp. 457–474). Dordrecht, Netherlands: Springer.

Michaelsen, L. K., Knight, A. B., & Fink, L. D. (2004). *Team-based learning.* Sterling, VA: Stylus

Michaelsen, L. K., & Sweet, M. (2011). Team-based learning. In W. Buskist & J. B. Groccia (Eds.), *Evidence-based teaching* (pp. 41–52). New Directions for Teaching and Learning, no. 128. San Francisco: Jossey-Bass.

Miller, R. (2009). Connecting beliefs with research on effective undergraduate education. *Peer Review, 11*(2), 4–8.

Millis, B. (2009). Becoming an effective teacher using cooperative learning: A personal odyssey. *Peer Review, 11*(2), 17–21.

Millis, B. (2010). *Cooperative learning in higher education.* Sterling, VA: Stylus.

Moon, J. (2006). *Learning journals: A handbook for reflective practice and professional development* (2nd ed.). New York: Routledge.

Mostrom, A. (2008). A unique use of concept maps as the primary organizing structure in two upper-level undergraduate biology courses: Results from the first implementation. In *Proceedings of the Third International Conference on Concept Maps 1* (pp. 76–83), Tallinn, Estonia, and Helsinki, Finland.

Mostrom, A., & Blumberg, P. (2012). Does learning-centered teaching promote grade improvement? *Innovative Higher Education, 37*(5), 397–405.

National Center for Education Statistics. (1995). *National assessment of college student learning: Identifying college graduates' essential skills in writing, speech, and listening, and critical thinking.* Washington, DC: US Department of Education.

National Research Council. (2001). In J. Pelligrino, N. Chudowsky, & R. Glaser (Eds.), *Knowing what students know: The science and design of educational assessment.* Washington, DC: National Academy Press.

Nilson, L. B. (2003). *Teaching at its best* (2nd ed.). Bolton, MA: Anker.

Nilson, L. B. (2007). *The graphic syllabus and the outcomes map.* San Francisco: Jossey-Bass.

Nilson, L. B. (2012). Time to raise questions about student ratings. In J. E. Groccia & L. Cruz (Eds.), *To improve the academy, vol. 31: Resources for faculty, instructional and organizational development* (pp. 213–228). San Francisco: Jossey-Bass.

Novak, G. M. (2011). Just-in-time teaching. In W. Buskist & J. E. Groccia, (Eds.), *Evidence-based teaching* (pp. 63–64). New Directions for Teaching and Learning, no. 128. San Francisco: Jossey-Bass.

Novak, J. D. (1998). *Learning, creating, and using knowledge.* Mahwah, NJ: Erlbaum.

Nygren, K. (2007). *Faculty guidebook.* Plainfield, IL: Pacific Crest Publications.

O'Neill, N. O. (2010). Internships as high-impact practice: Some reflections on quality. *Peer Review, 12*(4), 4–8.

Palsole, S. V., & Brunk-Chavez, B. L. (2011). The digital academy: Preparing faculty for digital course development. In J. E. Miller & J. E. Groccia (Eds.), *To improve the academy, vol. 30: Resources for faculty, instructional and organizational development* (pp. 17–30). San Francisco: Jossey-Bass.

Paris, S. C. (1998). Why learner-centered assessment is better than high stakes testing. In N. M. Lambert & B. L. McCombs (Eds.), *How students learn* (pp. 189–210). Washington, DC: American Psychological Association.

Pascarella, E. T., & Terenzini, P. T. (2005). *How college affects students, vol. 2: A third decade of research.* San Francisco: Jossey-Bass.

Perry, R. C., & Smart, J. C. (2007). *The scholarship of teaching and learning in higher education: An evidence-based perspective.* Dordrecht, Netherlands: Springer.

Pintrich, P. (2000). The role of goal orientation in self-regulated learning. In M. Boekarts, P. P. Pintrich, & M. Zeidner (Eds.), *Handbook of self-regulation* (pp. 451–502). San Diego, CA: Academic Press.

Prince, M. J. (2004). Does active learning work? A review of the research. *Journal of Engineering Education, 93*(3), 223–231.

Prince, M. J., & Felder, R. M. (2006). Inductive teaching and learning methods: Definitions, comparisons, and research bases. *Journal of Engineering Education, 95*(2), 123–138.

Prosser, M., & Trigwell, K. (1999). *Understanding learning and teaching: The experience in higher education.* London: Society for Research into Higher Education and the Open University Press.

Qualters, D. M. (2010). Engaging faculty colleagues in experiential education. In D. M. Qualters (Ed.), *Experiential education: Making the most of learning outside the classroom.* New Directions for Teaching and Learning, no. 124. (pp. 95–99). San Francisco: Jossey-Bass.

Raelin, J. A. (2010). Work-based learning: Valuing practice as an educational Event. In D. M. Qualters (Ed.), *Experiential education: Making the most of learning outside the classroom* (pp. 39–46). New Directions for Teaching and Learning, no. 124. San Francisco: Jossey-Bass.

Ramsden, P. (2003). *Learning to teach in higher education* (2nd ed.). London: Routledge Falmer.

Reddy, Y., & Andrade, H. (2010). A review of rubrics' use in higher education. *Assessment and Evaluation in Higher Education, 35*(4), 435–448.

Resnick, L. B. (1987). The 1987 Presidential Address: Learning in school and out. *Educational Researcher, 16*(9), 13–20.

Resnick. L. B. (1991). Shared cognition. In L. Resnick, J. Levine, & S. Teasley (Eds.), *Perspectives on socially shared cognition* (pp. 1–20). Washington, DC: American Psychological Association.

Rice, R. E., & Sorcinelli, M. D. (2002). Can the tenure process be improved? In R. Chait (Ed.), *The questions of tenure* (pp. 101–124). Cambridge, MA: Harvard University Press.

Richlin, L. (2001). Scholarly teaching and the scholarship of teaching. In C. Kreber (Ed.), *Scholarship revisited: Perspectives on the scholarship of teaching* (pp. 57–68). San Francisco: Jossey-Bass.

Rodgers, C. (2002). Defining reflection: Another look at John Dewey and reflective thinking. *Teachers College Record, 104*(4), 842–866.

Roth, M. T., & Zlactic, T. D. (2009). Development of student professionalism. *Pharmacotherapy, 29*(6), 749–756.

Sackett, D., Richardson, W., Rosenberg, W., & Haynes, R. (2000). *Evidence based medicine: How to practice and teach evidence-based medicine* (2nd ed.). New York: Churchill Livingstone.

Schön, D. (1987). *Educating the reflective practitioner.* San Francisco: Jossey-Bass.

Seldin, P. (1999). Current practices—good and bad—nationally. In P. Seldin (Ed.), *Changing practices in evaluating faculty: A practical guide to improved faculty performance and promotion/tenure decisions* (pp. 1–24). Bolton, MA: Anker.

Seldin, P., Miller, J. E., & Seldin, C. A. (2010). *Successful use of teaching portfolios* (4th ed.). San Francisco: Jossey-Bass.

Shepard, K. F., & Jensen, G. M. (2002). *Handbook of teaching for physical therapists* (2nd ed.). Woburn, MA: Butterworth Heinemann.

Shulman, L. S. (2004a). *Teaching as community property.* San Francisco: Jossey-Bass.

Shulman, L. S. (2004b). *The wisdom of practice: Essays on teaching, learning and learning to teach.* San Francisco: Jossey-Bass.

Simkins, S. M., & Maier, M. H. (2010). *Just-in-time teaching across the disciplines, across the academy.* Sterling, VA: Stylus.

Slocum, T., Spencer, T., & Detrich, R. (2012). Best available evidence: Three complementary approaches. *Education and Treatment of Children, 32*(2), 153–181.

Smith, R. (2001). Formative evaluation and the scholarship of teaching and learning. In C. Knapper & P. Cranton (Eds.), *Fresh approaches to the evaluation of teaching* (pp. 51–62). New Directions for Teaching and Learning, no. 88. San Francisco: Jossey-Bass.

Smither, J. W., London, M., & Reilly, R. R. (2005). Does performance improve following multi-source feedback? A theoretical model, meta-analysis and review of empirical findings. *Personnel Psychology, 58*, 33–36.

Spencer, T., Detrich, R., & Slocum, T. (2012). Evidence-based practice: A framework for making effective decisions. *Education and Treatment of Children, 53*(2), 127–151.

Spring, B. (2007). Evidence-based practice in clinical psychology: What it is, why it matters; what you need to know. *Journal of Clinical Psychology, 63*(7), 611–631.

Springer, L., Stanne, M., & Donovan, S. (1999). Effects of small-group learning on undergraduates in science, mathematics, engineering, and technology (health sciences): A meta-analysis. *Review of Educational Research, 69*(1), 21–51.

Stevens, D. D., & Cooper, J. E. (2009). *Journal keeping: How to use reflective writing for learning, teaching, professional insight and positive change.* Sterling, VA: Stylus.

Suskie, L. (2004). *Assessing student learning.* Bolton, MA: Anker.

Theall, M. (2010). Evaluating teaching: From reliability to accountability. In M. Svinicki & C. Wehlburg (Eds.), *New directions for teaching and learning: 123 Landmark Issues in Teaching and Learning* (pp. 85–96). San Francisco: Jossey-Bass.

Tomlin, G., & Borgetto, G. (2011). Research pyramid: A new evidence-based practice model for occupational therapy. *The American Journal of Occupational Therapy, 65*(2), 189–196.

Trierweiler, S. J. (2006). Training the next generation of psychologist clinicians: Good judgment and methodological realism at the interface between science and practice. In C. Goodheart, A. F. Kazdin, & R. J. Sternberg (Eds.), *Evidence-based psychotherapy: Where practice and research meet* (pp. 211–238). Washington, DC: American Psychological Association.

US Department of Education. (2012). *Education resources information center (ERIC).* Retrieved from www.eric.ed.gov

US Department of Education, Office of Policy, Evaluation, and Policy Development. (2010). *Evaluation of evidence-based practices in online learning: A meta-analysis and review of online learning studies.* Retrieved from www.ed.gov/rschstat/eval/tech/evidence-based-practices/finalreport.pdf

Vernon, D., & Blake, R. (1993). Does problem-based learning work? A meta-analysis of evaluative research. *Academic Medicine, 68*, 550–563.

Vonderwell, S. (2003). An examination of asynchronous communication experiences and perspectives of students in an online course: A case study. *The Internet and Higher Education, 6*(1), 77–90.

Wainwright, S. (2009). Using self-assessment to assess the effectiveness of learner-centered instructional design and delivery. *Journal of Faculty Development, 23*(3), 23–29.

Walvoord, B. E. (1998). *Effective grading.* San Francisco: Jossey-Bass.

Wehlburg, C. (2010). Assessing learning: From accountability to transformation. In M. Svinicki & C. Wehlburg (Eds.), *New directions for teaching and learning: 123 landmark issues in teaching and learning: A look back at new directions for teaching and learning* (pp. 45–50). San Francisco: Jossey-Bass.

Weimer, M. (2006). *Enhancing scholarly work on teaching and learning.* San Francisco: Jossey-Bass.

Weimer, M. (2010). *Inspired college teaching.* San Francisco: Jossey-Bass.

Weimer, M. (2013). *Learner-centered teaching* (2nd ed.). San Francisco: Jossey-Bass.

Wittrock, M. (1998). Cognition and subject matter learning. In N. M. Lambert & B. L. McCombs (Ed.), *How students learn* (pp. 143–152). Washington, DC: American Psychological Association.

Worsham, L. (2011). Fast-food scholarship: Do your job better. *The Chronicle of Higher Education, 58*(17), A26.

Wulff, D. H. (Ed.). (2005). *Aligning for learning: Strategies for teaching effectiveness.* Bolton, MA: Anker Publishing.

Zimmerman, B. J. (2000). Attaining self-regulation: A social cognitive perspective. In M. Boekarts, P. R. Pitrich, & M. Zeidner (Eds.), *Handbook of self-regulation: Theory, research and applications* (pp. 13–39). San Diego: Academic Press.

Zull, J. E. (2002). *The art of changing the brain.* Sterling, VA: Stylus Publishing.

APPENDIX: RUBRICS FOR SELF-ASSESSMENT OF TEACHING: TOOLS FOR IMPROVING DIFFERENT TYPES OF TEACHING

This appendix contains three parts:

- Orientation to the rubrics: a description of where to find more information about each aspect of the rubrics and how to follow the rubrics format
- Rubric set for improving classroom, laboratory, or online teaching for autonomous instructors
- Rubric set for mentoring undergraduate students, graduate students, or postdoctoral fellows in research or an engineering design projects

The categories are:

A   Rubrics for Improving Face-to-Face, Laboratory, or Online Teaching for Autonomous Instructors (shown in this appendix)

B   Rubrics for improving Face-to-Face, Laboratory, or Online Teaching for Instructors with Limited Autonomy

C   Rubrics for Improving the Mentoring of Students in Research or Engineering-Type Design Projects (shown in this appendix)

D   Rubrics for Improving Teaching in Experiential Settings

E   Rubrics for Improving Teaching in the Visual or Graphic Arts

F   Rubrics for Improving Teaching in the Performing Arts

G   Rubrics for Improving the Direction of Experiential Education

All of the rubrics can be accessed at www.josseybass.com/go/Blumberg. The password is *josseybasshighered*.

TABLE A.1 Where to Locate Information Relating to the Rubrics

Topic	Where to Locate More Information on This Topic
Explanation for the constructs common to all rubrics: Essential aspects of teaching	Table A.2 Chapters 2, 3
Rationale for the constructs for teaching in experiential context rubrics	Chapter 10
Support for the overall hierarchical model assessing teaching leading to the rubrics levels	Figure A.1 Chapters 8, 9
Template for all rubrics	Chapter 9, in "Rubric Template" section
Explanation for the rubric page format, rubrics criteria or assessment standards, and aspects of each rubrics page	Table A.3
Tips for completing these rubrics	Chapter 10, in "Using the Self-Assessment Rubrics Effectively" section

TABLE A.2 Where to Locate Explanations and Support for the Rubric Constructs

Construct	Where This Idea Is Discussed	Sections of Chapter Where This Idea Is Discussed
Guiding principle	Chapter 1	Strategy 1: Define the Essential Aspects of Teaching
Guiding principle of structure for teaching and learning	Chapter 3	Structure for Teaching and Learning
Guiding principle of instructional design responsibilities	Chapter 3	Instructional Design Responsibilities
Guiding principle of learning outcomes	Chapter 3	Assessment of Learning Outcomes
Criterion Common to All Rubrics		
Guiding Principle of Structure for Teaching and Learning		
Provide feedback to students	Chapter 3	Feedback to Students to Foster Learning
Provide reflection opportunities for students	Chapter 3	Student Reflections on Their Learning
Use consistent policies and processes to assess students	Chapter 3	Assessment Policies, Methods, and Process
Guiding Principle of Instructional Design Responsibilities		
Conduct reviews and revisions of teaching	Chapter 3	Reflect on Teaching as Part of a Review and Revision Process
Guiding Principle of Learning Outcomes		
Students demonstrate learning outcomes of acquisition of knowledge, skills, or values	Chapter 3	Assessment of Knowledge, Skills, or Values
Students demonstrate higher-order thinking and skills expressed in distinctive ways depending on the context	Chapter 3 Chapter 10	Assessment of Higher-Order Thinking Skills: Application, Critical Thinking, and Problem Solving Table 10.3
Students demonstrate learning skills, self-assessment	Chapter 3	Assessment of Learning and Self-Assessment Skills

Note: This table describes the criterion common to all rubrics and not the criteria that are unique to specific rubrics.

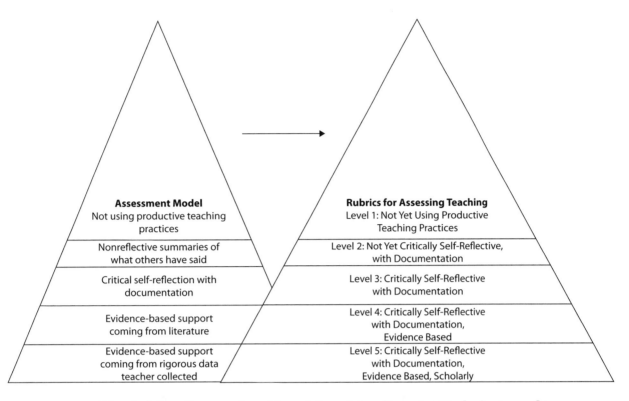

FIGURE A.1   Model for Assessing Teaching Leading to Rubric Levels

Throughout this book I used a pyramid figure to represent the hierarchical model of support for teaching. This hierarchical model corresponds to an assessment model. Figure A.1 illustrates the correspondence between the pyramid levels on the hierarchical assessment model and the rubric levels. The rows on the pyramid lead to the levels on the rubrics.

Rubric Page Template

The rubric page template follows logically from the rationale for the rubric levels as shown in Figure A.1. This template shows where to find explanations for the rubric page format and aspects of the rubrics page. Italics indicate where in this book you will find the rationale and further descriptions.

Guiding Principle: *Chapters 3, 9, 10*

Self-Assessment Criterion: *Chapters 3, 9, 10*

Rubric Quality Levels

❏ Not Yet Using Productive Teaching Practices (I have received feedback)

    Chapter 9

❏ Not Yet Critically Self-Reflective with Documentation (this is the current normative practice)

    Chapters 4, 9, 10

❏ Critically Self-Reflective with Documentation (satisfactory teaching occurs at this level and at the next two levels)

    Chapters 4, 9, 10

❏ Critically Self-Reflective with Documentation, Evidence Based (this must meet everything in previous level)

    Chapters 5, 9, 10

❏ Critically Self-Reflective with Documentation, Evidence Based, Scholarly (this must also meet everything in previous level and the following)

    Chapters 5, 9, 10

Further Clarification or Example of Criterion

Chapter 3

Suggested Sources for Documentation

Chapters 4, 9, 10. See table 9.2.

Rationale for Your Rating

Additional sheets can be attached. Please indicate where the evidence can be found on attached syllabi, student products, or your scholarly products or other documents.

Evidence to Support This Rating

When appropriate, document literature with citations or data collected at your institution to support decisions or action. Cite professional practice guidelines or standards if used.

    Chapters 5, 9

A
Rubrics for Improving Face-to-Face, Laboratory, or Online Teaching for Autonomous Instructors

Contents

A12 Students Demonstrate Learning Skills and Self-Assessment Skills

Optional Criteria

Rubric for the Organizing Principle of Structure for Teaching and Learning

A13 Help Students to Acquire or Use Intrinsic Motivation to Learn

Rubrics for the Organizing Principle of Instructional Design Responsibilities

A14 Creativity in Teaching

A15 Development of New or Unique Courses or Revision of Existing Ones

A16 Contribute to the Enhancement of Instructional Programs or Accreditation Process

Course Alignment Table

THE RUBRICS
Essential Criteria

Rubrics for the Organizing Principle of the Structure for Teaching and Learning

A1 Develop Learning Outcomes and Use Them to Select Teaching/ Learning Methods

Guiding Principle: Structure for teaching and learning

Self-Assessment Criterion: Develop challenging yet reasonable learning outcomes for the acquisition of knowledge, skills, or values, and use them to select appropriate teaching/learning methods and educational technologies—An Essential Criterion

Rubric Quality Levels

❑ Not Yet Using Productive Teaching Practices (I have received feedback)

I do not have specified learning goals <u>or</u>
I do not use appropriate or active learning activities to facilitate learning <u>or</u>
I use methods that are in conflict with the learning goals

❑ Not Yet Critically Self-Reflective with Documentation (this is the current normative practice)

I do not critically reflect on the relationship between my learning outcomes or teaching/learning methods and technologies

❑ Critically Self-Reflective with Documentation (satisfactory teaching occurs at this level and at the next two levels)

I use a variety of teaching/learning methods and technologies that are appropriate for student learning goals <u>and</u>
I create a respectful environment to foster learning (as defined by sensitivity to ethnic and cultural diversity) <u>and</u>
I critically reflect on the relationship between my learning outcomes or teaching/learning methods and technologies

❑ Critically Self-Reflective with Documentation, Evidence Based (this must meet everything in the previous level)

Literature or data from students inform my choice of the selected teaching/learning methods or educational technologies to foster mastery of learning outcomes (cite literature references)

❑ Critically Self-Reflective with Documentation, Evidence Based, Scholarly (this must meet everything in the previous level)

I provide

- A clear rationale for my choice of my teaching/learning methods and technologies <u>and</u>
- Evidence from student products that my teaching/learning methods facilitate students reaching learning goals

Further Clarification or Example of Criterion

Use of laboratory activities that require only one correct answer is a conflict when the goal of the course is inquiry learning

Suggested Sources for Documentation

- Higher education literature, either in general or discipline specific (e.g., epistemology of the discipline)
- Professional organizations devoted to higher education (e.g., AAC&U) or discipline-specific organizations that define learning outcomes of undergraduate, graduate, or professional education in general or in a discipline (e.g., American Society for Engineering Education)
- Regional accreditation, professional, or discipline accreditation agencies
- Review how students did on higher-order thinking activities
- Self-review of course materials that include a summary statement illustrating that the teaching/learning methods are appropriate for the student learning goals; course materials may include course syllabi, assignments, teaching/learning activities
- Reports from students, audio or video recording of student performance, or explanation of it
- Student course evaluations (i.e., information from standard or course-specific form)
- Self or peer review of student products (peer reviewed is preferred)
- Feedback from teaching assistants
- Rationale for your rating

Rationale for Your Rating

Additional sheets can be attached. Please indicate where the evidence can be found on attached syllabi, student products, or your scholarly products or other documents.

_____

_____

_____

Assessing and Improving Your Teaching: Strategies and Rubrics for Faculty Growth and Student Learning by Phyllis Blumberg. Copyright © 2014 by John Wiley & Sons, Inc. Reproduced by permission of Jossey-Bass, a Brand of Wiley. www.wiley.com.

Specify Student Learning Goals

_____

_____

_____

Specify Learning Methods Used

_____

_____

_____

Evidence to Support This Rating

If this evidence comes from syllabi or other documents, please indicate where the evidence can be found on these documents. When appropriate, document literature with citations or data collected at your institution to support decisions or action. Cite professional practice guidelines or standards if used.

_____

_____

_____

_____

A2 Promote Higher-Order Thinking

Guiding Principle: Structure for teaching and learning

Self-Assessment Criterion: Use teaching/learning methods that promote the achievement of challenging yet reasonable learning outcomes, understanding of content, the ability to apply the content, use critical thinking, and solve problems related to this discipline—An Essential Criterion

Rubric Quality Levels

❑ Not Yet Using Productive Teaching Practices (I have received feedback)

I provide content such that students can learn material by mostly memorizing without meaning and associations <u>or</u>

I do not provide enough opportunities for students to learn content with understanding or solve problems <u>or</u>

I provide a limited range of experiences that allow the student to grow <u>or</u>

I do not develop adequate guidelines and policies <u>or</u>

I have difficulty explaining the relationships between different learning experiences

❑ Not Yet Critically Self-Reflective with Documentation (this is the current normative practice)

I do not critically reflect on the relationship between my teaching/learning methods and the ability to acquire higher-order learning

❑ Critically Self-Reflective with Documentation (satisfactory teaching occurs at this level and at the next two levels)

I document that I

• Provide opportunities for all students, including the low-performing students, to learn content, develop an understanding of the content, an ability to solve problems, and grow <u>and</u>

• Provide challenging yet reasonable expectations for student learning <u>and</u>

• Recognize when students have not met learning outcomes <u>and</u>

• Develop adequate guidelines and policies <u>and</u>

• Critically reflect on the relationship between my teaching/learning methods and the ability to acquire higher-order learning

❑ Critically Self-Reflective with Documentation, Evidence Based (this must meet everything in the previous level)

Literature or data from students inform my choice of the selected:

• Teaching/learning methods to promote understanding, problem-solving skills, or ability to apply the content <u>and</u>

• Special efforts to help low-performing students to achieve (cite literature references) <u>and</u>

I articulate a clear and explicit rationale for the methods to develop them

❑ Critically Self-Reflective with Documentation, Evidence Based, Scholarly (this must meet everything in the previous level)

I create a scholarly product based on data about the teaching/learning used to promote the understanding of the content, the ability to apply the content, use critical thinking, and solve problems related to this discipline

Suggested Sources for Documentation

- Self-review of course materials, including course syllabi, assignments, teaching/learning activities, assessment methods, and activities
- A summary statement illustrating that the teaching/learning and assessment methods promote understanding, ability to apply the content, and solve problems
- Audio or video recording of student performance or explanation of it
- Self- or peer review of student products and personal statements (peer reviewed is preferred)
- Reports from students, student course evaluations (i.e., information from standard or course-specific form)
- Peer-reviewed presentation or publication
- Feedback from teaching assistants

Rationale for Your Rating

Additional sheets can be attached. Please indicate where the evidence can be found on attached syllabi, student products, or your scholarly products or other documents.

_____

_____

_____

Evidence to Support This Rating

When appropriate, document literature with citations or data collected at your institution to support decisions or action. Attach draft or completed scholarly product. Cite professional practice guidelines or standards if used.

_____

_____

_____

A3   Provide Feedback to Students to Foster Greater Learning

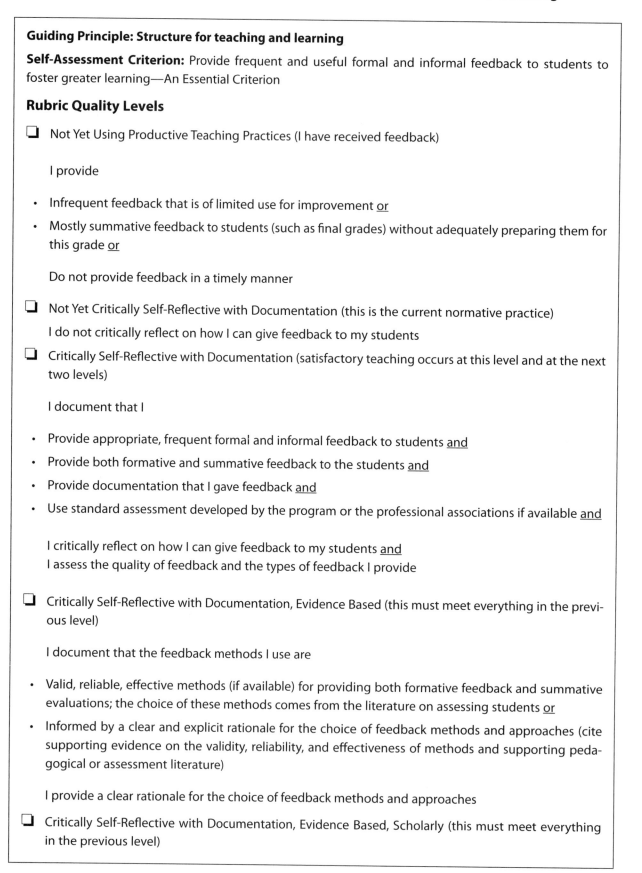

Guiding Principle: Structure for teaching and learning

Self-Assessment Criterion: Provide frequent and useful formal and informal feedback to students to foster greater learning—An Essential Criterion

Rubric Quality Levels

❑   Not Yet Using Productive Teaching Practices (I have received feedback)

I provide

•   Infrequent feedback that is of limited use for improvement <u>or</u>
•   Mostly summative feedback to students (such as final grades) without adequately preparing them for this grade <u>or</u>

Do not provide feedback in a timely manner

❑   Not Yet Critically Self-Reflective with Documentation (this is the current normative practice)
I do not critically reflect on how I can give feedback to my students

❑   Critically Self-Reflective with Documentation (satisfactory teaching occurs at this level and at the next two levels)

I document that I

•   Provide appropriate, frequent formal and informal feedback to students <u>and</u>
•   Provide both formative and summative feedback to the students <u>and</u>
•   Provide documentation that I gave feedback <u>and</u>
•   Use standard assessment developed by the program or the professional associations if available <u>and</u>

I critically reflect on how I can give feedback to my students <u>and</u>
I assess the quality of feedback and the types of feedback I provide

❑   Critically Self-Reflective with Documentation, Evidence Based (this must meet everything in the previous level)

I document that the feedback methods I use are

•   Valid, reliable, effective methods (if available) for providing both formative feedback and summative evaluations; the choice of these methods comes from the literature on assessing students <u>or</u>
•   Informed by a clear and explicit rationale for the choice of feedback methods and approaches (cite supporting evidence on the validity, reliability, and effectiveness of methods and supporting pedagogical or assessment literature)

I provide a clear rationale for the choice of feedback methods and approaches

❑   Critically Self-Reflective with Documentation, Evidence Based, Scholarly (this must meet everything in the previous level)

I provide evidence from student products that they improved based on this feedback

Suggested Sources for Documentation

- Documented use of standardized assessment tools or valid and reliable instructor-created assessments
- Documentation using critical incident observations
- Self-assessment tools
- Peer assessments on team projects, student peer feedback
- Review of assessment exercises or analysis from performance on classroom assessment techniques
- Provide feedback to students to foster greater learning
- Review of student products, drafts, and revisions
- Review of student portfolios/e-portfolios
- Higher education literature, either in general or discipline specific (e.g., epistemology of the discipline)
- Notes of meetings with students, personal progress notes on students, documentation from calendar, appointments
- Reports from students
- Checkpoints, feedback on progress of larger projects, comments or tracked changes in documents
- Audio or video recording of student performance or explanation of it
- Student course evaluations (i.e., information from standard or course-specific form)
- Self- or peer review of student products (peer reviewed is preferred)
- Student self-assessment on which feedback methods worked well for them of it
- Feedback from teaching assistants

Rationale for Your Rating

Additional sheets can be attached. Please indicate where the evidence can be found on attached syllabi, student products, or your scholarly products or other documents.

_____

_____

_____

Evidence to Support This Rating

When appropriate, document literature with citations or data collected at your institution to support decisions or action. Cite professional practice guidelines or standards if used.

_____

_____

_____

_____

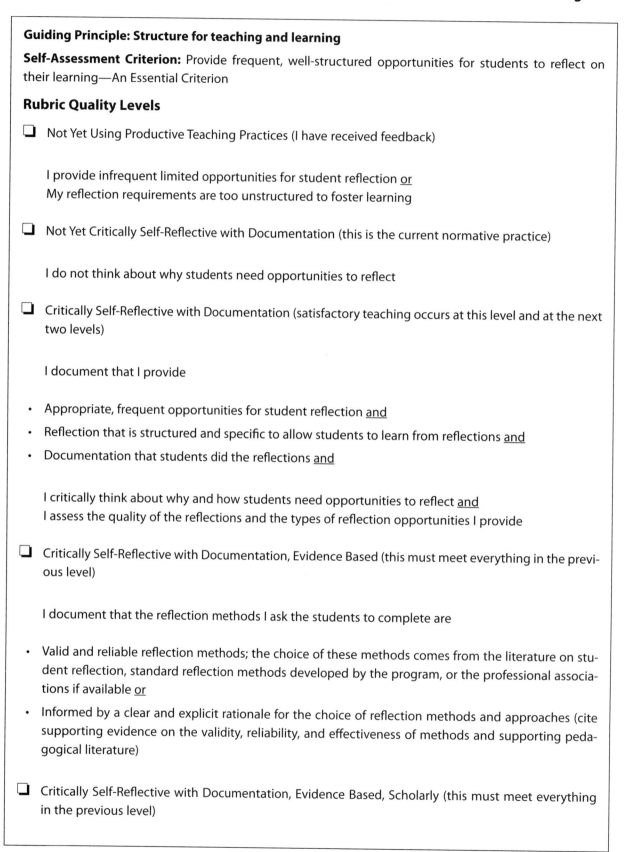

A4   Provide Opportunities for Students to Reflect on Their Learning

Guiding Principle: Structure for teaching and learning

Self-Assessment Criterion: Provide frequent, well-structured opportunities for students to reflect on their learning—An Essential Criterion

Rubric Quality Levels

❏ Not Yet Using Productive Teaching Practices (I have received feedback)

    I provide infrequent limited opportunities for student reflection <u>or</u>
    My reflection requirements are too unstructured to foster learning

❏ Not Yet Critically Self-Reflective with Documentation (this is the current normative practice)

    I do not think about why students need opportunities to reflect

❏ Critically Self-Reflective with Documentation (satisfactory teaching occurs at this level and at the next two levels)

    I document that I provide

- Appropriate, frequent opportunities for student reflection <u>and</u>
- Reflection that is structured and specific to allow students to learn from reflections <u>and</u>
- Documentation that students did the reflections <u>and</u>

    I critically think about why and how students need opportunities to reflect <u>and</u>
    I assess the quality of the reflections and the types of reflection opportunities I provide

❏ Critically Self-Reflective with Documentation, Evidence Based (this must meet everything in the previous level)

    I document that the reflection methods I ask the students to complete are

- Valid and reliable reflection methods; the choice of these methods comes from the literature on student reflection, standard reflection methods developed by the program, or the professional associations if available <u>or</u>
- Informed by a clear and explicit rationale for the choice of reflection methods and approaches (cite supporting evidence on the validity, reliability, and effectiveness of methods and supporting pedagogical literature)

❏ Critically Self-Reflective with Documentation, Evidence Based, Scholarly (this must meet everything in the previous level)

I provide

- A clear rationale for the choice of reflection methods and approaches <u>and</u>
- Evidence from student products that they learned as a result of these reflections

Suggested Sources for Documentation

- Copies of reflection assignments given to the students and their answers
- Student-generated evaluations of experiences (i.e., information from standard or course-specific form)
- Notes of meetings, conferences with students, memos sent to students
- Student reflections, evaluations, blogs, surveys
- Student assessment data
- Review of student products
- Reports from students
- Higher education literature, either in general or discipline specific (e.g., epistemology of the discipline)
- Documented use of standardized reflection tools
- Critical incident observations
- Student portfolios/e-portfolios
- Valid and reliable assessments that the instructor creates
- Concept maps
- End-of-semester student reflections on whether they achieved the goals or outcomes of the course and how they achieved them, reflections on learning

Rationale for Your Rating

Additional sheets can be attached. Please indicate where the evidence can be found on attached syllabi, student products, or your scholarly products or other documents.

_____

_____

_____

Evidence to Support This Rating

When appropriate, document literature with citations or data collected at your institution to support decisions or action. Cite professional practice guidelines or standards if used.

_____

_____

_____

A5   Use Consistent Policies and Processes to Assess Students

Guiding Principle: Structure for teaching and learning

Self-Assessment Criterion: Use consistent policies and processes to assess students—An Essential Criterion

Rubric Quality Levels

❏ Not Yet Using Productive Teaching Practices (I have received feedback)

I assign final grades without providing student with a rationale for the grades <u>or</u>
I do not grade and return student work in a timely way with feedback provided <u>or</u>
I use inconsistent or unexplained methods to assess students

❏ Not Yet Critically Self-Reflective with Documentation (this is the current normative practice)
I do not critically reflect on my selection of policies and processes on assessment

❏ Critically Self-Reflective with Documentation (satisfactory teaching occurs at this level and at the next two levels)

I document that I consistently

*   Use specified grading standards, such as grading rubrics and predetermined weights of projects or assignments, to assign grades <u>and</u>
*   Maintain fair and consistent standards of grading <u>and</u>
*   Grade and return student work in a timely way with feedback provided <u>and</u>
*   Critically think about my policies and process to assess students

❏ Critically Self-Reflective with Documentation, Evidence Based (this must meet everything in the previous level)

I provide documentation that grading standards for all of the students are used appropriately and consistently <u>or</u>
I use professional literature on assessing students

❏ Critically Self-Reflective with Documentation, Evidence Based, Scholarly (this must meet everything in the previous level)

I provide evidence from students that they believe their grades accurately reflect grading standards <u>or</u>
I create a scholarly product based on data about assessment of students

Suggested Sources for Documentation

*   Review of assessment plans
*   Review of comments made to students on their projects

Assessing and Improving Your Teaching: Strategies and Rubrics for Faculty Growth and Student Learning by Phyllis Blumberg. Copyright © 2014 by John Wiley & Sons, Inc. Reproduced by permission of Jossey-Bass, a Brand of Wiley. www.wiley.com.

- Review of assessment tools
- Self-reflections
- Peer-reviewed presentation or publication

Rationale for Your Rating

Additional sheets can be attached. Please indicate where the evidence can be found on attached syllabi, student products, or your scholarly products or other documents.

_____

_____

_____

Evidence to Support This Rating

When appropriate, document literature with citations or data collected at your institution to support decisions or action. Attach draft or completed scholarly product. Cite professional practice guidelines or standards if used.

_____

_____

_____

A6 Ensure Students Have Successful Learning Experiences through My Availability and Accessibility

Guiding Principle: Structure for teaching and learning

Self-Assessment Criterion: Ensure students have successful learning experiences through my availability and accessibility—An Essential Criterion

Rubric Quality Levels

❑ Not Yet Using Productive Teaching Practices (I have received feedback)

I am not available or accessible to students for one-on-one consultation or to answer questions

❑ Not Yet Critically Self-Reflective with Documentation (this is the current normative practice)

I do not reflect on how I ensure that students have successful learning experiences through availability and accessibility given they may be in different time zones and do not meet with me in person

❑ Critically Self-Reflective with Documentation (satisfactory teaching occurs at this level and at the next two levels)

I document that I am available or accessible for one-on-one consultation or to answer questions <u>and</u> I critically reflect on how I ensure that students have successful learning experiences through availability and accessibility even in distance learning situations given that students may be in different time zones and do not meet with me in person

❑ Critically Self-Reflective with Documentation, Evidence Based (this must meet everything in the previous level)

I document (through documentation of appointments with students, self-reflection, and electronic conversations) how I am available for students and help them have successful learning experiences

❑ Critically Self-Reflective with Documentation, Evidence Based, Scholarly (this must meet everything in the previous level)

I provide documentation from students that I was routinely available, accessible, and very instrumental in providing successful learning experiences

Suggested Sources for Documentation

- Notes of meetings with students
- Personal progress notes on students
- Documentation from calendar, appointments, electronic discussions
- Reports from students

- Student course evaluations (i.e., information from standard or course-specific form)
- Review of student products
- Audio or video recording of student project or explanation of it

Rationale for Your Rating

Additional sheets can be attached. Please indicate where the evidence can be found on attached syllabi, student products, or your scholarly products or other documents.

_____

_____

_____

Evidence to Support This Rating

When appropriate, document literature citation or data collected at this institution to support decisions or action. Cite professional practice guidelines or standards if used.

_____

_____

_____

_____

Rubrics for the Organizing Principle of Instructional Design Responsibilities

A7 Align Learning Outcomes

Guiding Principle: Instructional design responsibilities

Self-Assessment Criterion: Align learning outcomes: Internally with teaching and learning activities and assessments and within an educational program—An Essential Criterion

Rubric Quality Levels

❑ Not Yet Using Productive Teaching Practices (I have received feedback)

I do not align objectives, teaching/learning methods, and assessments in terms of cognitive process level required

❑ Not Yet Critically Self-Reflective with Documentation (this is the current normative practice)

I do not critically reflect on concepts of learning outcome alignment

❑ Critically Self-Reflective with Documentation (satisfactory teaching occurs at this level and at the next two levels)

I show (on a table or figure) how planned objectives, teaching/learning methods, and assessment methods both within a course and across the educational program are aligned or misaligned and
I have a plan to make them aligned if misalignment occurs and
I critically reflect on concepts of learning outcome alignment

❑ Critically Self-Reflective with Documentation, Evidence Based (this must meet everything in the previous level)

Literature or data inform my choice of consistent cognitive process level for the objectives, teaching/learning methods, and assessment methods (cite literature references) and
I provide evidence that objectives, teaching/learning methods, and assessment are explicitly, coherently, and consistently aligned in my syllabus and delivery

❑ Critically Self-Reflective with Documentation, Evidence Based, Scholarly (this must meet everything in the previous level)

I have data to show that the course is aligned between and across courses in the curriculum in terms of prerequisites or more advanced courses and
I provide an evidence-based rationale supported by student learning for my choice of consistent levels of cognitive process for the objectives, teaching/learning, and assessment

Further Clarification or Example of Criterion

Objectives, teaching/learning, and assessment methods are at a consistent cognitive process level on a learning taxonomy hierarchy (i.e., from remember through apply to create).

Suggested Sources for Documentation

- Self-review of course materials that include a summary statement illustrating that the course is aligned; course materials may include syllabi, assignments, teaching/learning methods and activities, assessment methods, and activities
- Plot or table showing alignment (see the alignment table on the last page of this rubric set for a way to plot alignment)
- Peer or self-review of alignment data
- Peer or self-review of levels of learning outcomes, learning activities, and assessments

Rationale for Your Rating

Additional sheets can be attached. Please indicate where the evidence can be found on attached syllabi, student products, or your scholarly products or other documents.

_____

_____

_____

Evidence to Support This Rating

Attach an alignment plot or figure, if used, such as given at the end of the rubrics set.
When appropriate, document literature with citations or data collected at your institution to support decisions or action. Cite professional practice guidelines or standards if used.

_____

_____

_____

_____

A8   Organize All Educational Experiences to Facilitate Learning

Guiding Principle: Instructional design responsibilities

Self-Assessment Criterion: Organize all educational experiences to facilitate learning—An Essential Criterion

Rubric Quality Levels

❏ Not Yet Using Productive Teaching Practices (I have received feedback)

I do not develop adequate syllabi <u>or</u>
I am disorganized in teaching <u>or</u>
I do not meet deadlines

❏ Not Yet Critically Self-Reflective with Documentation (this is the current normative practice)

I do not critically reflect on the organization of the educational experiences

❏ Critically Self-Reflective with Documentation (satisfactory teaching occurs at this level and the next two levels)

I document that as perceived by students or peers and my own review of the syllabus and other course material that

• All course materials and course delivery are organized <u>and</u>
• I meet deadlines <u>and</u>
• I return student work in a timely way with feedback provided <u>and</u>
• Students have opportunities to learn from graded work <u>and</u>

I critically reflect on the organization of the educational experiences

❏ Critically Self-Reflective with Documentation, Evidence Based (this must meet everything in the previous level)

I provide a rationale to support organization and delivery. Course organization is informed by

• Student achievement or feedback <u>or</u>
• Evidence-based understanding of the content such as using overarching, organizing themes of the discipline

❏ Critically Self-Reflective with Documentation, Evidence Based, Scholarly (this must meet everything in the previous level)

I provide evidence from student products that students understand content well because

- Students have integrated into their thinking the organizing themes of the discipline <u>or</u>

- Students use the organizing themes as scaffolds on which they built further learning <u>or</u>

  I create a scholarly product based on data about organization of teaching

Further Clarification or Example of Criterion

An overarching, organizing theme is a discipline-specific conceptual framework that helps experts integrate much of the material. Experts use these themes to learn new material: for example, the relationship of structure and function is an organizing theme of biology, homeostasis is an organizing theme in physiology, and the drive to modernity is an organizing theme in history.

Suggested Sources for Documentation

- Higher education literature, either in general or discipline specific (e.g., epistemology of the discipline)

- Self-review of course materials that includes a summary statement illustrating the overall organization and organizing themes; course materials may include course syllabi, assignments, teaching/learning activities, assessment activities

- Audio or video recording of student performance or explanation of it

- Report from chair from an annual evaluation, class observation, or ongoing discussions

- Student course evaluations (i.e., information from standard or course-specific form)

- Reflections from students

- Concept map integrating entire course

- Review of how I explain to students how entire course (in-class work, assignments, assessments) is integrated

- Self- or peer review of student products (peer reviewed is preferred)

- Feedback from teaching assistants

Rationale for Your Rating

Additional sheets can be attached. Please indicate where the evidence can be found on attached syllabi, student products, or your scholarly products or other documents.

_____

_____

_____

Evidence to Support This Rating

List the organizing schemes you used, if any.

_____

_____

_____

When appropriate, document literature with citations or data collected at your institution to support decisions or action. Cite professional practice guidelines or standards if used.

_____

_____

_____

_____

A9   Conduct Reviews and Revisions of Teaching

Guiding Principle: Instructional design responsibilities

Self-Assessment Criterion: Engage in self-analysis and reflection of teaching as part of a review and revision process including appraisal of content currency and accuracy—An Essential Criterion

Rubric Quality Levels

❑ Not Yet Using Productive Teaching Practices (I have received feedback)

I do not

- Collect or analyze course assessment data <u>or</u>
- Conduct self-analysis or reflections on my teaching <u>or</u>
- Change a course as a result of consistent feedback or reviews or changes in content <u>or</u>
- Share these reflections on annual performance reviews or other assessments of me <u>or</u>

I have received feedback that I lack knowledge and/or I do not use accurate and current content

❑ Not Yet Critically Self-Reflective with Documentation (this is the current normative practice**)**

I do not critically analyze or reflect on how and why I can review or revise teaching, including content currency and accuracy

❑ Critically Self-Reflective with Documentation (satisfactory teaching occurs at this level and at the next two levels)

I collect assessment data or feedback data from the students <u>and</u>
I conduct self-analysis or reflections on my teaching as part of a review and revision process to

- Identify areas for improvement <u>and</u>
- Change experience or expectations as a result of consistent feedback or reviews or changes in content <u>and</u>
- Share these reflections or other assessments as necessary <u>and</u>

I recognize when students have not met learning outcomes <u>and</u>
I have adequate knowledge and I use accurate and current content

❑ Critically Self-Reflective with Documentation, Evidence Based (this must meet everything in the previous level)

I use assessment data, self-analysis, reflection, or pedagogical literature to

- Propose or implement significant changes to courses if necessary <u>or</u>
- Show why the contents should be kept the same <u>or</u>
- Offer a rationale for not incorporating suggested changes

❑ Critically Self-Reflective with Documentation, Evidence Based, Scholarly (this must meet everything in the previous level)

I provide evidence through assessment data showing students learning and that the learning outcomes are met <u>or</u>

I provide evidence to show how teaching has changed and improved as a result of assessment or self-analysis <u>or</u>

I create a scholarly product (i.e., peer-reviewed publication) that demonstrates student learning using course assessment data, reflection, revisions of teaching, course planning, and reflection on teaching

Suggested Sources for Documentation

- Personal reflections or journals
- Student course evaluations (i.e., standard or course-specific form)
- Course assessment data (e.g., pre- and postcourse assessment data)
- Higher education literature, either in general or discipline specific (e.g., epistemology of the discipline)
- Audio or video recording of student performance or explanation of it
- Peer assessment data, discussions with peers or debriefings after assessment, peer coaching, peer observation
- Peer-reviewed presentation or publication
- Chair report from an annual evaluation, class observation, or ongoing discussions
- Feedback from teaching assistants
- Teaching portfolios
- Notes after grading each project with notes on what possible changes to make in the future
- Discussions from faculty learning communities

Rationale for Your Rating

Additional sheets can be attached. Please indicate where the evidence can be found on attached syllabi, student products, or your scholarly products or other documents.

_____

_____

_____

Evidence to Support This Rating

Cite pedagogical literature, professional practice guidelines, or standards if used to support your rationale. When appropriate, provide data collected by you or your department to support decisions or action. Attach draft or completed scholarly product.

_____

_____

_____

Rubrics for the Organizing Principle of Learning Outcomes

A10   Students Achieve Learning Outcomes of Acquisition of Knowledge, Skills, or Values

Guiding Principle: Learning Outcomes

Self-Assessment Criterion: Students achieve challenging yet reasonable learning outcomes of acquisition of knowledge, skills, or values—An Essential Criterion

Rubric Quality Levels

❑   Not Yet Using Productive Teaching Practices (I have received feedback)

I use assessments that show that students do not acquire knowledge <u>or</u> skills <u>or</u> values <u>or</u> I do not assess students on these criteria

❑   Not Yet Critically Self-Reflective with Documentation (this is the current normative practice)

I do not critically reflect on why and how students achieve learning outcomes of knowledge, skills, or values

❑   Critically Self-Reflective with Documentation (satisfactory teaching occurs at this level and at the next two levels)

I provide assessment opportunities for students to demonstrate their acquisition of knowledge, skills, or values <u>and</u>
I document that most students, including low-performing students, acquire knowledge <u>or</u> skills <u>or</u> values <u>and</u>
I critically reflect on why and how students achieve learning outcomes of knowledge, skills, or values; the choice of the knowledge, these skills, or the values might be based on departmental or college expectations or accreditation agencies

❑   Critically Self-Reflective with Documentation, Evidence Based (this must meet everything in the previous level)

I articulate a clear, explicit, and rationale for choice of the specific knowledge, skills, and values the students demonstrate (cite literature references to support the rationale; if this rationale is based on departmental or college expectations or accreditation agencies, cite these expectations)

❑   Critically Self-Reflective with Documentation, Evidence Based, Scholarly (this must meet everything in the previous level)

I provide

· Evidence from student products that students have gained competence in this knowledge, these skills, or these values and have mastered relevant learning outcomes <u>or</u>

- Create a scholarly product (i.e., peer-reviewed publication) that demonstrates students acquired the knowledge, developed skills, and values

Suggested Sources for Documentation

- Self- or peer review of student products (peer reviewed is preferred)
- Audio or video recording of student performance or explanation of it
- Higher education literature, either in general or discipline specific (e.g., epistemology of the discipline)
- Student performance on standardized discipline exams such as ETS or GRE discipline exams
- Follow-up of how students did in more advanced courses that build on what they learned in my course
- Feedback from teaching assistants
- Student performance on competency or practical skills exams
- Student portfolios/e-portfolios

Rationale for Your Rating

Additional sheets can be attached. Please indicate where the evidence can be found on attached syllabi, student products, or your scholarly products or other documents.

_____

_____

_____

What Knowledge, Skills, or Values Were Achieved?

_____

_____

_____

Evidence to Support This Rating

When appropriate, document literature with citations or data collected at your institution to support decisions or action. Cite professional practice guidelines or standards if used.

_____

_____

_____

_____

A11   Students Demonstrate Higher-Order Thinking

Guiding Principle: Learning outcomes

Self-Assessment Criterion: Students demonstrate the ability to apply the content, use critical thinking, and solve problems related to this discipline at a level that is expected and appropriate for the course—An Essential Criterion

Rubric Quality Levels

❏ Not Yet Using Productive Teaching Practices (I have received feedback)

I use assessments that show that students

- Learn content as isolated facts without meaning and associations <u>or</u>
- Learn content but are unable to apply the content, use critical thinking, or solve problems <u>or</u>
- Fail to learn <u>or</u>

I do not assess the students' understanding, problem solving, or application

❏ Not Yet Critically Self-Reflective with Documentation (this is the current normative practice)

I do not critically reflect on why and how students achieve higher-order learning outcomes

❏ Critically Self-Reflective with Documentation (satisfactory teaching occurs at this level and at the next two levels)

I provide assessment opportunities for students to demonstrate their ability to apply content, think critically, or solve problems <u>and</u>
I document that most students, including low-performing students, acquire some abilities to apply the content, use critical thinking, or solve problems <u>and</u>
I critically reflect on why and how students achieve higher-order learning outcomes

❏ Critically Self-Reflective with Documentation, Evidence Based (this must meet everything in the previous level)

I articulate a clear, explicit, and evidence-based rationale for choice of the application, critical thinking, and problem-solving skills the students demonstrate (cite literature references to support the rationale; if this rationale is based on departmental or college expectations or accreditation agencies, cite these expectations)

❏ Critically Self-Reflective with Documentation, Evidence Based, Scholarly (this must meet everything in the previous level)

I provide evidence through student products that students can apply the content, use critical thinking, and solve problems <u>or</u>
I create a scholarly product based on data showing that students achieved these objectives

Suggested Sources for Documentation

- Self- or peer review of student products (peer reviewed is preferred)

- Audio or video recording of student performance or explanation of it

- Higher education literature, either in general or discipline specific (e.g., epistemology of the discipline)

- Feedback from teaching assistants

- Writing an authentic document to be used outside class, for example, a letter to a newspaper editor or a brief for legislators on an issue covered in class

- Review of how students did on authentic problems

- Student portfolios/e-portfolios

- Follow-up of how students did in more advanced courses that build on what they learned in my course

Rationale for Your Rating

Additional sheets can be attached. Please indicate where the evidence can be found on attached syllabi, student products, or your scholarly products or other documents.

_____

_____

_____

An Example of the Kinds of Problems Students Can Solve

_____

_____

_____

Evidence to Support This Rating

When appropriate, document literature with citations or data collected at your institution to support decisions or action. Cite professional practice guidelines or standards if used.

_____

_____

_____

_____

A12   Students Demonstrate Learning Skills and Self-Assessment Skills

Guiding Principle: Learning outcomes

Self-Assessment Criterion: Students demonstrate learning skills that can transcend disciplinary content (e.g., time management or knowing where to look for information) and self-assessment skills (assessment of strengths/weaknesses or of own learning abilities)—An Essential Criterion

Rubric Quality Levels

❏   Not Yet Using Productive Teaching Practices (I have received feedback)

   I do not assess students on whether they have acquired learning skills <u>or</u> can self-assess their own ability to learn <u>or</u> of their strengths and weaknesses <u>or</u>
   I do not assess students on these criteria

❏   Not Yet Critically Self-Reflective with Documentation (this is the current normative practice)

   I do not critically reflect on why and how students can demonstrate learning skills

❏   Critically Self-Reflective with Documentation (satisfactory teaching occurs at this level and at the next two levels)

   I provide assessment opportunities for students to demonstrate learning and self-assessment skills <u>and</u>
   I document that most students, including the low-performing students, acquire some learning and self-assessment skills <u>and</u>
   I critically reflect on why and how students can demonstrate learning skills; the choice of these skills might be based on departmental or college expectations or accreditation agencies

❏   Critically Self-Reflective with Documentation, Evidence Based (this must meet everything in the previous level)

   I document that most students, including low-performing students, demonstrate their mastery of learning-to-learn skills and self-assessment skills <u>and</u>
   I articulate a clear, explicit, and evidence-based rationale for choice of the specific skills the students demonstrate (cite literature references to support the rationale; if this rationale is based on departmental or college expectations or accreditation agencies, cite these expectations)

❏   Critically Self-Reflective with Documentation, Evidence Based, Scholarly (this must meet everything in the previous level)

   I provide evidence from student products that students have gained competence in these skills and have mastered relevant learning outcomes <u>or</u>
   I create a scholarly product (i.e., peer-reviewed publication) that demonstrates students developed learning skills

Further Clarification or Example of Criterion

These skills are also called process outcomes or metacognitive skills. Learning skills include time management, self-monitoring, goal setting, how to do independent reading, determining a personal need to know more, knowing whom to ask or where to seek information, determining when the need is met, and development of self-awareness of own learning abilities. Self-assessment skills include assessment of learning abilities and assessment of strengths and weaknesses.

Suggested Sources for Documentation

- Self- or peer review of student products (peer reviewed is preferred)
- Audio or video recording of student performance or explanation of it
- Higher education literature, either in general or discipline specific (e.g., epistemology of the discipline)
- Feedback from teaching assistants
- Student portfolios/e-portfolios
- Authentic assessments where the students need to use these learning skills
- Follow-up of how students did in more advanced courses that build on what they learned in my course

Rationale for Your Rating

Additional sheets can be attached. Please indicate where the evidence can be found on attached syllabi, student products, or your scholarly products or other documents.

_____

_____

_____

What Learning Skills Were Developed?

_____

_____

Evidence to Support This Rating

When appropriate, document literature with citations or data collected at your institution to support decisions or action. Cite professional practice guidelines or standards if used.

_____

_____

_____

_____

Optional Criteria
Rubric for the Organizing Principle of Structure for Teaching and Learning

A13   Help Students to Acquire or Use Intrinsic Motivation to Learn

Guiding Principle: Structure for teaching and learning

Self-Assessment Criterion: Help students to acquire or use intrinsic motivation to learn (i.e., personal desire to learn, seeing relevance for individual student goals) while recognizing their extrinsic reasons to earn grades—An Optional Criterion. *Note:* This may not be appropriate in all types of courses.

Rubric Quality Levels

❑ Not Yet Using Productive Teaching Practices (I have received feedback)

I extensively use extrinsic motivators to get students to earn grades or engage in course activities

❑ Not Yet Critically Self-Reflective with Documentation (this is the current normative practice)

I do not critically reflect on why and how students should acquire intrinsic motivation to learn

❑ Critically Self-Reflective with Documentation (satisfactory teaching occurs at this level and at the next two levels)

I provide some opportunities for students to become intrinsically motivated to learn by connecting student goals with educational outcomes, nurturing a personal desire to achieve, and using some extrinsic motivators to get students to engage in course activities <u>and</u>
I critically reflect on why and how students should acquire intrinsic motivation to learn

❑ Critically Self-Reflective with Documentation, Evidence Based (this must meet everything in the previous level)

I articulate how my enthusiasm, abilities, teaching style, or methods provide many opportunities for students to become intrinsically motivated to learn even when the course appears not to fit their personal goals <u>or</u>
I am nominated by students for a teaching award

❑ Critically Self-Reflective with Documentation, Evidence Based, Scholarly (this must meet everything in the previous level)

I provide evidence through student comments or evaluations that my efforts to motivate, inspire, and encourage students have led students to become intrinsically motivated and confident to learn even when the course appears not to fit their personal goals <u>or</u>
I win a teaching award that involves student nominations or input

Suggested Sources for Documentation

- Self- or peer review of student products (peer reviewed is preferred)
- Reports from students
- Audio or video recording of student performance or explanation of it
- Student course evaluations (i.e., information from standard or course specific form)
- Personal reflection
- Peer assessment data
- Feedback from teaching assistants
- Student portfolios/e-portfolios

Rationale for Your Rating

Additional sheets can be attached. Please indicate where the evidence can be found on attached syllabi, student products, or your scholarly products or other documents.

_____

_____

_____

Evidence to Support This Rating

When appropriate, document literature citations or data collected at your institution to support decisions or action. Attach nomination or notification letter for award. Cite professional practice guidelines or standards if used.

_____

_____

_____

Rubrics for the Organizing Principle of Instructional Design Responsibilities

A14   Creativity in Teaching

Guiding Principle: Instructional design responsibilities

Self-Assessment Criterion: Creativity in the way the course is taught or how students are evaluated—An Optional Criterion

Rubric Quality Levels

❑ Not Yet Using Productive Teaching Practices (I have received feedback)

I use very limited creative or innovative inquiry or approaches to teach the course or evaluate the students

❑ Not Yet Critically Self-Reflective with Documentation (this is the current normative practice)

I do not critically reflect on why and how my teaching should be creative

❑ Critically Self-Reflective with Documentation (satisfactory teaching occurs at this level and at the next two levels)

Where appropriate, I use creative or innovative methods, including instructional methods, teaching techniques, or integrating educational technologies to teach courses or evaluate the students <u>and</u> I critically reflect on why and how my teaching should be creative

❑ Critically Self-Reflective with Documentation, Evidence Based (this must meet everything in the previous level)

These creative or innovative methods are informed by literature or data and foster increased student learning and motivation (cite literature references) <u>or</u>
I am nominated by others for an award for teaching innovation

❑ Critically Self-Reflective with Documentation, Evidence Based, Scholarly (this must meet everything in the previous level)

Creates a scholarly product informed by assessment data that the creativity in the way the course is taught or how the students are evaluated achieves increased student learning and motivation <u>or</u>
I have won an award for teaching innovation

Further Clarification or Example of Criterion

Creativity, defined as innovative for the discipline, uses innovative activities or assessments that improve learning.

Suggested Sources for Documentation

- Higher education literature, either in general or discipline specific (e.g., epistemology of the discipline) Self-review of course materials that includes a summary statement illustrating the creativity in the way the course is taught; course materials may include course syllabi, assignments, teaching/learning activities, assessment methods, and activities

- Report from chair from an annual evaluation, memo, or ongoing discussions

- Reports from students

- Student course evaluations (i.e., information from standard or course-specific form)

- Self- or peer review of student products (peer reviewed is preferred)

- Peer-reviewed presentation or publication

Rationale for Your Rating

Additional sheets can be attached. Please indicate where the evidence can be found on attached syllabi, student products, or your scholarly products or other documents.

_____

_____

_____

Evidence to Support This Rating

Attach draft or completed scholarly product or nomination or notification letter for award. If this evidence comes from syllabi or other documents, indicate where the evidence can be found on these documents. When appropriate, document literature with citations or data collected at your institution to support decisions or action. Cite professional practice guidelines or standards if used.

_____

_____

_____

_____

A15   Development of New or Unique Courses or Revision of Existing Ones

Guiding Principle: Instructional design responsibilities

Self-Assessment Criterion: Development of new or unique courses or revision of existing ones, if appropriate—An Optional Criterion

Rubric Quality Levels

❏ Not Yet Using Productive Teaching Practices (I have received feedback)

My course materials were not developed or not developed on time <u>or</u>
Another instructor was asked to assist me to complete the course <u>or</u>
My course design elements are not clear to the students

❏ Not Yet Critically Self-Reflective with Documentation (this is the current normative practice)

I do not critically reflect on how I can develop new or revised courses

❏ Critically Self-Reflective with Documentation (satisfactory teaching occurs at this level and at the next two levels)

I document that

• Course materials were developed on time <u>and</u>
• Material is appropriate and current <u>and</u>
• Design elements were clear to the students <u>and</u>

I critically reflect on how I can develop new or revised courses

❏ Critically Self-Reflective with Documentation, Evidence Based (this must meet everything in the previous level)

I develop or revise course design based on evidence coming from previous course evaluations or literature in higher education (cite literature references) <u>and</u>
I critically reflect on student evaluations to improve teaching and learning

❏ Critically Self-Reflective with Documentation, Evidence Based, Scholarly (this must meet everything in the previous level)

I conduct classroom research to investigate how to teach this course or investigate why the students are learning <u>or</u>
I show evidence that new or revised courses foster student mastery of learning outcomes

Suggested Sources for Documentation

- Classroom research data
- Report from course director
- Peer report or peer review of products developed
- Chair report from an annual evaluation, memo, or ongoing discussions
- Student course evaluations (i.e., information from standard or course-specific form)
- Higher education literature in general or discipline specific (e.g., epistemology of the discipline)

Rationale for Your Rating

Additional sheets can be attached. Please indicate where the evidence can be found on attached syllabi, student products, or your scholarly products or other documents.

_____

_____

_____

Evidence to Support This Rating

When appropriate, document literature with citations or data collected at your institution to support decisions or action. Cite professional practice guidelines or standards if used.

_____

_____

_____

_____

A16   Contribute to the Enhancement of Instructional Programs or Accreditation Process

Guiding Principle: Instructional design responsibilities

Self-Assessment Criterion: Contribute to the enhancement of instructional programs and improvement of the education of the students by developing or revising any of the following: educational programs, educational technology, instructional manual or textbook; submit education proposals; or play a leadership role in the educational accreditation process—An Optional Criterion

Rubric Quality Levels

❏ Not Yet Using Productive Teaching Practices (I have received feedback)

   I did not contribute to

- Enhancing instructional programs <u>or</u>
- Improving the education of students <u>or</u>
- The accreditation process

❏ Not Yet Critically Self-Reflective with Documentation (this is the current normative practice)

   I do not critically reflect on how I can enhance instructional programs

❏ Critically Self-Reflective with Documentation (satisfactory teaching occurs at this level and at the next two levels)

   I document that I contribute to the enhancement of instructional programs and improvement of the education of students through any of the examples listed under the definition of this criterion <u>or</u>
   I document that I play a leadership role in the educational accreditation process <u>and</u>
   I critically reflect on how I can enhance instructional programs

❏ Critically Self-Reflective with Documentation, Evidence Based (this must meet everything in the previous level)

   I have evidence, from either published literature or assessment data, to support my rationale for choices for these contributions, indicating that students have mastered learning outcomes as a result of this work (cite literature references)

❏ Critically Self-Reflective with Documentation, Evidence Based, Scholarly (this must meet everything in the previous level)

   I create a scholarly product based on the

- Enhancement of instructional programs <u>or</u>
- Improvement of the education of students <u>or</u> the accreditation process

Suggested Sources for Documentation

- Review of products developed for educational programs such as
  - Materials for online education or learning activities
  - Instructional manuals, or textbooks
- Review of proposals to improve the educational process
- Peer-reviewed presentation or publication
- Self- or peer review of student products (peer reviewed is preferred)

Rationale for Your Rating

Additional sheets can be attached. Please indicate where the evidence can be found on attached syllabi, student products, or your scholarly products or other documents.

_____

_____

_____

Evidence to Support This Rating

Attach draft or completed scholarly product or nomination or notification letter for award. If this evidence comes from syllabi or other documents, please indicate where the evidence can be found on these documents. When appropriate, document literature with citations or data collected at your institution to support decisions or action. Cite professional practice guidelines or standards if used.

_____

_____

_____

_____

Course Alignment Table

This table shows the alignment of level of learning outcome, teaching, or learning methods, and assessment methods (Blumberg, 2009). What overarching organizing theme of your discipline does this objective relate to?

Directions

1. Use a separate table for each major course learning outcome.

2. Along the learning outcomes row, briefly list one learning outcome in the correct cell(s) according to the level of cognitive process or verb listed.

3. Along the teaching and learning row, briefly list the teaching and learning methods in the correct cell(s) by determining what level of cognitive process the students need to use during the teaching and learning activities.

4. Along the assessment row, briefly list the assessment task requirements in the correct cell(s) by determining what level of cognitive process the students need to use during the assessment tasks.

5. Draw a line or lines connecting the cells marked in these three columns.

   - A straight, vertical line connecting all rows means this is an aligned.
   - One or more diagonal lines, without a corresponding vertical line connecting the learning outcome, illustrates that the course is misaligned.

What level is each of the following?	Aspect is not included in the course	Low level (recognize, recall knowledge)	Medium level (apply, organize, or analyze)	High level (synthesize, critique, or evaluate)
Learning outcome				
Teaching/learning methods				
Assessment task requirements				

C
RUBRICS FOR IMPROVING THE MENTORING OF STUDENTS IN RESEARCH OR ENGINEERING-TYPE DESIGN PROJECTS

These rubrics are for instructors who mentor students in undergraduate, graduate, or postdoctoral research or engineering-type design projects.

Contents

C12 Conduct Reviews and Revisions of Mentoring

Rubrics for the Organizing Principle of Learning Outcomes

C13 Students Achieve Learning Outcomes of Acquisition of Knowledge and Skills

C14 Students Demonstrate Higher-Order Thinking

C15 Students Demonstrate Learning Skills and Continue to Do Research or Design Projects

C16 Results or Products of Research or Project Design Experience for Mentoring Undergraduate Students

C17 Results or Products of Research or Project Design Experience for Mentoring Graduate Students or Postdoctoral Fellows

Optional Criteria

Rubric for the Organizing Principle of Structure for Teaching and Learning

C18 Help Students to Acquire or Use Intrinsic Motivation to Learn

Rubric for the Organizing Principle of Instructional Design Responsibilities

C19 Enhance the Research Experience for All Students

THE RUBRICS
Essential Criteria for Excellent, Effective Mentoring

Rubrics for the Organizing Principle of the Structure for Teaching and Learning

C1   Institute Well-Defined Expectations and Roles for Students

Guiding Principle: Structure for teaching and learning

Self-Assessment Criterion: Institute well-defined expectations and roles for students while engaged in research or project. For all levels of students—An Essential Criterion

Rubric Quality Levels

❏   Not Yet Using Productive Teaching Practices (I have received feedback)

   I do not

- Develop clearly defined expectations for the students <u>or</u>
- Provide an adequate orientation to the research environment and experiential expectations <u>or</u>
- Have realistic expectations for what students can do

❏   Not Yet Critically Self-Reflective with Documentation (this is the current normative practice)

   I do not critically reflect on the student roles and expectations

❏   Critically Self-Reflective with Documentation (satisfactory teaching occurs at this level and at the next two levels)

   I provide an adequate orientation to the environment and research or project expectation <u>and</u>
   I use insight into the research or project to inform my choices in the development of clearly defined expectations for students in different situations <u>and</u>
   I have realistic expectations for what students can do based on level of student and previous research experiences <u>and</u>
   I critically reflect on the student roles and expectations

❏   Critically Self-Reflective with Documentation, Evidence Based (this must meet everything in the previous level)

   Literature or data from students or about the student abilities and experiences inform my choices in the development of student expectations and responsibilities. Cite references for literature.

Assessing and Improving Your Teaching: Strategies and Rubrics for Faculty Growth and Student Learning by Phyllis Blumberg.
Copyright © 2014 by John Wiley & Sons, Inc. Reproduced by permission of Jossey-Bass, a Brand of Wiley. www.wiley.com.

❑ Critically Self-Reflective with Documentation, Evidence Based, Scholarly (this must meet everything in the previous level)

I provide

- A clear rationale for choice of expectations and responsibilities <u>and</u>
- Evidence from student products that expectations and responsibilities are met

Suggested Sources for Documentation

- Personal reflection
- Student-generated evaluations of experiences (i.e., information from standard or course-specific form)
- Student assessment data (e.g., pre- and postassessment data)
- Audio or video recording of student presentation or explanation of it
- Lab notebooks
- Higher education literature, either in general or discipline specific (e.g., epistemology of the discipline)
- Peer assessment data
- Chair or unit director report from an annual evaluation, observation at site, or ongoing discussions

Rationale for Your Rating

Additional sheets can be attached. Please indicate where the evidence can be found on attached syllabi, student products, or your scholarly products or other documents.

_____

_____

_____

Specify the Expectations for the Students

_____

_____

_____

Evidence to Support This Rating

When appropriate, document literature with citations or data collected at your institution to support decisions or action. Cite professional practice guidelines or standards if used.

_____

_____

_____

_____

C2   Plan and Implement Individualized Research or Project Experiences

Guiding Principle: Structure for teaching and learning

Self-Assessment Criterion: Plan and implement individualized research or project experiences. For all levels of students—An Essential Criterion

Rubric Quality Levels

❏   Not Yet Using Productive Teaching Practices (I have received feedback)

   I do not individualize research or project experience to account for individual difference among students <u>or</u>
   I use the same mentoring style with all students regardless of their level and abilities

❏   Not Yet Critically Self-Reflective with Documentation (this is the current normative practice)

   I do not critically reflect on how I plan <u>and</u> implement individualized research or project experiences

❏   Critically Self-Reflective with Documentation (satisfactory teaching occurs at this level and the next two levels)

   I implement individual research or project experiences that are appropriate for the students <u>and</u>
   I recognize when students have not met learning outcomes <u>and</u>
   I adjust mentoring style to ensure student success <u>and</u>
   I critically reflect on how I plan <u>and</u> implement individualized research or project experiences

❏   Critically Self-Reflective with Documentation, Evidence Based (must meet everything in the previous level)

   I reflect on why individual plans were appropriate, show how adjustments were made when necessary, and provide documentation on these reflections (cite literature if appropriate)

❏   Critically Self-Reflective with Documentation, Evidence Based, Scholarly (this must meet everything in the previous level)

   I provide documentation from students that they realize how their research or project experience changed, improved during the course of the research, or was developed to meet their individual needs

Suggested Sources for Documentation

- Personal reflection
- Student-generated evaluations of experiences (i.e., information from standard or course-specific form)
- Student assessment data (e.g., pre- and postassessment data)
- Audio or video recording of student performance or explanation of it

- Higher education literature, either in general or discipline specific (e.g., epistemology of the discipline)
- Peer assessment data
- Chair or research director report from an annual evaluation, observation at site, or ongoing discussions

Rationale for Your Rating

Additional sheets can be attached. Please indicate where the evidence can be found on attached syllabi, student products, or your scholarly products or other documents.

_____

_____

_____

Specify How the Experience Was Individualized

_____

_____

_____

Evidence to Support This Rating

Attach student evidence. If this evidence comes from documents, please indicate where the evidence can be found on these documents. When appropriate, document literature with citations or data collected at your institution to support decisions or action. Cite professional practice guidelines or standards if used.

_____

_____

_____

_____

C3   Provide Opportunities for Students to Learn by Doing

Guiding Principle: Structure for teaching and learning

Self-Assessment Criterion: Provide supervised opportunities for students to learn by doing through modeling. For all levels of students—An Essential Criterion

Rubric Quality Levels

❏ Not Yet Using Productive Teaching Practices (I have received feedback)

I do not provide supervised opportunities for students to learn by doing or perform independently when ready

❏ Not Yet Critically Self-Reflective with Documentation (this is the current normative practice)

I do not critically reflect on how I can provide supervised opportunities for students to learn by doing

❏ Critically Self-Reflective with Documentation (satisfactory teaching occurs at this level and at the next two levels)

I provide a variety of real research or project experiences that accomplish the learning objectives based on understanding of student and the research or project challenge <u>and</u>
I document experiences and the students' assessment of the performance <u>and</u>
I critically reflect on how I can provide supervised opportunities for students to learn by doing

❏ Critically Self-Reflective with Documentation, Evidence Based (must meet everything in the previous level)

I identify experiences and responsibilities based on literature or data (cite references for literature or provide the data) <u>and</u>
I help students grow by increasing expectations

❏ Critically Self-Reflective with Documentation, Evidence Based, Scholarly (this must meet everything in the previous level)

I provide a clear rationale for the learning opportunities and expectations <u>and</u>
Students show evidence that they have risen to increased challenges commensurate with level expected

Suggested Sources for Documentation

- Personal reflection
- Student-generated evaluations of experiences (i.e., information from standard or course-specific form)
- Student assessment data (e.g., pre- and postassessment data)
- Audio or video recording of student presentation or explanation of it

- Higher education literature, either in general or discipline specific (e.g., epistemology of the discipline)
- Peer assessment data
- Chair or unit director report from an annual evaluation, observation at site, or ongoing discussions

Rationale for Your Rating

Additional sheets can be attached. Please indicate where the evidence can be found on attached syllabi, student products, or your scholarly products or other documents.

_____

_____

_____

Evidence to Support This Rating

When appropriate, document literature with citations or data collected at your institution to support decisions or action. Cite professional practice guidelines or standards if used.

_____

_____

_____

_____

C4   Ensure My Availability and Accessibility

Guiding Principle: Structure for teaching and learning

Self-Assessment Criterion: Ensure students have successful research or project experiences through my availability and accessibility. For all levels of students—An Essential Criterion

Rubric Quality Levels

☐ Not Yet Using Productive Teaching Practices (I have received feedback)

I am not available or accessible for one-on-one consultation or to answer questions <u>or</u>
I do not provide an appropriate alternative teacher (i.e., advanced students, professionals/practitioners in the field)

☒ Not Yet Critically Self-Reflective with Documentation (this is the current normative practice)

I do not reflect on how I ensure that students have successful learning experiences through availability and accessibility of appropriate alternative teachers, especially when I am not available

☐ Critically Self-Reflective with Documentation (satisfactory teaching occurs at this level and at the next two levels)

I am available or accessible for one-on-one consultation or to answer questions <u>or</u>
I provide an appropriate alternative mentor (i.e., advanced graduate students, other professors, or researchers in the field) <u>and</u>
I critically reflect on how I ensure that students have successful learning experiences through availability and accessibility of appropriate alternative teachers, especially when I am not available

☐ Critically Self-Reflective with Documentation, Evidence Based (this must meet everything in the previous level)

I document (through documentation of appointments with students, self-reflection) how I am available for students and help students have successful research or project experience

☐ Critically Self-Reflective with Documentation, Evidence Based, Scholarly (this must meet everything in the previous level)

I provide documentation from students that I was routinely available, accessible, and very instrumental in providing for their successful research or project experience

Suggested Sources for Documentation

- Notes of meetings with students
- Personal progress notes on students
- Documentation from calendar, appointments
- Reports from students

- Student course evaluations (i.e., information from standard or course-specific form)
- Review of student products
- Audio or video recording of student project or explanation of it

Rationale for Your Rating

Additional sheets can be attached. Please indicate where the evidence can be found on attached syllabi, student products, or your scholarly products or other documents.

_____

_____

_____

Evidence to Support This Rating

When appropriate, document literature citation or data collected at this institution to support decisions or action. Cite professional practice guidelines or standards if used.

_____

_____

_____

_____

C5   Help Undergraduate Students Understand the Research or Project Design Process and the Decision-Making Criteria

Guiding Principle: Structure for teaching and learning

Self-Assessment Criterion: Help students understand the research or project design process and decision-making criteria. For mentoring undergraduate students—An Essential Criterion

Rubric Quality Levels

❏   Not Yet Using Productive Teaching Practices (I have received feedback)

I do not help students see the difference between work done in laboratory courses and research or products <u>or</u>
I do not explain the purpose and desired outcomes resulting from activities <u>or</u>
I allow students to constantly ask if they are correct because they think there is a correct answer

❏   Not Yet Critically Self-Reflective with Documentation (this is the current normative practice)

I do not critically reflect on how I can

- Help students understand the research or project design process <u>or</u>
- Explain decision-making criteria

❏   Critically Self-Reflective with Documentation (satisfactory teaching occurs at this level and at the next two levels)

I critically reflect on how I help students identify and suggest ways to test appropriate hypotheses or problems in the research or design project <u>and</u>
I reflect on how I explain the purpose and desired outcomes resulting from activities

❏   Critically Self-Reflective with Documentation, Evidence Based (this must meet everything in the previous level)

I document how I help students identify possible solutions to authentic research or design problems; the literature helps to identify these authentic problems <u>and</u>
I use evidence-based literature and guidelines to explain decision making (cite references for literature) <u>and</u>
I discuss implementation of decisions and policies developed

❏   Critically Self-Reflective with Documentation, Evidence Based, Scholarly (this must meet everything in the previous level)

I document how I help students function independently in research or project design at a level that is appropriate for the student yet being mindful of when to intervene <u>and</u>
I provide evidence through student products that they understand decision-making criteria

Assessing and Improving Your Teaching: Strategies and Rubrics for Faculty Growth and Student Learning by Phyllis Blumberg. Copyright © 2014 by John Wiley & Sons, Inc. Reproduced by permission of Jossey-Bass, a Brand of Wiley. www.wiley.com.

Suggested Sources for Documentation

- Personal reflection
- Student-generated evaluations of experiences (i.e., information from standard or course-specific form)
- Personal progress notes on students
- Notes of meetings with students
- Student reflections, evaluations
- Memos sent to students
- Student assessment data
- Review of student products, including lab notebook, reports
- Reports from students
- Review of student presentations at internal lab or research meetings, journal club, or seminar
- Follow-up data on where student went after graduation, type of job, graduate school or postdoctoral fellowship, publications when no longer working with mentor, continuation of research on his or her own

Rationale for Your Rating

Additional sheets can be attached. Please indicate where the evidence can be found on attached syllabi, student products, or your scholarly products or other documents.

_____

_____

_____

Evidence to Support This Rating

When appropriate, document literature citation or data collected at this institution to support decisions or action. Cite professional practice guidelines or standards if used.

_____

_____

_____

_____.

C6   Help Graduate Students or Postdoctoral Fellows Understand the Research or Project Design Process and the Decision-Making Criteria

---

Guiding Principle: Structure for teaching and learning

Self-Assessment Criterion: Help students understand the research or project design process for mentoring graduate students or postdoctoral fellows—An Essential Criterion

Rubric Quality Levels

❑   Not Yet Using Productive Teaching Practices (I have received feedback)

   I do not

- Help students engage in an appropriate research or design projects <u>or</u>
- Explain the purpose and desired outcomes resulting from these activities

❑   Not Yet Critically Self-Reflective with Documentation (this is the current normative practice)

   I do not critically reflect on how I can

- Help students understand the research or project design process <u>or</u>
- Explain decision-making criteria

❑   Critically Self-Reflective with Documentation (satisfactory teaching occurs at this level and at the next two levels)

   I critically reflect on how I help students to develop research or project ideas and develop a plan to conduct the research or design the project <u>and</u>
   I critically reflect on how I explain the purpose and desired outcomes resulting from these activities

❑   Critically Self-Reflective with Documentation, Evidence Based (this must meet everything in the previous level)

   I document how I guide students to work independently yet being mindful of when to intervene <u>and</u>
   I use evidence-based literature and guidelines to explain decision making (cite references for literature) <u>and</u>
   I discuss implementation of decisions and policies developed

❑   Critically Self-Reflective with Documentation, Evidence Based, Scholarly (this must meet everything in the previous level)

   I provide documentation from students that they learned how to conduct independent research or design projects under my guidance <u>and</u>
   I provide evidence through student products that they understand decision-making criteria

Suggested Sources for Documentation

- Personal reflection
- Student-generated evaluations of experiences (i.e., information from standard or course-specific form)
- Personal progress notes on students
- Notes of meetings with students
- Student reflections, evaluations
- Memos sent to students
- Student assessment data
- Review of student products, including lab notebook, reports
- Reports from students
- Review of student presentations at internal lab or research meetings, journal club, or seminar
- Follow-up data on where student went after graduation, type of job, or postdoctoral fellowship publications when no longer working with mentor, continuation of research on his or her own

Rationale for Your Rating

Additional sheets can be attached. Please indicate where the evidence can be found on attached syllabi, student products, or your scholarly products or other documents.

_____

_____

_____

Evidence to Support This Rating

When appropriate, document literature citation or data collected at this institution to support decisions or action. Cite professional practice guidelines or standards if used.

_____

_____

_____

_____

C7   Adhere to Current Professional and Ethical Standards in Research or Project Design

Guiding Principle: Structure for teaching and learning

Self-Assessment Criterion: Adhere to current professional and ethical standards in research or project design; insist that the student avoid plagiarism, fabrication of data. For mentoring all levels—An Essential Criterion

Rubric Quality Levels

❑ Not Yet Using Productive Teaching Practices (I have received feedback)

   I do not adhere to all of the current professional and ethical standards for research or project design in this discipline

❑ Not Yet Critically Self-Reflective with Documentation (this is the current normative practice)

   I do not critically reflect on how or if I adhere to current professional and ethical standards in research or project design; I do not insist that the student avoid plagiarism, fabrication of data

❑ Critically Self-Reflective with Documentation (satisfactory teaching occurs at this level and at the next two levels)

   I critically reflect on how I adhere to all of the current professional and ethical standards for research or project design in this discipline <u>and</u>
   I ensure that the students also adhere to all of the current professional and ethical standards for research or project design in this discipline

❑ Critically Self-Reflective with Documentation, Evidence Based (this must meet everything in the previous level)

   I discuss professional and ethical standards for researchers and engineers with the student <u>and</u>
   I use professional literature on ethics for this discipline (cite references for literature)

❑ Critically Self-Reflective with Documentation, Evidence Based, Scholarly (this must meet everything in the previous level)

   I provide evidence through student products that students have gained competence in professional and ethical standards in this discipline

Suggested Sources for Documentation

* Documentation that instructor is current on all ethical considerations in conducting research through training or certification

* Documentation that all students are current on all ethical considerations in conducting research

* Observations of students that data are handled ethically

Rationale for Your Rating

Additional sheets can be attached. Please indicate where the evidence can be found on attached syllabi, student products, or your scholarly products or other documents.

_____

_____

_____

Evidence to Support This Rating

When appropriate, document literature citation or data collected at this institution to support decisions or action. Cite professional practice guidelines or standards if used.

_____

_____

_____

_____

C8   Provide Feedback to Students to Foster Greater Learning

Guiding Principle: Structure for teaching and learning

Self-Assessment Criterion: Provide frequent and useful formal and informal feedback to students. For all levels of students—An Essential Criterion

Rubric Quality Levels

❏   Not Yet Using Productive Teaching Practices (I have received feedback)

I provide

- Infrequent feedback that is of limited use for improvement <u>or</u>
- Mostly summative grades to the student without adequately preparing the student for this grade <u>or</u>

I do not provide feedback in a timely manner

❏   Not Yet Critically Self-Reflective with Documentation (this is the current normative practice)

I do not critically reflect on how I can give feedback to my students

❏   Critically Self-Reflective with Documentation (satisfactory teaching occurs at this level and at the next two levels)

I document that I

- Provide appropriate, frequent formal and informal feedback to students <u>and</u>
- Provide both formative and summative feedback to the students <u>and</u>
- Provide documentation that feedback was given <u>and</u>

I use standard assessment developed by the program or the professional associations, if available, <u>and</u>
I critically reflect on how I can give feedback to my students <u>and</u>
I assess the quality of feedback and the types of feedback I provide

❏   Critically Self-Reflective with Documentation, Evidence Based (this must meet everything in the previous level)

I document that the feedback methods I use are

- Valid, reliable, and effective methods (if available) for providing both formative feedback and summative evaluations, with the choice of these methods coming from the literature on assessing students <u>or</u>
- Informed by a clear and explicit rationale for the choice of feedback methods and approaches (cite supporting evidence on the validity, reliability, and effectiveness of methods and supporting pedagogical or assessment literature)

I provide a clear rationale for the choice of feedback methods and approaches

❑ Critically Self-Reflective with Documentation, Evidence Based, Scholarly (this must meet everything in the previous level)

I provide evidence from student products that they improved based on this feedback

Suggested Sources for Documentation

- Copies of informal formative assessments given to the students, self-assessment tools
- Copies of summative assessments
- Student-generated evaluations of experiences (i.e., information from standard or course-specific form)
- Progress notes shared with the students
- Notes of meetings with students, memos sent to students
- Student reflections, evaluations, reports from students
- Student assessment data
- Checkpoints, feedback on progress of larger projects, comments or tracked changes in documents
- Review of student products, drafts, and revisions
- Student self-assessment on which feedback methods worked well for them
- Higher education literature, either in general or discipline specific (e.g., epistemology of the discipline)
- Documented use of standardized assessment tools
- Documentation using critical incident observations
- Valid and reliable assessments that the instructor creates

Rationale for Your Rating

Additional sheets can be attached. Please indicate where the evidence can be found on attached syllabi, student products, or your scholarly products or other documents.

_____

_____

_____

Evidence to Support This Rating

When appropriate, document literature citation or data collected at this institution to support decisions or action. Cite professional practice guidelines or standards if used.

_____

_____

_____

_____

C9   Provide Opportunities for Students to Reflect on Their Experiences

Guiding Principle: Structure for teaching and learning

Self-Assessment Criterion: Provide frequent, well-structured opportunities for students to reflect on their experiences so they can link them to learning in their educational program. For mentoring all levels of students—An Essential Criterion

Rubric Quality Levels

❏ Not Yet Using Productive Teaching Practices (I have received feedback)

I provide only limited opportunities for student reflection <u>or</u>
My reflection requirements are too unstructured to foster learning

❏ Not Yet Critically Self-Reflective with Documentation (this is the current normative practice)

I do not think about why students need opportunities to reflect

❏ Critically Self-Reflective with Documentation (satisfactory teaching occurs at this level and at the next two levels)

I document that I provide

- Appropriate, frequent opportunities for student reflection <u>and</u>
- Reflection that is structured and specific to allow students to learn from reflections <u>and</u>
- Documentation that students did the reflections <u>and</u>

I critically think about why and how students need opportunities to reflect <u>and</u>
I assess the quality of the reflections and the types of reflection opportunities I provide

❏ Critically Self-Reflective with Documentation, Evidence Based (this must meet everything in the previous level)

I document that the reflection methods I ask the students to complete are

- Valid, reliable, and effective methods, with the choice of these methods coming from the literature on students' reflection, standard reflection methods developed by the program, or the professional associations, if available <u>or</u>
- Informed by a clear and explicit rationale for the choice of reflection methods and approaches (cite supporting evidence on the validity, reliability, and effectiveness of methods and supporting pedagogical or experiential learning literature)

❏ Critically Self-Reflective with Documentation, Evidence Based, Scholarly (this must meet everything in the previous level)

I provide

- A clear rationale for the choice of reflection methods and approaches <u>and</u>
- Evidence from student products that they learned as a result of these reflections

Suggested Sources for Documentation

- Copies of reflection assignments given to the students
- Student-generated evaluations of experiences (i.e., information from standard or course-specific form)
- Notes from reflections shared with the students
- Notes of meetings with students, memos sent to students
- Student reflections, evaluations
- Student assessment data
- Review of student products
- Higher education literature, either in general or discipline specific (e.g., epistemology of the discipline)
- Documented use of standardized reflection tools
- Documentation using critical incident observations
- Reflections on learning during and after their research experience
- Reports from students

Rationale for Your Rating

Additional sheets can be attached. Please indicate where the evidence can be found on attached syllabi, student products, or your scholarly products or other documents.

_____

_____

Evidence to Support This Rating

When appropriate, document literature citation or data collected at this institution to support decisions or action. Cite professional practice guidelines or standards if used.

_____

_____

_____

_____

C10   Use Consistent Policies and Process to Assess Students

Guiding Principle: Structure for teaching and learning

Self-Assessment Criterion: Use consistent policies and processes to assess students. For mentoring all levels of students—An Essential Criterion

Rubric Quality Levels

❏ Not Yet Using Productive Teaching Practices (I have received feedback)

I provide final grades without providing student with a rationale for the grades <u>or</u>
I do not grade and return student work in a timely way with feedback provided <u>or</u>
I use inconsistent or unexplained methods to assess students

❏ Not Yet Critically Self-Reflective with Documentation (this is the current normative practice)

I do not critically reflect on my selection of policies and processes on assessment

❏ Critically Self-Reflective with Documentation (satisfactory teaching occurs at this level and at the next two levels)

I document that I consistently use specified grading standards, such as grading rubrics, and predetermined weights of projects or assignments, to assign grades <u>and</u>
I critically reflect on my selection of policies and processes on assessment

❏ Critically Self-Reflective with Documentation (satisfactory teaching occurs at this level and at the next two levels)

I critically reflect on my selection of policies and processes on assessment

❏ Critically Self-Reflective with Documentation, Evidence Based (this must meet everything in the previous level)

I provide documentation that grading standards for all students are used appropriately and consistently <u>or</u>
I use professional literature on assessing students

❏ Critically Self-Reflective with Documentation, Evidence Based, Scholarly (this must meet everything in the previous level)

I provide evidence from students that they believe their grades accurately reflected grading standards <u>or</u>
I create a scholarly product based on data about assessment of students

Suggested Sources for Documentation

- Review of assessment plans
- Review of comments made to students on their projects
- Review of assessment tools
- Self-reflections
- Peer-reviewed presentation or publication

Rationale for Your Rating

Additional sheets can be attached. Please indicate where the evidence can be found on attached syllabi, student products, or your scholarly products or other documents.

_____

_____

_____

Evidence to Support This Rating

When appropriate, document literature citation or data collected at this institution to support decisions or action. Cite professional practice guidelines or standards if used. Attach draft or completed scholarly product.

_____

_____

_____

_____

Rubrics for the Organizing Principle of Instructional Design Responsibilities

C11 Organization and Delivery of Experiential Learning to Facilitate Learning

Guiding Principle: Instructional design responsibilities

Self-Assessment Criterion: Overall organization and delivery of experiential learning to facilitate learning. For mentoring all levels of students—An Essential Criterion

Rubric Quality Levels

❏ Not Yet Using Productive Teaching Practices (I have received feedback)

I provide a limited range of experiences that will allow students to grow or
I do not develop adequate guidelines and policies or
I do not meet deadlines or
I do not adequately connect learning experiences to learning objectives or
I do not help students master learning objectives

❏ Not Yet Critically Self-Reflective with Documentation (this is the current normative practice)

I do not critically reflect on the organization of the educational experience

❏ Critically Self-Reflective with Documentation (satisfactory teaching occurs at this level and at the next two levels)

As perceived by students or peers,

- I meet deadlines and
- I return student work in a timely way with feedback provided and
- Students have opportunities to learn from their research, graded work, and my assessments and
- I critically reflect on the organization of the educational experiences

❏ Critically Self-Reflective with Documentation, Evidence Based (this must meet everything in the previous level)

I provide a rationale to support organization and delivery; my organization is informed by

- Student achievement, feedback, or
- Evidence-based understanding of the content such as using overarching, organizing themes of the discipline

❏ Critically Self-Reflective with Documentation, Evidence Based, Scholarly (this must meet everything in the previous level)

I provide evidence from student products that students

- Have integrated into their thinking an organized and rational approach to problem solving <u>or</u>
- Use the organizing themes as scaffolds on which they built further learning <u>or</u>
- I create a scholarly product based on data about the organization of teaching in this setting

Further Clarification or Example of Criterion

An overarching, organizing theme is a discipline-specific conceptual framework that helps experts integrate much of the material. Experts use these themes to learn new material. The structure-function relationship is an organizing theme of biology, for example, and homeostasis is an organizing theme in physiology.

Suggested Sources for Documentation

- Higher education literature, either in general or discipline specific (e.g., epistemology of the discipline)
- Self-review of course materials that includes a summary statement illustrating the overall organization and organizing themes
- Audio or video recording of student presentation or explanation of it
- Self-report from chair from an annual evaluation, class observation, or ongoing discussions
- Student course evaluations (i.e., information from standard or course-specific form)
- Self- or peer review of student products (peer reviewed is preferred)
- Feedback from technicians
- Reflections from students
- Concept map integrating entire research project
- Review of how I explain to students how entire research project is integrated

Rationale for Your Rating

Additional sheets can be attached. Please indicate where the evidence can be found on attached syllabi, student products, or your scholarly products or other documents.

_____

_____

_____

Evidence to Support This Rating

When appropriate, document literature citation or data collected at this institution to support decisions or action. Cite professional practice guidelines or standards if used. Attach draft or completed scholarly product.

_____

_____

_____

C12   Conduct Reviews and Revisions of Mentoring

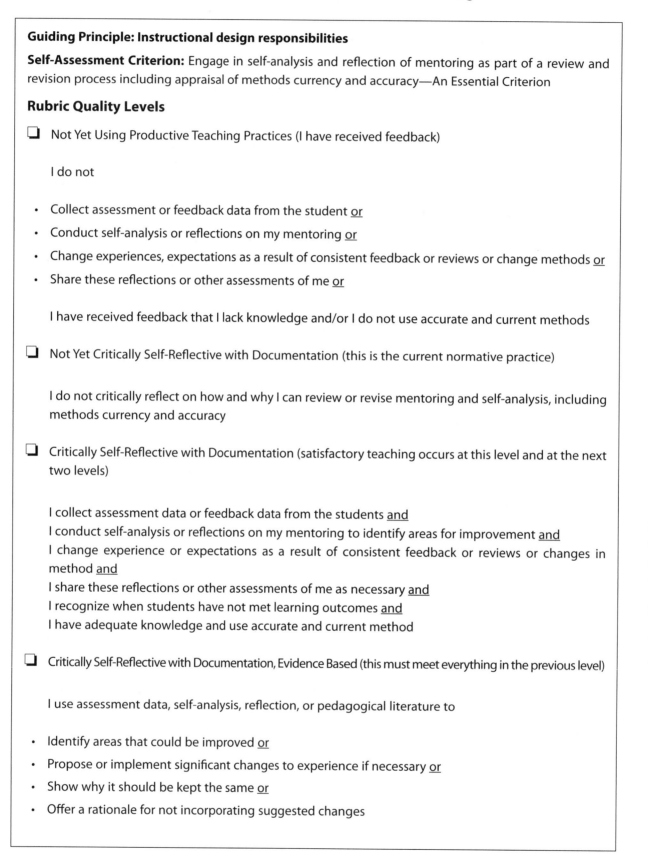

Guiding Principle: Instructional design responsibilities

Self-Assessment Criterion: Engage in self-analysis and reflection of mentoring as part of a review and revision process including appraisal of methods currency and accuracy—An Essential Criterion

Rubric Quality Levels

❏   Not Yet Using Productive Teaching Practices (I have received feedback)

   I do not

- Collect assessment or feedback data from the student <u>or</u>
- Conduct self-analysis or reflections on my mentoring <u>or</u>
- Change experiences, expectations as a result of consistent feedback or reviews or change methods <u>or</u>
- Share these reflections or other assessments of me <u>or</u>

   I have received feedback that I lack knowledge and/or I do not use accurate and current methods

❏   Not Yet Critically Self-Reflective with Documentation (this is the current normative practice)

   I do not critically reflect on how and why I can review or revise mentoring and self-analysis, including methods currency and accuracy

❏   Critically Self-Reflective with Documentation (satisfactory teaching occurs at this level and at the next two levels)

   I collect assessment data or feedback data from the students <u>and</u>
   I conduct self-analysis or reflections on my mentoring to identify areas for improvement <u>and</u>
   I change experience or expectations as a result of consistent feedback or reviews or changes in method <u>and</u>
   I share these reflections or other assessments of me as necessary <u>and</u>
   I recognize when students have not met learning outcomes <u>and</u>
   I have adequate knowledge and use accurate and current method

❏   Critically Self-Reflective with Documentation, Evidence Based (this must meet everything in the previous level)

   I use assessment data, self-analysis, reflection, or pedagogical literature to

- Identify areas that could be improved <u>or</u>
- Propose or implement significant changes to experience if necessary <u>or</u>
- Show why it should be kept the same <u>or</u>
- Offer a rationale for not incorporating suggested changes

❏ Critically Self-Reflective with Documentation, Evidence Based, Scholarly (this must meet everything in the previous level)

I provide evidence through assessment data showing students learning and that the learning outcomes are met <u>or</u>
I provide evidence to show how teaching has changed as a result of assessment or self-analysis <u>or</u>
I create a scholarly product using assessment data, reflection, revisions of experience, and reflection on experience

Suggested Sources for Documentation

- Personal reflection
- Student-generated evaluations of experiences (i.e., information from standard or course-specific form)
- Student assessment data (e.g., pre- and postassessment data)
- Higher education literature, either in general or discipline specific (e.g., epistemology of the discipline)
- Peer assessment data
- Peer-reviewed presentation or publication
- Chair report either from an annual review, class observation, or ongoing discussions

Rationale for Your Rating

Additional sheets can be attached. Please indicate where the evidence can be found on attached syllabi, student products, or your scholarly products or other documents.

_____

_____

_____

Evidence to Support This Rating

When appropriate, document literature citation or data collected at this institution to support decisions or action. Cite professional practice guidelines or standards if used. Attach draft or completed scholarly product.

_____

_____

_____

Rubrics for the Organizing Principle of Learning Outcomes

C13   Students Achieve Learning Outcomes of Acquisition of Knowledge and Skills

Guiding Principle: Learning outcomes

Self-Assessment Criterion: Students achieve challenging yet reasonable learning outcomes of acquisition of knowledge, research skills, or values. For mentoring all levels—An Essential Criterion

Rubric Quality Levels

❑ Not Yet Using Productive Teaching Practices (I have received feedback)

I use assessments that show that students do not acquire knowledge <u>or</u> skills <u>or</u> values <u>or</u> I do not assess students on these components

❑ Not Yet Critically Self-Reflective with Documentation (this is the current normative practice)

I do not critically reflect on why and how students achieve learning outcomes of knowledge, skills, or values

❑ Critically Self-Reflective with Documentation (satisfactory teaching occurs at this level and at the next two levels)

I provide assessment opportunities for students to demonstrate their acquisition of knowledge, skills, or values <u>and</u>
I document that most students, including low-performing students, acquire knowledge <u>or</u> skills <u>or</u> values <u>and</u>
I critically reflect on why and how students achieve learning outcomes of knowledge, skills, or values; the choice of the knowledge, these skills, or these values might be based on departmental or college expectations or accreditation agencies

❑ Critically Self-Reflective with Documentation, Evidence Based (this must meet everything in the previous level)

I articulate a clear, explicit, and evidence-based rationale for choice of the specific knowledge, skills, and values the students demonstrate (cite references for literature to support the rationale; if this rationale is based on departmental or college expectations or accreditation agencies, cite these expectations)

❑ Critically Self-Reflective with Documentation, Evidence Based, Scholarly (this must meet everything in the previous level)

I provide evidence from student products that students have gained competence in this knowledge, these skills, or these values and have mastered relevant learning outcomes <u>or</u>

I create a scholarly product (i.e., peer-reviewed publication) that demonstrates students acquired the knowledge and developed skills and values

Suggested Sources for Documentation

- Self- or peer review of student products (peer reviewed is preferred)
- Audio or video recording of student presentation or actual work or explanation of it
- Higher education literature, either in general or discipline specific (e.g., epistemology of the discipline)
- Student assessments
- Peer-reviewed presentation or publication
- Follow-up if students did further research

Rationale for Your Rating

Additional sheets can be attached. Please indicate where the evidence can be found on attached syllabi, student products, or your scholarly products or other documents.

_____

_____

_____

Evidence to Support This Rating

When appropriate, document literature citation or data collected at this institution to support decisions or action. Cite professional practice guidelines or standards if used.

_____

_____

_____

_____

C14   Students Demonstrate Higher-Order Thinking

Guiding Principle: Learning outcomes

Self-Assessment Criterion: Students demonstrate the ability to apply the content, use critical thinking, and solve problems related to this research or project design. For all levels of students—An Essential Criterion

Rubric Quality Levels

❏ Not Yet Using Productive Teaching Practices (I have received feedback)

I use assessments that show that

- Students learn content as isolated facts without meaning and associations <u>or</u>
- Students employ research methods in a rote manner but are unable to apply these methods. Students learn content but are unable to apply the content, use critical thinking, or solve problems <u>or</u>
- Students fail to learn <u>or</u>

I do not assess the students' understanding, problem solving, or application

❏ Not Yet Critically Self-Reflective with Documentation (this is the current normative practice)

I do not critically reflect on why and how students achieve higher-order learning outcomes

❏ Critically Self-Reflective with Documentation (satisfactory teaching occurs at this level and at the next two levels)

I provide assessment opportunities for students to demonstrate their ability to apply research methods, think critically, or solve problems <u>and</u>
I document that most students, including low-performing students, acquire some abilities to apply the research methods, use critical thinking, or solve problems <u>and</u>
I critically reflect on why and how students achieve higher-order learning outcomes

❏ Critically Self-Reflective with Documentation, Evidence Based (this must meet everything in the previous level)

I articulate a clear, explicit, and evidence-based rationale for choice of the application, critical thinking, and problem-solving skills students demonstrate (cite references for literature to support the rationale; if this rationale is based on departmental or college expectations or accreditation agencies, cite these expectations)

❏ Critically Self-Reflective with Documentation, Evidence Based, Scholarly (this must meet everything in the previous level)

I provide evidence through student products that students can apply the content, use critical thinking, and solve problems <u>or</u>

I create a scholarly product based on data showing that students achieved these objectives

Suggested Sources for Documentation

- Self- or peer review of student products (peer reviewed is preferred)
- Audio or video recording of student project or product or explanation of product
- Student portfolio
- Higher education literature, either in general or discipline specific (e.g., epistemology of the discipline)
- Student assessments
- Review of how students did on authentic problems
- Peer-reviewed presentation or publication
- Follow-up if students did further research

Rationale for Your Rating

Additional sheets can be attached. Please indicate where the evidence can be found on attached syllabi, student products, or your scholarly products or other documents.

_____

_____

_____

Evidence to Support This Rating

When appropriate, document literature citation or data collected at this institution to support decisions or action. Cite professional practice guidelines or standards if used.

_____

_____

_____

_____

C15 Students Demonstrate Learning Skills and Continue to Do Research or Design Projects

Guiding Principle: Learning outcomes

Self-Assessment Criterion: Students demonstrate an ability to continue to do research or design projects or ability to develop further relevant skills and to self-assess research or design skills and self-assessment of strengths/weaknesses. For mentoring all levels—An Essential Criterion

Rubric Quality Levels

❏ Not Yet Using Productive Teaching Practices (I have received feedback)

I do not assist students to acquire

- Research or project design skills <u>or</u>
- Self-assessment of their ability to do research or design projects or of their strengths and weaknesses <u>or</u>

I do not assess students on these components

❏ Not Yet Critically Self-Reflective with Documentation (this is the current normative practice)

I do not critically reflect on why and how students can demonstrate learning or self-assessment skills <u>or</u> I do not critically reflect on how and why students develop the ability to continue to do research or develop further skills

❏ Critically Self-Reflective with Documentation (satisfactory teaching occurs at this level and at the next two levels)

I provide assessment opportunities for students to demonstrate some further research or project design skills learning and self-assessment skills <u>and</u>
I provide opportunities for students to learn and demonstrate some further research or project design skills <u>or</u> self-assessment of their ability to do research or design projects or of their strengths and weaknesses; the choice of these skills might be based on departmental or college expectations or accreditation agencies <u>and</u>
I provide opportunities for students to succeed by minimizing risk in the research or design process <u>and</u>
I critically reflect on how and why students develop the ability to continue to do research or to develop further skills

❏ Critically Self-Reflective with Documentation, Evidence Based (this must meet everything in the previous level)

Most students, including low-performing students, demonstrate their mastery of research and learning to learn skills and self-assessment skills <u>and</u>
I articulate a clear, explicit, and evidence-based rationale for choice of the specific skills the students demonstrate (cite references for literature to support the rationale; if this rationale is based on departmental or college expectations or accreditation agencies, cite these expectations)

❑ Critically Self-Reflective with Documentation, Evidence Based, Scholarly (this must meet everything in the previous level)

I provide evidence from student products that students have gained competence in these skills and continue to do research or design projects <u>or</u>
I create a scholarly product (i.e., peer-reviewed publication) that demonstrates students developed research or project design skills (an assessment of the process or a document of the results)

Suggested Sources for Documentation

- Personal reflections, evaluations
- Student-generated evaluations of experiences (i.e., information from standard or course-specific form)
- Personal progress notes on students, notes of meetings with students, memos sent to students
- Student assessment data, reports from students
- Review of student products, recording of student products, or explanation of products
- Peer review of student research
- Higher education literature, either in general or discipline specific (e.g., epistemology of the discipline)
- Follow-up of how students did in further research
- Follow-up data on where student went after graduation

Rationale for Your Rating

Additional sheets can be attached. Please indicate where the evidence can be found on attached syllabi, student products, or your scholarly products or other documents.

_____

_____

_____

What Learning Skills Were Developed?

Provide a rationale for this rating.

_____

_____

_____

Evidence to Support This Rating

When appropriate, document literature citation or data collected at this institution to support decisions or action. Cite professional practice guidelines or standards if used.

_____

_____

_____

_____

C16 Results or Products of Research or Project Design Experience for Mentoring Undergraduate Students

Guiding Principle: Learning outcomes

Self-Assessment Criterion: Results or products of research or design experience. For mentoring undergraduate students—An Essential Criterion

Rubric Quality Levels

❑ Not Yet Using Productive Teaching Practices (I have received feedback)

I do not require students to develop any documentation of the research process or design experience

❑ Not Yet Critically Self-Reflective with Documentation (this is the current normative practice)

I do not critically reflect on why and how students should have results or products of experience

❑ Critically Self-Reflective with Documentation (satisfactory teaching occurs at this level and at the next two levels)

I require students to produce a lab notebook or report of work achieved or progress <u>and</u> I critically reflect on why and how students should have results or products of experience

❑ Critically Self-Reflective with Documentation, Evidence Based (this must meet everything in the previous level)

I show how the students and I together reflected on the lab notebook or report of work achieved or progress

❑ Critically Self-Reflective with Documentation, Evidence Based, Scholarly (this must meet everything in the previous level)

I guide students to prepare a presentation or publication in which the student appears as an author

Suggested Sources for Documentation

- Lab notebook, or research notes review
- Review of student presentations at internal lab or research meetings, journal club, or seminar
- Presentations/posters or recordings of them
- Abstracts
- Publications
- Follow-up if students continue doing further research
- Follow-up data on where student went after graduation, type of job, graduate school, or postdoctoral fellowship

Rationale for Your Rating

Additional sheets can be attached. Please indicate where the evidence can be found on attached syllabi, student products, or your scholarly products or other documents.

_____

_____

_____

Evidence to Support This Rating

When appropriate, document literature citation or data collected at this institution to support decisions or action. Cite professional practice guidelines or standards if used.

_____

_____

_____

_____

C17   Results or Products of Research or Project Design Experience for Mentoring Graduate Students or Postdoctoral Fellows

Guiding Principle: Learning outcomes

Self-Assessment Criterion: Results or products of research or project design experience. For mentoring graduate students or postdoctoral fellows—An Essential Criterion

Rubric Quality Levels

☐ Not Yet Using Productive Teaching Practices (I have received feedback)

I do not require students to develop any documentation of the research process or design experience or
I do not require students to prepare a presentation or publication in which the student appears as an author or
I do not give the student sufficient credit (i.e., authorship or acknowledgment) for work the student performed

☐ Not Yet Critically Self-Reflective with Documentation (this is the current normative practice)

I do not critically reflect on why and how students should have results or products of their experience

☐ Critically Self-Reflective with Documentation (satisfactory teaching occurs at this level and at the next two levels)

I guide student to prepare a presentation or publication in which the student appears as an author, either in an in-house or a non-peer-reviewed or a peer-reviewed venue, and
I critically reflect on why and how students should have results or products of experience

☐ Critically Self-Reflective with Documentation, Evidence Based (this must meet everything in the previous level)

I guide students to prepare a peer-reviewed presentation or publication in which the student appears as an author

☐ Critically Self-Reflective with Documentation, Evidence Based, Scholarly (this must meet everything in the previous level)

I guide students to prepare a referred (peer-reviewed) publication for which the student is the sole or first author

Suggested Sources for Documentation

- Lab notebook or research notes review
- Review of student presentations at internal lab or research meetings, journal club, or seminar
- Presentations/posters or recordings of them

- Abstracts
- Publications
- Follow-up if students continue doing research
- Follow-up data on where student went after graduation, type of job, or postdoctoral fellowship

Rationale for Your Rating

Additional sheets can be attached. Please indicate where the evidence can be found on attached syllabi, student products, or your scholarly products or other documents.

_____

_____

_____

Evidence to Support This Rating

When appropriate, document literature citation or data collected at this institution to support decisions or action. Cite professional practice guidelines or standards if used.

_____

_____

_____

_____

Optional Criteria
Rubric for the Organizing Principle of Structure for Teaching and Learning

C18   Help Students to Acquire or Use Intrinsic Motivation to Learn

Guiding Principle: Structure for teaching and learning

Self-Assessment Criterion: Help students to acquire or use intrinsic motivation to learn (i.e., personal desire to learn, seeing relevance for individual student goals) while recognizing their extrinsic reasons to earn grades. For undergraduate students. An Optional Criterion. *Note:* May not be appropriate in all types of settings.

Rubric Quality Levels

❏ Not Yet Using Productive Teaching Practices (I have received feedback)

   I extensively use extrinsic motivators to get students to earn grades or engage in research activities

❏ Not Yet Critically Self-Reflective with Documentation (this is the current normative practice)

   I do not critically reflect on why and how students should acquire intrinsic motivation to learn

❏ Critically Self-Reflective with Documentation (satisfactory teaching occurs at this level and at the next two levels)

   I critically reflect on how I provide some opportunities for students to become intrinsically motivated to learn by connecting student goals with educational outcomes, nurturing a personal desire to achieve, and using some extrinsic motivators to get students to engage in using some extrinsic motivators to initiate or engage in research activities

❏ Critically Self-Reflective with Documentation, Evidence Based (this must meet everything in the previous level)

   I articulate how my enthusiasm, abilities, teaching style, or methods provide many opportunities for students to become intrinsically motivated to learn even when the research or design project appears not to fit the student goals <u>or</u>
   I am nominated by students for a research mentoring award

❏ Critically Self-Reflective with Documentation, Evidence Based, Scholarly (this must meet everything in the previous level)

   I provide evidence through student comments or evaluations that my efforts to motivate, inspire, and encourage students have led students to become intrinsically motivated and confident to learn even when the research experience appears not to fit the students' original goals <u>or</u>
   I win a teaching award that involves student nominations or input

Suggested Sources for Documentation

- Self- or peer review of student products (peer reviewed is preferred)
- Reports from students
- Audio or video recording of student work or presentation or explanation of it
- Student course evaluations (i.e., information from standard or course-specific form)
- Personal reflection
- Peer assessment data
- Feedback from technicians

Rationale for Your Rating

Additional sheets can be attached. Please indicate where the evidence can be found on attached syllabi, student products, or your scholarly products or other documents.

_____

_____

_____

Evidence to Support This Rating

When appropriate, document literature citation or data collected at this institution to support decisions or action. Cite professional practice guidelines or standards if used. Attach student comments or nomination letter for award.

_____

_____

_____

_____

Rubric for the Organizing Principle of Instructional Design Responsibilities

C19   Enhance the Research Experience for All Students

Guiding Principle: Instructional design responsibilities

Self-Assessment Criterion: Develop or revise manuals for how to mentor student research or project design, educational technology to enhance research or project design experience, proposals to benefit student research or design projects. For mentoring all levels—An Optional Criterion

Rubric Quality Levels

❏   Not Yet Using Productive Teaching Practices (I have received feedback)

When asked to contribute, I did not contribute to

- The enhancement of instructional programs or research programs and improve the education of student researchers or designers <u>or</u>
- Improve the education of students

❏   Not Yet Critically Self-Reflective with Documentation (this is the current normative practice)

I do not critically reflect on how I can enhance the instructional program

❏   Critically Self-Reflective with Documentation (satisfactory teaching occurs at this level and at the next two levels)

I contribute to the enhancement of instructional programs and improvement of the education of students through any of the examples listed under the definition of this criterion <u>or</u>
I critically reflect on how I can enhance the instructional research program

❏   Critically Self-Reflective with Documentation, Evidence Based (this must meet everything in the previous level)

I have evidence, from either the published literature or assessment data, to support my rationale for choices for these contributions, indicating that students have benefited from the enhanced research or project design process (cite references for literature) <u>or</u>
I provide specific assessment data from research or project design experience

❏   Critically Self-Reflective with Documentation, Evidence Based, Scholarly (this must meet everything in the previous level)

I create a scholarly product based on enhancement of the research or design programs, skill development exercises, or improvement of the education of student researchers or designers

Suggested Sources for Documentation

- Review of products developed for educational programs such as
  - Materials for online education or learning activities
  - Instructional manuals or textbooks
- A protocol for the ethical treatment of humans or animals that other students follow
- Peer-reviewed presentation or publication on mentoring students in research or self- or peer review of student products (peer reviewed is preferred)
- Report from others on roles individual played in revising the research experience
- Review of proposals to improve the research process for students

Rationale for Your Rating

Additional sheets can be attached. Please indicate where the evidence can be found on attached syllabi, student products, or your scholarly products or other documents.

_____

_____

_____

Evidence to Support This Rating

When appropriate, document literature citation or data collected at this institution to support decisions or action. Cite professional practice guidelines or standards if used.

_____

_____

_____

_____

Index

Page numbers in italics refer to exhibits, figures, and tables.

Index